FOR LOVE OF THE FATHER

MERIDIAN

Crossing Aesthetics

Werner Hamacher

Editor

Stanford

University

Press

———————

Stanford

California

FOR LOVE OF THE FATHER

A Psychoanalytic Study of
Religious Terrorism

Ruth Stein

Stanford University Press
Stanford, California

Chapter 1 was originally published in *Psychoanalytic Dialogues*
12(3) (2002): 393–420, as "Evil as love and as liberation"; also
published in *Terrorism, Jihad, and Sacred Vengeance*, ed. Jerry
Piven, Chris Boyd, and Henry Lawton, pp. 38–61 (Giessen:
Psychosozial-Verlag, 2004); and in *Hating in the First Person
Plural: Psychoanalytic Essays on Racism, Homophobia, Misogyny,
and Terror*, ed. Donald Moss, pp. 281–310 (New York: Other
Press, 2003).

Portions of Chapter 2 were originally published in the *Psychoanalytic Review* 93(2) (2006): 201–29, as "Fundamentalism, father
and son, and vertical desire," used by permission of the National
Psychological Association for Psychoanalysis; and in *Studies in
Gender and Sexuality* 4(1) (2003): 38–58, as "Vertical mystical
homoeros: An altered form of desire in fundamentalism."

Chapter 4 was originally published in *The International Journal
of Psychoanalysis* 87(4) (2006): 1005–27, as "Father regression:
Theoretical reflections and clinical narratives."

Printed in the United States of America on acid-free, archival-
quality paper

Library of Congress Cataloging-in-Publication Data
Stein, Ruth, Ph. D.
  For love of the father : a psychoanalytic study of religious
terrorism / Ruth Stein.
    p. cm.—(Meridian : crossing aesthetics)
  Includes bibliographical references and index.
  ISBN 978-0-8047-6304-2 (cloth : alk. paper)—
ISBN 978-0-8047-6305-9 (pbk. : alk. paper)
  1. Terrorism—Psychological aspects. 2. Terrorists—Psychology.
3. Terrorism—Religious aspects--Islam. I. Title. II. Series:
Meridian (Stanford, Calif.)
  HV6431.S7285 2009
  363.32501'9—dc22   2009029788

Typeset by Classic Typography in 10.9/13 Adobe Garamond

For Gavriel

Contents

Acknowledgments

The subject of this book has never been easy to discuss. Annihilatory concepts, menacing violence, apocalyptic war, and the dark side of religion may be more likely to repel than attract interlocutors. Yet I have been most fortunate in having people close to me who were always ready to share, consider, and reconsider with me the difficult ideas in this study. They listened to me, catalyzed me, or otherwise enriched me during the years this book was written. The first person to hear my responses on reading the letter to the hijackers was Gavriel Reisner, my husband. I remember the places on our nightly walks where I paused to gasp over how the ideas that ground this book were coming together in my mind. My intimate reader, my candid critic, Gavriel, made things come alive and become valid and hearable.

Jessica Benjamin was intrigued by my idea of the process whereby diverse anxieties can be channeled into a single fear of God, and by the way I read Atta's letter, and she was the first to suggest I write it all up. Donald Moss invited me to present my germinating ideas on a panel we shared at the Southeast Asian Forum at the New York University Medical School a short time after 9/11. His invitation stimulated me to further articulate my thoughts. Rina Lazar listened to my stories, ideas, and the affects involved, and read my texts with her sharp mind and good heart.

Alan Bass mentioned to me Werner Hamacher, the editor of the Meridian Series at Stanford University Press, with which Alan has published his recent books. This put me in touch with Werner, a great scholar and a most generous, open-minded editor, whose warm reception encouraged me significantly over the years. Walter (Mac) Davis, whose intelligence and honesty are extraordinary, read most parts of the book, for which I am grateful. Jerry Piven has been a knowledgeable and enthusiastic interlocutor. So has been the group assembled through the initiative of Dan Hill, the director of the PsyBC Forums, who became interested in fundamentalism years ago and contacted me one day suggesting we begin studying this subject through reading and discussing two of my papers (what became Chapters 1 and 2). The distinguished group of discussants included, in addition to Dan, Werner Bohleber, Walter (Mac) Davis, Michael Eigen, Sue Grand, James (Jim) Jones, Richard Koenigsberg, Donald Moss, Ana-Maria Rizzuto, Moshe Spero, Charles (Chuck) Strozier, and Joel Whitebook. A group as strong-minded and as diverse as the above persons could not but generate much heat, which melded conceptual elaboration, emotional expression, and interpersonal debate in our attempts to sort out what we were thinking on fundamentalism. The readers who joined these passionate online discussions are too numerous to list here, but their contributions to thinking these topics are recorded with gratitude. These interchanges about terrorism, religion, clinical and applied psychoanalysis, and other topics can be found in the archives of the PsyBC Web site (www.psybc.com).

Ken Corbett, who was then editor of *Studies in Gender and Sexuality*, invited me to contribute a paper on fundamentalism to the journal, and then edited it with me, a process from which I learned a lot. The following summer, Lynn Schultz listened and edited the material then available in an effort to learn and to help me go forward with this slowly moving project. My Israeli friends and colleagues, Phillip (Yizhak) Bloom, Jocelyn Hatab, Yoram Hazan, Itamar Levy, and in particular, Yizhak Mendelsson, read the first two papers in their early stages. Michael Shoshani invited me to talk about the topic at a conference in Jaffa of the Tel Aviv Institute for Psychoanalysis, where Yossi Triest made some insightful comments. In addition to the NYU Medical School (2001) and the Tel Aviv Institute (2003), I gave talks about parts of the book at: the Karen Horney Institute in New York City (2002); the Institute for Psychoanalytic Training and Research (IPTAR) in New York City (2002); the NYU Postdoctoral Program in Psychotherapy and Psychoanalysis (2002); Yale Genocide Studies Program (2003); the annual conference of the German Psychoanalytic Society in Kassel (2004); the American Psychoanalytic Winter Meeting (2004); the international interdisciplinary conference on terror and violence at the German Foreign Ministry in Berlin (sponsored by the two German Psychoanalytic Societies) (2004); the Canadian Psychoanalytic Society in Montreal (2005); the Chicago Psychoanalytic Society (2006); John Jay College in New York City (2006); the International Psychoanalytic Congress in Berlin (2007); the Van Leer Institute in Jerusalem (2007); the Israel Psychoanalytic Society (2007) in Jerusalem; the Pulse of Death Now Conference at Columbia University (2008); the Seattle Psychoanalytic Society (2008); and the Israel Association for Psychotherapy, Tel Aviv (2008).

Chapter 1 has been translated and published in French, at the request of the late Janine Chasseguet-Smirgel (*Revue Française de Psychanalyse*, 2002), in Italian (*Psicoanalisi e Metodo*, 2003), and in German (*Psyche*, 2005). I recently translated it into Hebrew before delivering it in Jerusalem.

I thank Dr. Mehdi Abedi, volume editor of *Jihad and Shahadat*, for his generous permission to reprint Chapter 7 from his book as Appendix B.

I greatly appreciate the encouragement of Emily-Jane Cohen, acquisitions editor at Stanford University Press; the helpful guidance of Sarah Crane Newman in processing the manuscript into a book; and Mariana Raykov's helpful suggestions and gentle prodding to move along the production schedule. My copy editor, Andrew Frisardi, won my deep gratitude for his intelligent editing, which has been attuned to nuances of language and of meaning. Until I encountered through him this kind of work and the difference it makes, I never understood people's emotional reactions to their editors.

While writing this book I was nourished by the love I feel and receive from my wonderful big family, parts of which live in the United States, and parts of which have stayed in Israel, a family whose diversity in matters religious and political manages to be contained within the space of our bond.

Preface

On September 11, 2001, while my visual cortex was registering the endlessly replaying images of towers sliced by airplanes, then crumbling in orange-red fire and gray-black smoke against a white light and a blue sky, I also saw the shorn, wounded, vacuous horizon, and suddenly felt overwhelmed by the utter triumph and exhilarating power the planners must have been feeling at that very moment as they eyed the same landscape. Their jubilation and triumph, I imagined, must have been a milestone experience,[1] a sense of an obstacle removed, a limit erased. I imagined how, for them, the skies had now opened to heaven, clearing a direct path to God. I could feel the destroyer's gaze as it fastened on the mutilated skyline and I wondered whether my view was indeed a counterpart to the image that imprinted the dying terrorist's mind as he joyously became fire.

Even if my internal picture of the torn skyline is far from what went through the terrorists' brain in those unknowable moments of rushing toward death, this still could have been, I speculated, the terrorist's anticipatory fantasy before the event, or at the moment when he was assaulting the plane's passengers shouting *Allah-Hu-Akbar*, God is tremendous. That awesome moment brought home to me the vast proportions of a triumph, a joy, a sense of unbounded self-validation, a vindication, an otherworldly liberation, a feeling that the sky, far from being the limit, was the way to heaven. There was sense that this feeling was too dreadful to deal with; for a moment I had a sharp intuition that articulating this pleasurable emotion, this *jouissance*, was far worse than confronting the hatred that had led to these attacks. The feeling quickly vanished, but I realized that I had overstepped a boundary: I had entered for a moment the realm of the megalomaniac terrorist—his boundless triumph—and I had identified with it.

Perhaps it was my personal history that allowed this plunge of the imagination. I have vivid memories of Shiite devotees marching on the day of the Ashura (the day of collective mourning for the martyrdom of Hussein ibn-Ali, Modhammed's grandson, at the Battle of Karbala) in ecstasies of self-flagellation in the streets of Tehran, where I lived in my teenage years. Rows of men, mostly young, were marching and chanting rhythmically, their naked upper bodies becoming more and more blood-ied with each lashing of the iron chains they gave their chests and their backs, in a cascading frenzy, engulfed within this well-orchestrated orgias-tic ritual. They were commemorating Hussein's martyrdom, entranced by his pain, merging with his ecstatic torture.[2] On such days, foreigners were told not to stand out,[3] in fact not be visible at all to the celebrating crowd, who, I was told, would not hesitate to assault and injure any non-Muslim person.

Still earlier years in my life were redolent with narratives that recounted the perennial Jewish longing to follow the historical martyrs' celebratory overcoming of the self, and devout girls chanting, "Rabbi Akiva said, I have been praying my whole life for this command to come my way so I can fulfill it—oh, my Lord, when will it come?" Rabbi Akiva is the arch-martyr in Jewish history whose flesh was shredded by Roman iron combs for refusing to desist from acknowledging his God. The suffer-ing of this scholar-hero assumed fantastic proportions of joy in our vivid imaginations. Rabbi Akiva represented the epitome of self-realization and joy through self-sacrifice, the highest goal in life, "Oh, Lord, when will this command find me and I fulfill it?" Emotions are strongest when they deal specifically with mental pain. Emotions are also more poignant the more they reverse the feelings that precede them. Our imagination was electrified by the frisson that accompanied the triumphant conversion of scenes of capitulation into moments of victory. Was there an affinity be-tween these events, the scenes recounted in my childhood in their Jewish context, and the humiliation of terrorists that is patiently nurtured into a meticulously planned reversal, a triumph proportionate to the insult? Most probably. After all, horrific religious acts can transform wretched-ness into ecstasy; indeed, the victory of overcoming a sense of helplessness is enormously magnified when it is transposed into the service of an all-powerful God. Was there an affinity between the thinking of the group of bright, accomplished Jewish fundamentalists I came to know in my young adulthood and the way militant Islamic fundamentalists think and reason? I admit that the similarities are staggering, encompassing reasoning; moral convictions; the sense of brotherhood; and the allocation of trust and distrust toward the government, society, moderate co-religionists, or those outside of the religion. Some of the phrases the religious terrorists put their ideas into sound chillingly familiar, as does the hope of a redeeming future in an apocalyptic restoration of a golden past, and in the enveloping, jubilant sense of rightness and devotion. With all the cultural differences, the psychological structures of the two groups are the same,[4] and so is their reliance on a God who benevolently takes the believer's enemies and makes them His own adversaries, whom He will eventually defeat in an apocalyptic denouement if the group of loyal believers just does the right things.

This study is impacted by the background mentioned above, a background that made itself painfully felt on that Tuesday morning, September 11, 2001, in Manhattan, where I found myself just a few days after leaving Israel, a country torn by fundamentalism and terrorism. The reflection that began on that day became a constant accompaniment, almost an alternative world, to my predominantly clinical work, and commanded much of my emotional and intellectual energy for the following years. It took several years, including several hiatuses, to write this book, a much longer time than I had anticipated. During those years I read a great deal of material about Islam and Islamic theology and history (all the while resonating with many of the Arabic words whose affinity with Hebrew one's ear learns to gradually pick up). I read the Quran and the jihad manifestos, viewed innumerable video clips and longer videotapes of speeches and sermons of Islamic leaders to their congregations and to outsiders, as well as apologistic and propagandist productions designed for non-Muslim consumption. I also poured over various analyses of these phenomena that attempted to explain them from the most diverse perspectives. This gave me a more solid sense of how these developments came about, historically and politically, even as I hardly incorporated any references to those readings into this book, since I focus here on a specific vantage point, that of the emotional vicissitudes of the zealot seen through a psychoanalytic lens.

The good fortune in completing this book now, years after I had planned to, is that at present there are incomparably more translations from the Arabic of messages and articles from Web sites (which is where globalist jihad publishes most of its communications), broadcast speeches, and compilations of sourcebooks. All these materials are now made accessible to non-Arabic speakers. They seem to largely support the intuition that the motives explicitly stated in the various projects, covenants, and plans of Islamic terrorist organizations are predominantly *theological*, and since fundamentalists and terrorists believe that there can be no political organization that is not religious, their plans and discourses are *theologico-political*. This spate of translations helps us to gradually come to terms with what we had difficulty recognizing earlier, namely, that suicidal terrorism and murderous killings and executions are specifically *religious* phenomena.

The writing in this book assumes various stances. The introduction is a more general, even if somewhat polemical, preparation for the more specific subsequent chapters. What follows the introduction is an analysis, interspersed with narratives, some of them clinical, some textual, of the phenomenon of religious terrorism in terms that are mostly taken from psychoanalytic discourse. The constitutive and to me perennially enigmatic relationship between father and son is at the heart of a network of ideas which I endeavored to make cohere.

The reflections in Chapters 1 through 4 are followed in the last chapter by an analysis of evil. Informed by philosophical notions on evil, this chapter seeks to articulate some psychoanalytic ideas that might clarify some of the complexities in this area. My fantasy and ardent wish is for readers to think with me and against me, and to continue the reflection, urgently needed, on a subject that does not leave us in peace.

FOR LOVE OF THE FATHER

Introduction

I began writing this book after I had read the letter found in Moham-med Atta's luggage on September 11, 2001.[1] What fascinated me was the letter's tone of calm serenity and its counterintuitive appeal. How could a statement inciting its receivers to kill, to destroy and be destroyed, I won-dered, exude such solemn serenity? The utter strangeness of this docu-ment captivated me. If given attentive reading and decoding, I felt, it promised to open a window to a mind otherwise hermetically closed and enigmatic to us.

Reading the letter, I sensed that the contrast between the presumed function of the letter and its emotional tone held the key, or at least one of the keys, to the mystery of what lay behind the attacks. As always, when reason and feeling seem disjointed, or even clash, what counts, what is believed by the receiver—whether observer, listener, or reader—is the feeling tone. This is what needed to be attended to first. Obviously, the affective register of the letter in no way expresses the mental state we would expect it to express. Direct hatred and fury, condemnation of the people who were to be killed, and a pitch made to hit them hard—all these were missing. The letter carried an altogether different mood. What this different mood was, how it was generated, and what its psychic pur-pose was, will be one of the focuses of this book.

Psychoanalytic Understanding

Although drawn from various sources, this work is primarily psychoana-lytic. Reading the letter through the prism of psychoanalysis, with attention to some of its surrounding cultural and political contexts, proved quite fruitful, and led to further thoughts and then to more connections. My thoughts were mostly embedded in psychoanalytic concepts that enable us to think about people's mental states, their motives, and the influences that go into making them perceive themselves and others in certain ways rather than in others. Psychoanalytic thought also has much to say about the relation between the individual and the group, and about collective processes that are steeped in group emotions and perceptions. Psychoanalysis is singularly equipped to investigate human action through its conceptualizations of inner processes and structures that are generated by internalized interactions and identifications with other persons. Clinical experience and its theorized concepts, in tandem with knowledge that is gained through identification and empathy with other minds, steeping oneself imaginatively in the emotional states of the others' and of one's own interiority, makes it possible to understand something about those states of mind. A great part of psychoanalytic theories and concepts of human psychodynamics are based on the knowledge gained from one's trained inner experience while entering another person's mind during psychoanalytic work in a therapeutic setting. Immersion in another person's states of mind, and concurrently in one's own resonant emergent forms of awareness, tapping into the parts of oneself that correspond to the psyche one wishes to know, modulated and articulated with other kinds of knowledge, lead to the grasping of links between subjective experience and mental processes. Obviously such an idiographic and attuned approach is very different from the nomothetic procedure of taking another person to be an object of knowledge by assessing and measuring the *behavior* of that person or that person's group. External observation is a perennial source of knowledge, but it is enormously augmented by attending to the ways one is *impacted* by the other to be known. Heinrich Racker,[2] Heinz Kohut, or Thomas Ogden, are a few among many psychoanalysts who have written illuminatingly about these issues. A cultivated, reflective, "mentalizing" mode, in which we perceive the other person as an intentional subject with a unique interior world, makes it possible to trace the most diverse and the most unexpected ways of thinking. Extensive brain and infant research has yielded a corpus of knowledge regarding the centrality of affect in providing knowledge about other people (cf. Joseph LeDoux, Colwyn Trevarthen, Edward Tronick).[3]

The need to identify with the mind of the religious terrorist in order to understand it poses enormous problems, since the effort to emotionally understand such a person entails an act of partially identifying with an individual whose cultural and ideological background is not only quite alien to the one undertaking this task, but, most pointedly, whose professed intention is to annihilate her. Note that I use *terrorist* deliberately, even as I am aware of the controversies regarding political differences and questions of values, embodied as they are in the saying that one person's terrorist is another's freedom fighter. I use the term *terrorist* since I believe that Islamist extremists are not freedom fighters, nor politically oriented negotiators, but are mainly preoccupied with disseminating the terror of death and with dying and killing, that is, with taking life. I call them religious terrorists because the matrix for their mentality, their underlying mode of thinking and language, is religious. Yet terrorists are also human beings and as such need to be understood for their own sake—as human beings. At the same time, they and their environment also need to be understood on pragmatic grounds, so as to be defeated, as terrorists want and plan to destroy us. In effect, the curiosity to understand the terrorist's mind per se is superseded by the pressing urgency to comprehend one's enemy.

The Difficulties of Identificatory Knowledge

There are two possible kinds of objection to the claim to know, however partially, the mind of a terrorist. One is methodological, the other affective. The methodological argument claims that we cannot know an absent person, whether nonpresent, uncooperative, or dead. The other objection touches on the formidable affective difficulty of identifying with minds of deadly enemies. First, let us look at the methodological objection that claims that in order to gain knowledge of an individual, one has to speak to him—that is, to interview, or better, to psychoanalyze him. This can be countered by pointing to the productive tradition of writings in which the attempt is made to psychoanalytically understand historical figures that the author never met personally. Freud's writings on Leonardo, and Erikson's on Martin Luther, Gandhi, and Hitler, are a few among many other testimonies to the fact that valuable knowledge can be gathered from oral and written materials, culled from rituals, documents, or artistic objects, as long as one approaches such productions from various perspectives within oneself and lets them resonate with the subject of contemplation. Texts or textlike products can be analyzed, further constructions can be hypothesized, which then can be deconstructed and read against themselves. Informed, intuitive-imaginative synthesizing of various and contradictory sites of knowledge, supported by psychoanalytic theory, enables us to project ourselves into the minds that dwell behind the written, televised, or otherwise mediated expression. As to the liability of reading one's own fears and desires into the other, this can only be answered by the judgment of the reader as to whether the interpretation offered is coherent and adequate enough to make sense and illuminate the *interpretans*, or if, on the contrary, the interpreter's subjectivity functioned as a distorting lens and produced a tendentious or unconvincing account.

This links the methodological issue with the affective one. The emotional intensity involved in our having to think the mind of someone who desires and has sworn to annihilate us (and who may increasingly possess the means to do so), a mind, that, furthermore, is at least partially immersed in trance or in other altered states of consciousness—hypervigilant yet numbed, calculating yet dissociated—creates formidable barriers to understanding. These issues were intensely debated among the analysts, sociologists, and literary critics who gathered on the PsyBC Internet site in 2004 to discuss what later became two of the chapters of this book (Chapters 1 and 2). Our discussion concerned the possibility of thinking under conditions of terror and hatred—the terror and hatred coming toward us, the participants, from the direction of the object and subject of our thinking. The awareness of how one is perceived by such a mind—whether as an intensely targeted, particular goal for destruction, or as a faceless, impersonal source of evil—seemed to be nearly intolerable to some of us.[4] To fathom the psyche of the terrorist, we have to enter states of mind that may be terrifying, foreign, and hateful. The refusal to identify with convictions that aim at one's own annihilation is all too understandable. There is a powerful desire to alienate oneself from such sinister registers, to split them off, to amputate horror from one's awareness so that it is not felt to be part of oneself. Creating distance from unmitigated hostility aimed at oneself is needed for the sake of sanity and balance. Achieving significant identification with annihilatory intent toward the self may feel dangerous, deeply aversive, even perverse.

But it is not only the anxiety attendant on the imagining of explosive hatred and violence against the self that may make thinking ineffective. There is also the shame of being helpless in the face of such violence, the insult of our total vulnerability and the shattering of our belief in warranted safety, coupled with the shame at being so hated, all contributing to the reluctance to look at the contours of the terrorist mind and identify with it from the inside. The effort that may be needed to overcome this resistance may be compensated by a certain painful fascination as well as by the anticipation of the mastery over shock and fear that comes with understanding. The ambivalent desire to enter the inimical sensibility of the terrorist, the need to know and temporarily make the antagonistic mind our own and share it to some extent, was one of the motives for writing this book. After all, the terrorists not only inflict physical violence and instill fear in us, they also attempt to impose their own fantasy on a world that is now forced to confront this inimical vision without itself being heard or believed.[5]

September 11 and the other suicide bombings are spectacular, grand-scale acts of communication that use the media to send messages in a war of ideas that is going on at present. Osama bin Laden's messages to the world are cast in terms of justice and punishment; he speaks about the West feeling what the oppressed Muslims feel: fear and humiliation. The mechanism by which he intends to mete out this punishment involves processes of identification: Westerners will come to share the bitter taste dishonored Muslims carry, that is, they will identify with the fury and helplessness of the oppressed and violated inhabitants of the House of Islam (*Dar al-Islam*).

But the stakes are higher than notions of revenge and punishment. Bin Laden wants to punish and humiliate America for profaning the sacred places of Islam in Saudi Arabia, Jerusalem, and elsewhere by its very presence—not necessarily as a colonizing force, not even as a commercial or diplomatic presence. Any non-Muslim presence in Muslim lands is a profanation. This expressly *religious* intention sees the purging of Muslim lands from non-Muslim presence, together with the toppling of not-properly-Muslim Arab, African, and Asian governments, as first steps in the campaign of spreading the (s)word of Islam to a world that is deeply sunk in hypocrisy, lies, corruption, and darkness.[6] Thus, on the fourth anniversary of 9/11, Dr. Ayman al-Zawahiri gave an interview to As-Sahab (the media production house of al-Qaeda) that was subsequently released on various Islamist Web sites. After explaining to Americans that their culture is defunct, Zawahiri invited them to Islam: "[We call upon Americans] to be honest with themselves and to realize that their current creed—which is composed of materialistic secularism, the distorted Christianity that has nothing to do with Jesus Christ, the hereditary Crusader hatred, and their submission to Zionist hegemony over money and politics—this creed, this mixture, will only lead them to destruction in this world, and torments in the Hereafter."[7] Bin Laden differs from al-Zawahiri's call to conversion, assuming a different position: he issues a call "by Allah's leave" to every Muslim individual to fulfill his religious obligation in any country he can, "to kill Americans and their allies . . . and seize their money wherever and whenever they find them." He calls on Muslim *ulema* (legal scholars), leaders, youths, and soldiers to launch the raid on the Devil's army, the Americans and their allies "from the supporters of Satan."[8] In a letter to the Saudis, bin Laden writes that "there are only three choices in Islam: either willing submission; or payment of the *jizya* [which signifies economic, though not spiritual, submission to the authority of Islam];[9] or the sword—for it is not right to let him [the infidel] live."[10] The matter is summed up for every person alive: either convert to Islam or submit and live under the suzerainty of Islam, or die.

Ironically, there is a grim parallel between the terrorist ideological attempt to erase the habitual modes of belief and mental existence of non-Muslims or not-good-enough Muslims, and the individual career of a terrorist who erases his individuality when he enters the physical milieu of training and the psychical mindset of indoctrination that prepares him to sacrifice himself to God. Once the would-be suicide bomber becomes part of a totalitarian group, in the training camps of Afghanistan or elsewhere, he enters a system that works against individuality, memory, and continuous personal history. The parallel between this silencing and the desire to mute the masses of infidel enemies cannot be ignored. Terrorism aims at destroying thinking and personal existence on both sides of the religious-ideological divide.

When an analyst attends to her own fantasies and reveries while intensely listening to a patient, noting the flow of thoughts, feelings, and images that come up in her as a running commentary on the patient's speaking and emoting, she tacitly works with the assumption that the human mind is endowed with exquisite, built-in mechanisms (mirror-neurons, recently discovered and elaborated, being but a small portion of these mechanisms) for apprehending the other's state.[11] Spinning such fantasies, like dreaming, like committing parapraxes and slips of the tongue, like performing symbolic actions, means creating end products pulled together from moments of learning and inference, subliminally organized in piecemeal fashion. These then become indicators that can be used to obtain meanings not accessible in other ways, in a kind of knowledge that supplements theoretical and more objective knowledge. Spontaneous acts of imaginative visualization, such as the one I described in the Preface, illustrate this kind of perception, capturing a moment that can overcome the difficulties in thinking and imagining this topic.

Cultural Criticism

The difficulties in thinking are not only individual but also sociocultural. It seems to me that we have to rethink our cultural, critical, and action-oriented tools to encompass this kind of violence. A telling example of such a shift is the case of cultural critic Teresa de Lauretis.[12] Responding to a query about a possible end of critical theory, de Lauretis looks back on her involvement in the 1960s in "militantly critical"—that is, feminist, gender, and queer—theories, as well as her later contributions to the coming-to-voice of so-called "subjugated knowledge," in women's, African-American, ethnic, and postcolonial studies. She reminisces on the ways people in those days regarded the ideas produced in these fields of discourse as theorized practices of an armed struggle against a deceptive and disappointing liberal-democratic state and its apparatuses. These discursive practices no longer serve her (or us), she writes, since they constitute contemporary Western forms that are at present incommensurable with manifestations of terrorism such as those that struck the Twin Towers in New York and other monuments of Western power. The destructive violence that erupts throughout the political space reveals the world's stubborn "resistance to discursification . . . or negotiation," and creates "the enigma of the now" that is due to the fact that "our theories, discourses, and knowledges are incompatible with [the] . . . forms and means of expression [of this] destructive violence."[13]

The difficulty of thinking about suicidal terrorism is thus substantial, not only personally and psychoanalytically, but also on contemporary ethical and discursive levels. The realization of this difficulty puts one in the problematic position of trying to understand phenomena of religious terrorism in terms that are not reducible to materialistic or even political (including multicultural or postcolonial) explanations. At the same time they need to resist the lure of romanticizing the spiritual or ethical positions adumbrated by violent fundamentalism. In other words, the attitude required in this situation is to resist *both* reductive materialistic *and* romanticizing, self-idealizing accounts. Political philosopher Roxanne Euben exemplifies this difficulty.[14] Euben criticizes the ways Western liberals consider fundamentalist ideas as merely a function of economic or political frustrations, and finds similarities between fundamentalist ethics and Foucauldian and Saidian critiques of modernity that condemn Western rationalism for its exploitative reason and hypocritical wielding of power. I believe Euben may be right, though not in the way she intended. It is true that, in their critiques of Western culture, both Islamic fundamentalists and thinkers like Foucault or Said often indiscriminately vilify humanist accomplishments, holding them in scathing mistrust. Both Islamist theologians and certain extremist proponents of postmodernism overgeneralize the liabilities and faults of contemporary culture, rephrasing them as products of disciplinary, exploitative, or colonizing power operations.

But these partial similarities do not cancel the vast differences between the postmodern critiques of reifying, profit-driven, exploitative reason and the fanatically intolerant rejection of universal human affinity and human otherness that is a hallmark of violent fundamentalism. The two cannot be considered equivalent critiques of modernism. The postmodern articulation and support of the ubiquity and validity of multiplicity, heterogeneity, and difference is distinctly opposed to the fundamentalist proclamation of the exclusivity and unity of one's Truth. For Islamic fundamentalism amounts to a conviction that each particular human existence is homogeneous and subjected to a superior immutable will, while insisting, in diametrical opposition to postmodernism, on the sameness of the right way of life for every person. Most important, the postmodernist rejection of foundationalism, grand narratives, and metaphysical truth stands in stark contrast to the pronounced foundationalism and authoritarianism of fundamentalism. Postmodern and fundamentalist critiques of modernism are comparable and become somewhat similar only in those cases where postmodern thinking functions in a defensive, narcissistic mode that eventually becomes contemptuous of rationality, democracy, and the need for law and government.[15]

I have dwelt on the differences between postmodernism and fundamentalism so as to call attention to the risk of confounding the two, as well as the confusion among some postmodern thinkers regarding fundamentalism, such as their ignorance regarding the utter seriousness with which violent Islamic fundamentalists mean the bloody messages they transmit, and the consistency with which they intend to act on them.[16] Against these tendencies, I propose we step up our efforts to understand forms of fundamentalist terrorism with the aid of variegated tools and conceptions. Some of these tools and conceptions reach beyond functional, utilitarian modes of commentary and critical thinking on sociocultural disenfranchisement; they go beyond the discourse of the racially underprivileged "wretched of the earth,"[17] or the resistance of subversive groups to capitalist evil and state power.[18] The latter critical practices deal with deterritorialized peoples who are disenfranchised;[19] they hold discourses on madness,[20] and seek to provide a postmodern response to the demise of positivistic religion.[21] But postmodern discourse on racial and ethnic oppression, on the individual's subjection to the power of the state, or on positivistic epistemology and, relatedly, on capitalist values, valuable and important as such discourse is for us, cannot fill the lack of a much-needed critical discourse on *religious* fanaticism and *religious* suicidal terrorism. Using postmodern, post-Marxist, secular terminology to explain religious terrorism does not do justice to its specifically religious and spiritual aspects, and in particular, it does not fully contend with the unique power religious ideas and sentiments hold for contemporary fanatical groups,[22] indeed, it minimizes the part religion plays in them.

The foregoing assertion needs to be qualified by the recognition that there are numerous contemporary, often postmodernist writings that deal specifically with the question of religion and God. This recognition is, however, tempered by the fact that these writings often, and increasingly, equate religion with an ethical stance *tout court*, and emphasize notions of ethics rather than cult and ritual. These writings are inspired by notions taken from what Slavoj Žižek cogently describes as the "neo-Jewish" thought of Emmanuel Lévinas or Jacques Derrida, a kind of thought that addresses post-theistic forms of religion, a direction which is obviously inappropriate to the phenomena addressed here.[23] These approaches ignore the powerful psychologically archaic and destructive nature of contemporary religious terrorism, and, since they address issues such as the idea of God in a post-Nietzschean world, their terminology is incommensurate with the theistic and more archaic forms of fundamentalism, where God as a supreme being is considered the foundation of everything. Obviously, the archaic yet starkly present and contemporaneous forms of religion represented in militant coercive fundamentalism call for different ways of thinking. Cultural critic Terry Eagleton (who likewise believes that terrorism is not political in any conventional sense of the term) notes that the left "is at home with imperial power and guerrilla warfare, but embarrassed on the whole by the thought of death, evil, sacrifice, or the sublime."[24]

Indeed, death, evil, sacrifice, and the sublime are important elements in the desire of Islamic extremists to reinstate the Islamic caliphate of the seventh century abolished eighty years ago by Kemal Atatürk. Death, evil, sacrifice, and the sublime are also important elements in the worldviews and plans of fundamentalist fringe groups in Israel to rebuild the Third Temple, or the worldviews and plans of Hamas and Hezbollah members to Islamicize all of Israel,[25] and they feature in the desire of American Christian fundamentalists to accelerate the second coming of Jesus Christ as prophesized in the Book of Revelation. In the face of these phenomena, we need to enlarge and adapt our linguistic and conceptual tools to encompass *the archaically omnipotent, transgressive, and regressive dimensions* of contemporary religious extremism. In particular, we need to take into account the characteristic *concreteness and literalization* of sacralized discourses. Psychoanalytic thinking offers a rich vocabulary for the tensions between the archaic and the rational, and for processes whereby the symbolic dimension of human experience can become concretized and enacted while fueled by psychological motives that sponsor religious suicidal terrorism.

Psychoanalysis and Suicidal Terrorism

We have said that new conceptual and terminological tools need to be added to the various forms of understanding through which the phenomenon of contemporary Islamic extremism is presently being studied and interpreted. At this point I have in mind the irrational, or seemingly irrational, nonutilitarian dimension of religious suicidal thinking. Totalitarian mass movements, such as extremist Islamism, function according to Max Weber's value rationality, which involves "commands" or "demands" that are binding, as well as the willingness to accept the inordinate risks and costs that may be implicated in adhering to those values.[26] Fundamentalist movements are not utilitarian; their totalistic projects are rarely fought for the sake of material gains or to free people from oppressive regimes. They have no coherent economic project, and their political plans comprise vague, world-embracing visions such as fighting the West, or rather, the whole world until it is brought to its knees.[27] Their acts of random decimation of human beings do not focus on any immediate goals of instrumental gains and profits, but are rather committed for religious ends, seeking to actualize final redemptive scripts.[28]

We know that these nonutilitarian, nonpragmatic policies and actions stem from the specific relationship between the political and the religious aspects of life, which have never been separated in Islam. As has often been noted, the political and the religious overlap in Islam to a great extent, and there cannot be any notion of political power that is not religious, since according to Islamic law (*shari'a*), all earthly sovereignty belongs to God alone and *shari'a* means the abolition of man-made laws.[29] This is what makes every political agenda infused with religious intentionality. In contrast to classical secular terrorist organizations that aim at overthrowing the nation-state, the goal of Islamic terrorism is to transform more and more secular governments into theocratic ones.[30] The means for attaining these ambitions pass through cultures of death, nurtured over centuries by theological writings.[31] The militant version of Islam has always existed in its theological thinking but has come to occupy center stage again in the past eighty years or so.

It needs to be emphasized that in my analysis I do not include all of the Islamic faith or all Muslims, and it would be totally wrong to generalize from these extremist violent strands to all of religion and all the different creeds. I single out for study the most violent, jihadist, militant streak in this religion. At the same time, and this needs to be said as well, I am not sure whether Islam, and religion in general, are not very seriously implicated in surrounding and presaging such intentionality, particularly in their blend of submission to God and militantism on His behalf. The cults of death such as we are witnessing in Islamic jihadism involve the transcendence cum erasure of the individual, whose particularity is dismantled in the service of producing unified action.[32] In working to reestablish theocracies, these movements aim to undo the painstaking work of centuries of civilization, whose accomplishments we are accustomed to take for granted.[33]

Extremist religious groups, such as the jihadists, cohere around a transcendent, divine project and drive the religious impulse *ad absurdum*. They obey what Hannah Arendt calls a Superlaw,[34] whose archaic patterns are reanimated by charismatic leaders and promoted by cultural crises into the idiom of totalitarian religion. The frame of instrumental political strivings in which they are couched is misleading and conceals their totalistic, redemptive bent. The divorce of Islamist terrorist policies from Realpolitik becomes apparent in view of their inaccessibility to direct political arbitration. Michael Ignatieff distinguishes between terrorists who can be engaged politically, seeking emancipation or recognition, and terrorists who seek nonpolitical goals,[35] and Avishai Margalit elucidates in this vein the difference between "politics as economics" and "politics as religion." Margalit suggests that politics-as-economics is based on the generic economic idea of substitution and exchange, since everything within this paradigm is subject to negotiation and hence to compromise. Economics-as-religion, by contrast, is powered by the idea of the holy. The notion of the holy is by definition absolute, setting strict limits on what humans are entitled to negotiate and compromise, since compromise in this realm is equivalent to betrayal of the holy cause.[36] In contrast to the pragmatism of economy-based politics, the politics of the holy is strongly irredentist (revenge-seeking) and aims at the eventual reacquisition, in a future war, of what has been compromised at the present. It thus never relents on its projects, and every compromise or truce is seen as a merely temporary necessity, to be reversed when the time comes and the opportunity presents itself for redemption or reconquest of what has been given up.

The other side of the reliance on the holy and the divine is the mistrust of human values and of the binding power of mutual obligations. Such mistrust breeds tremendous underlying nihilism. Ian Buruma and Avishai Margalit, in their study of the totalitarian roots of the hatred of the secular West,[37] speak of the "spiritual politics" that are led by these movements against a culture that is seen by them as materialistic, coldly mechanical, luridly promiscuous, and poisonous for the soul.[38] In more direct language, Paul Berman calls these views "a politics of mass mobilization for unachievable ends."[39] Based on my studies of Islamic writings and manifestos, I resonate with the parallel many contemporary thinkers see between Islamic extremism and European totalitarian movements of the last century.[40] Common to both is the valorization of strong passions, talk about "the soul" of the nation or the movement, patriarchal honoring of the Leader, and contempt for petty earthly concerns such as comfort or benefit or pleasure, embodied in the bourgeoisie, or in secular liberal democratic ways of life or in things concretely or symbolically feminine.[41]

Why the Slow, Belated Understanding?

The idea that religious devotion rather than material advance inspires Islamic terrorism has been slow to enter our awareness. One reason for this obliviousness has already been mentioned earlier, namely, our rationalistic epistemological hubris, which has been biased toward thinking primarily in terms of materialistic gains and rational politics and which abhors the recognition of how much in human affairs is irrational and ideological. With all this, however, the growing evidence of the meager correlation between, on the one hand, the factors of poverty, oppression, and territorial occupation, and on the other hand, the acts of the religious terrorists, is gradually sinking into our consciousness, making us aware of what is involved.[42]

In addition to authors who research or explore the geopolitical evidence for the assumption that poverty does not cause terrorism, and that prosperity does not cure it,[43] there is accumulating evidence from a different perspective for this notion. Islamic scholar Mary Habeck is an important researcher who documents how jihadist ideology goes back nearly seven hundred years to the writings of Ibn Taymiyya, long before the rise of European colonialism, the state of Israel, the founding of the United States, or the development of the global economy.[44] Both geopolitical, economic research and textual scholarly research thus clearly point to the religious nature of present suicidal terrorism.

Juxtaposed Poles, Hybrid Discourse

All this is to say that it might be useful to examine at closer quarters the meaning of what we could call, for lack (at present) of a better term, religious rationality, or the religious rationale. One of the most conspicuous aspects of this rationale is the religious rephrasing of death as life and life as death. In these rephrasings, religious sensibility seeks to create a continuity and perhaps even an interchangeability between the two. This desire for a strong continuity beyond life and a transformation of death seeks to overcome a limit, and to do it in a more or less concrete way.

Understanding this desire for concrete continuity may be well served, I suggest, by a psychoanalytically dynamic understanding that relies on a hybrid discourse, a hyphenation,[45] a juxtaposition of the archaic with the contemporary, the political with the religious, the messianic with the manipulative, the historical with the apocalyptic, and variegated forms of cohabitation of high-technical tools with archaic worldviews.[46] The present "holy terror," where terrorist groups strive to wield sophisticated weapons of mass destruction, forces us to generate new conceptions and to explore, even identify with, unaccustomed ways of thinking and modes of feeling that are produced by mindsets different from, and inimical to, our own. Some of the notions grounding terrorist acts are historically old. Images are back again of life under religious dominion, ferocious crusades and holy wars, and catastrophic clashes of ideologies. Such images animate a rhetorical discourse the likes of which most of us believed we could only find in the Bible or in ancient scriptural and historical texts. We are forced to think anew phenomena that we erroneously believed were on the wane in an Enlightenment and post-Enlightenment world. This world, thought to be increasingly secularized and "disenchanted," was ostensibly heading toward a Fukuyaman end of its history via an omnicultural melding into a common Westernized prosperous, peaceful denouement. Clearly, such a vision of the imminent homogenization of the world cannot be sustained. The old-new amalgams, the heterogeneity of the phenomena we are dealing with, adds to the spectral character, the science-fictional, quasi-virtual tone of fantastically destructive scripts that increasingly circulate in our mind, their mind, cyberspace, a bizarre fusion of Quranic verses and computer simulations. We are required to hold together disparate areas of knowledge, bridging something ancient begun in the very distant past and resurfacing in the immediate present, and synchronized with instant communication chatrooms and cellphone chatter. Prospects of biological warfare, such as those that were looming in the days of the anthrax scare shortly after September 11, or chemical warfare, such as those that were found in some homemade laboratories in Europe, brought home the disheartening need to begin investigating anew the lethal diseases, specters of the Dark Ages, of dread and misery that we thought we had permanently eradicated from the face of the earth. Sadly, while in the past these diseases were Nature's making (or were believed to have been sent by God), they have recently become humanly inflicted calamities. At the same time, the possibility of terrorist attacks in the form of cyberwars has been articulated as well. While some scholars think its threat is overstated, others see it as a worrisome possibility.[47]

I propose that these archaisms and asynchronicities lend themselves to psychoanalytic reflection, since psychoanalysis takes for granted the coexistence of archaic and modern forms of mental processing. It assumes that unconscious fantasies and archaic wishes and fears seek manifold venues for their actualization, including the most recent contemporary forms of expression. In a sense, this is how psychoanalysis works anyway; it holds both the archaic past and the volatile present within a synchronizing view, since unconscious modes of mental processing conflate temporalities, making the past lose its irrevocability and coaxing the future, at least partially, to yield some of its uncontrollability. This is not easy to follow or implement. In the present case, it demands of us the strong realization of a cultural and human world "out there," or rather within us, that is violently opposed to the pride and security we take in the achievement we have attained of democratic liberalism. This is a world, indeed, that sees the values of democratic liberal culture as the acme of corruption, selfishness, and lack of honor, faith, heroism, and honesty, and that wants to see us as a mortal enemy in order to fight these vices through us.

A spate of translations of extreme Islamic, particularly jihadist, literature, mostly disseminated electronically,[48] has made the views of this movement more transparent, presenting us with sobering evidence of an unending struggle to establish domination over eternal enemies, a struggle that is put in theological rather than in tactical terms. These statements may accelerate our attainment of lucidity in this area, helping us to see through the distinctly bilingual nature of fundamentalist communication. Extremist Islam, perceiving itself as being at war with dangerous enemies, speaks in two languages: one aimed at the outside world, the other reserved for insiders. The language used toward the outside rationalizes and specifies conditions in a manner that is geared to being acceptable to foreign (enemy) ears, whereas the language spoken to insiders expresses the intentions and beliefs in their unveiled form.[49] Hans Kippenberg, a German Islamist, traces the behavior and appearance of the 9/11 hijackers, describing in detail how in the West, in a world of lies, in Satan's Kingdom, it was necessary for them to conceal their true identity as God's warriors, as servants of the highest Might.[50] The phenomenon of doublespeak is structurally common to all fundamentalist groups, which, as Israeli Islamist Emanuel Sivan has shown,[51] are innovative and adaptive manipulators of language and imagery. Islamic fundamentalists,[52] Sivan writes, can be psychologically sophisticated strategists who are efficacious in alternatively concealing and amplifying passionate attachments in accordance with the target audience. The secular, rationalizing, retributive language (i.e., the war on America is a punishment for occupation) fundamentalist groups often use to conceal their religious motives contributes to the ease with which we hear a language with which we are familiar rather than the language they actually speak. If we add to these factors the refusal to believe that such things can happen to America,[53] we get a fuller measure of our torpor in grasping the situation and its significance.

The Psychodynamic Approach

Psychodynamics is the study of human emotions and representations. It takes place in the context of an awareness that psychopathology is not only an individual matter, but that it is also dependent on the specific culture. This means that behaviors that would be judged abnormal in one culture or tradition can be deemed normal in another culture or tradition with a different mental stand. Islamists Hans Kippenberg and Tilman Seidenstricker see the September 11 attacks as "committed by groups who understand themselves as communities that reenact the struggle for an Islamic state."[54] In an important sense, this self-understanding may sound perfectly rational, particularly if we are willing to acknowledge that certain Islamic subcultures are not discordant with the psychological makeup of radical Islamists. The embeddedness of Islamist radicals in their culture is analogous to the way American fundamentalists are members of a particular subculture that is grounded in a specific American tradition,[55] and to the way other radical groups are embedded in theirs. Thus, certain human psychodynamics are similar across cultures, and particularly so given our common basic existential human condition—namely that we are all subject to mortality. At the same time, there are distinct cultural prisms through which a culture, or a subculture, functions to maintain itself and to foster the mental well-being of its members. The quandary of whether whole cultures or subcultures can be judged nonethical (some appellations for them are "cultures of death," "cultures of violence," or "cultures of cruelty") can thus become more complicated than individual cases of mental disorder. It seems to me that educational practices are critical, as well as, concomitantly, the choices a culture makes as to what is deemed as giving a human strength and self-esteem. Is it honor or the prevention of shame? The honor of the group or of the individual? Is it individuality? Is it the experience and capacity for intimacy? Is it achievement? And what is it that is singled out culturally as causing suffering, or as preventing it? More studies are needed concerning the relations between individuals and their respective cultures, as well as the relations between cultures. An important assumption that I believe should ground such studies is the notion that a culture is a mutually consented, convened container, a venue for the expression of conscious and unconscious fantasies and affects, and that different cultures devise different ways to contain fantasies and affects and to express them. According to this view, we create culture in order to structure our chaos and soothe our fears, and cultures differ as to what are the tools, ideas, and beliefs that are foregrounded as endowing life with structure and meaning.

This view of culture that is cognizant of the deeply emotional and ultimately "irrational" but pressing and exigent layers that subtend human groups in no way negates the more rationalistic view that sees cultural institutions as social contracts. The superstructure of a "social contract" is a necessary guarantee against the Hobbesian nightmare of the killing of everyone by everyone. A social contract is also a cautionary means against the romanticized, totalitarian visions of absolute affiliative oneness of all humans; after all, such visions can easily escalate into a group utopia that may hail the death of the individual. I am talking here of something different than the pragmatic reasons for social conventions and contracts by referring to the level at which cultural structures, symbols, and objects have been manufactured over human history to provide meaning, solace, and rules that hold individuals together against fears of the dangers threatening them, especially against the greatest threat of all, extinction. Existentialist anthropologist Ernst Becker theorized, and his followers empirically demonstrated, that culture is organized against the human anxiety over death.[56] On this view, *human culture, or human society is not entirely separate from psychic structure,*[57] but bears some correspondence with it; psychodynamic analysis of fundamentalist terrorism, therefore, is part of the psychoanalysis of culture. Such an approach calls not only for substantial moderation in the belief in human rationality and in the orderliness of the world, it also calls for embracing the tragic dimension that suffuses human life, a life rampant with irresolvable conflicts, strife, regret, and death.[58] Attempts to come to terms with this tragic shadow involve the recognition of destructive forces that act in the human mind, most poignantly the temptation to overcome death anxiety by "killing" death, so to speak. Resisting the temptation to overcome death by killing others, through immortality projects, through religion and war, means seeing through the illusion that is embodied in the magical fantasy that by killing a person who is "destined" to die, or "deserves" to die, one is spared death oneself and/or regains an eternal afterlife. Rejecting the excitement that may arise in the face of violence, death, and destruction, as well as opposing the enticement to submit masochistically and to self-destroy, means renouncing magical illusions of omnipotent invulnerability.

In considering the temptation that the absurd and the violent may hold for the human psyche, we often witness the guise of procedural correctness and efficacy that a profoundly irrational, mad action can take. In the face of this rationalized irrationality, we need to use a mode of thinking, such as psychoanalysis, that will bridge the mythic and symbolic with the emotional and individual, and will strictly abstain from pathologizing or even diagnosing the individual actors of such dramas. Such thinking will forgo the error of dubbing terrorists as madmen, at the same time as it will strive, however partially and temporarily, to account for a destructive culture that may or may not be self-destructive.

I hope that it is clear from the above that a psycho*dynamic* approach is not synonymous with the psycho*diagnostic* one. One should not diagnose or ascribe this or that psychopathology to individuals or even to groups in the case of a cultural phenomenon such as religious terrorism, since pathology, to reiterate, is largely relative to its cultural context. The stance to assume is rather psychodynamic, which means that it addresses inner psychic constellations of conflicts and affects, internalized relations among representations of self and others, and other dimensions we call psychic reality. All these configurations are observed and traced in a way that involves minimal judgment as to whether they are pathological or not. Whereas the psychopathological refers to *specific* categories of psychic sickness in *individuals* (and is to a considerable extent relative to culture), the psychodynamic deals with a reality that, in being formed by unconscious fantasies and perduring in mindsets, constitutes a general order of psychic life. This psychic order is both general and yet is often different from "objective" reality. Unconscious fantasies are generated by the internal representations of self and others; the fantasies undergo transformations and alterations and are then externalized and realized in relationships with actual human others. In brief, when we speak psychodynamically, we deal with the unconscious operations that regulate and shape psychic life *in general*.

Observing certain emotional dynamics of religion through a psychoanalytic prism, tracing some of the more corrupt variations in the human quest for purity, dignity, and purpose, we realize the crucial role that *identificatory love* plays in this figuration.[59] Identificatory love is love for the ideal found in another, an ideal with which one wishes to identify (this notion will be discussed particularly in Chapters 1, 3, and 4). The subjection and wish to merge with a remote, superhuman entity, particularly as it is depicted in the religions of the One God,[60] with no humanizing and no feminizing features, is a constituting element in human-human and divine-human relations. This relationship will be discussed in Chapters 1 and 2. Seen within this framework, religious terrorism, particularly in its lower echelons of the suicidal-homicidal missionaries and their fraternity formations, has a distinct logic of its own. This logic is marked by the transcendence of material and political interests toward horizons of utter solace whereby the distance that is perceived to separate the aspirant from the absolutely superior divinity can be bridged through religious sacrificial acts of humans, of the human. The means to attain this bliss is holy war, the jihad that was declared on the West several times, notably by bin Laden in 1996 on the United States,[61] and seven hundred years before him by Ibn Taymiyya, an Islamic scholar, whose elaboration of the concept of jihad as war won him a venerated place in Islamic history and made him a source of inspiration for religious terrorists.[62] Seeing every aspect of life in terms of religion and the loving feelings that are associated with taking life are unfamiliar to most of us, but we need to see them and hear them. As in the holy wars of the Old Testament, a holy war here is a conquest that aggrandizes God's name and a demonstrative deadly ritual that seeks to annihilate or dominate the other in God's name. The desire for a spectacular demonstration of symbolic religious acts in an ongoing holy war explains the highly allegorical nature of this kind of terrorism.[63] The act of 9/11 was a performative act of communication. It was not aimed to show America that it should "repent its imperial hubris, rethink its support of the corrupt Saudis, re-evaluate its policy towards Israel, do penance for the injustice of a global economy," as Michael Ignatieff puts it. Instead, he adds, "what we are up against is apocalyptic nihilism," since "terror does

not express a politics, but a metaphysics, a desire to give ultimate meaning to time and history through ever-escalating acts of violence which
culminate in a final battle between good and evil."[64]

This absolutist, all-or-nothing stance of religious struggles, an attitude
that is not interested in the adjudication of differences or in presenting
demands that can be answered in negotiation with enemies, strives to
achieve the dominion of one faith over all of mankind. Such an attitude
insists on imposing the emotional and cognitive beliefs, the deep-seated
existential mode of religious subjection, on the entire world. It not only
denies the right of the other to have opposing or even different beliefs;
it denies the right of those who hold such beliefs to exist at all.[65] Pragmatism, compromise, negotiation, weighing and averaging, giving and
taking, play no role in this project, and media communication and pro-
paganda serve merely to aid and accelerate the anticipated redemption
of the world through Islam. At the same time, while the televised broadcasts of al-Qaeda leaders comprise religious enunciations to the world,
their insider speech seems to address their believers who are increasingly
deterritorialized and globalized, fortifying their faith and resolve for action. Whatever the audience, these messages often seem to function like
enunciatory acts for the imminent reign of the deity, thereby testifying
to the eschatological sources of the terrorist program. This inexorable,
all-or-nothing stance mimics the absoluteness of death, and death in various modes of resolution features largely in the killings committed by this
movement, and will be discussed in this book in various places, but particularly in Chapters 2 and 3.

Violent acts of sacralized murder, "death, evil, sacrifice, or the sublime,"
in the words of Terry Eagleton mentioned earlier, slowly begin to enter
our discourse. I realize this on rereading, now in 2009, some of the lines I
wrote here immediately after September 11. Yet we are still groping, years
after this event, to grasp this particular convergence of political militancy
and submissive piety, a piety whose psychological roots will be discussed
in Chapter 4, whereas its ethical structure will be explored in the last
chapter of this book.

§1 Evil as Love and as Liberation

The Mind of a Suicidal Religious Terrorist

The letter to the hijackers that was found in Mohammed Atta's luggage in the car that was left at Logan Airport before the World Trade Center attack is a striking document.[1] A highly revelatory testimony, it may provide us with some understanding of how the mind of a suicide killer works. As psychoanalysis, indeed society, faces the emergence of new kinds of mass-destructive attacks on human beings, we must seek whatever additional knowledge we can about the states of mind that are conducive to such attacks. In particular, I believe, we should try to comprehend the mentality behind intensely religious self-sacrifice. We need to learn more about the psychodynamic issues involved in a decision that caused (and may go on causing) horrible suffering and grief to masses of people. We need to inquire what are the themes linked with and explanatory of this kind of evil.

In their anthology of studies by religious theorists and political scientists who authenticated and translated the letter from the Arabic, Hans Kippenberg and Tilman Seidenstricker describe the letter as a collection of rituals. The purpose of the letter and the mandated rituals, in their view, was to transform a young Muslim into a warrior, instilling spiritual motives that create inner peace, fearlessness, obeisance, and lack of feeling during the killing.[2] But the letter is more than a document tracing the initiation and transformation of a man into a warrior. Had it only been a means of contacting and fortifying the minds of terrorists about to commit an act of mass destruction, we would expect such a document to be filled with a raging rhetoric of hate, a cry to destruction and annihilation. Instead, we hear a voice that reassures, calms, calls for restraint and thoughtful control, and appeals for a heightened consciousness in its readers. One might say that this is the voice of a wise father, instructing his sons in the steps they are to take on a mission of great importance, and reminding them of the attitude suited to accomplishing that mission. The letter calls for the terrorists to wash and perfume their bodies; to clean and to polish their knives; to be serene, confident, patient, and smiling; and to remember and renew their intentions. It reminds them that the task before them demands their attentiveness and, even more, their devoted adherence to God.

The letter frequently mentions love of God and God's satisfaction with the act to be accomplished. Essentially, it details some things that have to be done in order for the terrorists to gain entry into God's eternal paradise. We know that these acts involve the murder of human beings, those who are considered the enemies of God, as well as the self-annihilation of the terrorists themselves, who are going to be tools for the elimination of other humans. But the letter does not spell this out. While doing the work of killing and destruction, the doer, God's faithful servant, must remember to make supplications to God wherever he finds himself and whatever he does. Basically, the letter describes a ritual at the end of which the supplicant is to receive God's approval by doing what pleases God—purifying the world of contaminating infidels. Again, this is not mentioned in the letter. What is indeed stressed is that, if one is to merge with God, the most elevated Being human thought can envision, one has to perform the act accurately and mindfully.

How can we explain the tone of the letter? Can it teach us something about the state of mind in which the terrorists were steeped, either by themselves or by others (by special "training," including the formulating and reading of the letter we are studying)? What is the mental atmosphere of anticipating and preparing for such a destruction of other and self? What is the place and role of a smiling, calm, confident state of mind with which one passes from life into death, a state of mind so diametrically inverse to the turmoil, terror, and rage that would be the expected accompaniments to committing such destruction?

The Son's Supplicating Love for the Father

I have always been deeply impressed by the intimate, loving discourse a believer holds with God while praying and supplicating. Particularly poignant to me is the theme of a son praying to his God-father. One can practically hear the sweet plaintive murmur of the Psalmist, "My God, so numerous became those who hunt me, so many are those who stand over me, who say to my soul, you have no redemption in God, and You, my God, giveth back to me my breath and saveth me with Thy love."[3] And one is riveted not only by the music but also by the lyrics of Jesus Christ's love songs to God in Bach's *Passion According to St. Matthew*, "Dein Mund hat mich gelabet mit Milch und süßer Kost" (Your mouth has fed and replenished me with milk and the sweetest nourishment). Both the psalm and St. Matthew are profound works of great beauty and inspiration, where joy and pain intertwine.

The letter to the terrorists does not speak of hatred. It is past hatred. Absurdly and perversely, it is about love. It is about love of God. We can palpably sense the confident intimacy of a son close to his father and the seeking of a love that is given as promised and no longer withheld. If this feeling is sustained inside one, it does not have to be demonstrated externally. The letter is a reminder: "Everywhere you go say that prayer and smile and be calm, for God is with the believers. And the angels protect you without you feeling anything"; and, "You should feel complete tranquility, because the time between you and your marriage [in heaven] is very short." Inasmuch as nothing further is said about that marriage, and particularly whom one will marry (the famous paradisiacal virgins are not mentioned at this point), the idea that the marriage is that of the son(s) to God does not sound absurd at all.[4]

The thought that there might be a root affinity between the theme of a son's love for his divine father and the underlying theme of the letter feels quite unpleasant. Do these motifs of religious devotion and intimate communion and of using "God" to inflict mass killing and destruction spring from the same psychic source? And do they bear on the image of the father as the one who opens windows to the outer world, and who offers—to his daughter as well as to his son—liberation from domesticity and the mother's absolute power? Is there any similarity between the father of freedom and creativity and the father who loves those who kill his enemies and chooses those killers as his accepted sons? In both cases, the "father" not only dispenses empowerment and inspiration, he also imparts a sense of joy and fulfillment, the joy of deliverance from a too-enclosing life and the opportunity to identify with ideals. Jessica Benjamin's words thus acquire an added resonance: "Identificatory love is the

relational context in which, for males, separation and gender identification occur. The strong mutual attraction between father and son allows
for recognition through identification, a special erotic relationship. . . .
The boy is in love with his ideal. This homoerotic, identificatory love
serves as the boy's vehicle of establishing masculine identity and confirm-
ing his sense of himself as subject of desire."[5]

What we have here however, is identificatory love that goes awry and
is amplified and perverted by divine aloofness and difference. The state of
ecstasy that comes with doing God's will and the rapture of merging with
Him is known to be a joyous experience. "Those who dismiss 'evil cults'
have no idea how rapturous this state can be and how no other pleasure
can compare with it," said a disciple in Bhagwan Shree Rajneesh's community, when describing "true bliss and abundant joy."[6] William James
called the ecstasy found in doing God's will the "joy which may result . . .
from absolute self-surrender."[7] Such a religious experience of transcendence bathes one in a sense of truth that is absolutely convincing and sublime. And it usually involves both a disciple and a guide in "the ecstatic
merger of leader and follower."[8] Obviously, the shadow of an anonymous
guide and leader who issues loving paternal injunctions falls upon the
letter and is part of the liminal state of transcendence we are dealing with
here. Being immersed in such an altered state of attention and receptiv-
ity engenders a sense of profound psychic unity and ineffable illumina-
tion. Such a state can be so intense and all-encompassing that it makes
time and death disappear. Human beings have always sought such states,
often through religious or secular mysticism, with the help of cultural
rites, drugs, oxygen deficit (through rapid breathing), sleep deprivation,
or some other form of an imposed ordeal. These states may also be experienced in such familiar activities as song, dance, sexual love, childbirth,
aesthetic effort, mechanical flight, artistic and intellectual creation—and
going to war. We know that in such states the self feels uniquely alive,
integrated, and in touch with larger, cosmic forces. We also know that
one who creates rituals for manufacturing experiences of transcendence
can thereby create a bond that allows group-sanctioned action, including
violence and even murder, to be committed with ease and even joy.

Such a smooth passage from life to death obscurely connects in our
minds with a mutation, a sweetening of dying, either by loss of self or by
"well-intentioned" killing, in a sickening marriage of love and murder (a

combination we read about in the reports of some serial killers and murderers). When such a state of mind prevails, love can smoothly glide into murder. We are faced with a most hateful action that is performed in a spirit of devotion, a kind of beatitude that culminates in literally killing, not only others but also the self. Obviously, this is not the misfortune of being killed during a battle, or an outburst of murderous rage. Neither is it the choice a martyr makes to sacrifice his life when being assaulted by heathen torturers.[9] What we have here is martyrdom that is murderous; militancy that is sacralized; a symbiotic, simultaneous killing and dying, where approaching intimacy with God the Father requires becoming one with one's victims, "marrying" them in death and destruction. The language of the letter belies explanations for the terrorist acts as secular political actions, pointing to a transcendent mystical experience of a special nature. This mystical experience, I suggest, hosts *the transformation of self-hatred and envy into love of God*, a Love-of-God that promotes the obliteration of those parts of the self that are antagonistic to the sense of compulsory purity.

Robert Jay Lifton, in his illuminating study of what he calls "death imagery," talks about universal symbols of pollution and defilement as signifying being contaminated and soiled with "death-taint and total severance." Purity, on the other hand, signifies "life-continuity and unbroken connection." The process of purification would then represent the transformation from death to life.[10] In the cases where purification means killing—paradoxically, by purifying the defiling elements so as to wrest life out of death—one arrives at death once again (I talk about these phenomena at greater length in the next chapter). The detachment from and contempt for human life displayed by the terrorists, coupled with a fervent, extreme love for God, is substantially different from the "love" many a serial killer has professed feeling for his victim(s). Serial killers speak about their inchoate longing to enter the other, particularly the other's body, even (or especially) after the victim's death.[11] Sheikh Ahmed Yassin, the Hamas leader who inspired the momentum of the suicide bombers against Israel, seems to articulate the difference between the serial killer and the suicide bomber: "Love of martyrdom is something deep inside the heart. But these rewards are not in themselves the goal of the martyr. *The only aim is to win Allah's satisfaction.* That can be done in the simplest and speediest manner by dying in the cause of Allah."[12]

The Father, Hypermasculinity, and the Disappearing Woman

Let us consider again the transformation of (self-) hatred into love of God. We know from the press that Mohammed Atta had an overbearing, self-confident, successful, moderately religious father, who, on being told what his son had been involved with, expressed disbelief at the idea that his son, whom he used to scorn for not being manly enough, could execute such an act.[13] People who knew him, the press tells us, say that Atta was painfully shy with women. We read in his will, written in 1996, that he requests that no pregnant woman or other unclean person should approach his body, and that his genitalia be washed with gloved hands. In the years leading to the attack, taciturn, humorless, introverted Mohammed Atta had become increasingly pious and austere, frequenting Hamburg's Big Mosque. He was, witnesses tell us, a dour presence in school and in the house of his German hosts.[14] Atta, who was often repulsed by people's small pleasures, was also harsh and demanding toward himself in matters of religious observance, with no smile to lighten his sullen face. In particular, everything having to do with the sexual body was felt by him to be defiled and therefore untouchable.

One afternoon I found myself in a massive mujahideen demonstration in Trafalgar Square in London in November 2000, where a young British convert to Islam was holding a speech. The argument this man employed to explain why he had converted to Islam and joined the mujahideen had to do, as I had anticipated, with sexuality. He stridently lashed out at the rottenness of Western society, a society "poisoned by homosexuality, adultery, fornication, sexual license." He was screaming, with rage and fear, that sexual sinning must come to an end for it destroys the world. The new light he was seeing, the Truth he found in Islam, he said, helped him find a remedy to the sexual ills of British society. His discourse, centered on sexuality, was antisexual, antiheterosexual, and manifestly antihomosexual. As Catherine Liu put it: "Mohammed Atta's phobic reaction to sexually integrated society is a symptom of his being both inside and outside of secular modernity. It is his negation and wish to annihilate this complex configuration that becomes the measure of absolute violence. . . . Atta's murderous mindset has everything to do with contempt for women. The cult of purity is maintained psychically at the expense of real women."[15]

Clearly, women do not exist in this "masculine" letter (even the famous virgins are mentioned here in one auxiliary phrase that speaks of their waiting for the heroes in their beautiful clothes, hardly a very sexual or intimate description). The culture of hypermasculinity and the ideal of warriors who purify the world of contaminants (whom bin Laden contemptuously equates with women), absolve these men of the need to articulate the desirability and potential power of women.[16] If there is no acknowledged emotional need for woman, there is no dependency and no envy.[17] There is only a liberation from the primordial fear of being tempted to lean on a woman and thereby become softened, engulfed, and emasculated. Modern, strong women typify a world out of order and threaten the sexual security of these men. The banishment of women reinforces the pervasive homoerotic grouping among Islamic extremists, where the desired loss of individuation that is feared with women is given free reign and finds its place in a devout submission to God. This shift (from women to homoerotic bonding around an idealized male divinity) marks a specific regressive-transcendent trajectory that is altogether different than falling into an engulfing maternal womb. The frightful sliding "down" toward the feminine and maternal can be replaced—or even, shall we say, superseded—by an ecstatic soaring "upward," toward the heavenly Father, who is imagined to be waiting there to redeem his sons' troubled souls and sweep away the doubts of their former selves. It seems as if the primitive father of Freud's primal horde has been resuscitated or, better, is still alive, and has come to embrace his sons—provided they unite against "woman," that is, against the feminine principle of pleasure and softness (found both in Islamic women and in Western society, which is seen as feminized). Instead of rebelling against the oppressive Father and against the frenzied death the Father demands, there is a giving up of oneself to Him, a total submission.[18]

The Letter: A Second Look

In our first attempt to apprehend the atmosphere of the letter we came upon a generalized mood of loving reverence of God and an overarching desire to unite with Him (in prayer, in the right action while living one's last hours of life, and in concrete union with Him in paradise). In our second look at the letter, we search for the particulars. We observe that the letter is a blend of precise technical details and meticulous preparations (although clearly the detailed planning was made and learned earlier and at this stage is assumed to have been mastered and internalized).

The technical preparations were meant to be coupled with spiritual rituals, on which the letter adds repeated reassurances and promises. The text seems to be a last-minute message, a reminder to fortify the spirit and to rehearse once again the sequence of the religious acts that have to be performed at each stage, from the night before the attack until the moments of taking over the plane and its passengers. Thus we find interwoven a sacred ritual of self-consecration and of preparation of the body, formulated with an air of festivity and grave devotion; itemized details alternate with metaphysical language, in turn followed by still more particulars. The small details (e.g., how to wear one's shoes, how to tighten one's clothes) are far from being mere behavioral indications: they are all taken from ancient laws and are heavily laden with religious significance.[19] Most important, the addressees of the letter (always referred to in the plural, as a group of brotherly peers) are constantly reminded of a very special kind of *knowledge* they possess, exclusively and omnipotently; they are called upon to renew their "intention" and to elevate their spirits and minds to a higher plane.[20]

We have noted the conspicuous absence in the letter of hateful expressions or of any overt rage and violence; on the contrary, it contains expectant, even loving, imagery. Gradually, however, we become aware of a different state of mind, one that is not merely a joyous mood suffused with the desire to affiliate with God. We realize that, by their being told to pray incessantly, to occupy their minds with repetitive mantras of the One and Only God, and inwardly to articulate thousands of supplications to Him, the terrorists must be transported into a state of self-hypnosis and merger, a continuous trance, an intense, depersonalized relating to the godly object. They are immersed in a state of total alienation from the outer world, which has become a "thing," as the letter commands: "Completely forget something called 'this world' [or 'this life']." This state metamorphoses the passage from life to death, normally experienced as fatefully final and irrevocable, into a smooth, weightless step, as if one were passing from one train car to another, from one room to the next. The felt shift in the sense of death is both frightening and exhilarating. Death, the irreversible cessation of one's life, the ultimate dark unknown that inspires in us horror (or a peaceful or not-so-peaceful withdrawal into ourselves, occasionally coupled with a sense of continuity with living humanity), ceases to be death. It becomes a smooth, weightless passing over a threshold toward the light.

The words that describe this transition into the "real (immortal) life" in God's paradisiacal lap convey the heady, intoxicating taste of omnipotence. Assuring the terrorists that it is only a matter of moments and of some actions that remain to be done, the letter entreats them: "The time for play is over and the serious time is upon us," indicating that real existence is yet to come; the group has almost reached it.[21] A powerful sense of fraternal communion adds to the joyous radiance of the impending event. The writer rhetorically asks, "Shouldn't we take advantage of these last hours to offer sacrifices and obedience?"[22] As the approaching future is visualized, there is a crescendo of hope, an opening toward rebirth: "because the time between you and your marriage [in heaven] is very short. Afterward begins the happy life, where God is satisfied with you, and eternal bliss." The passage between inferior, wasteful life and the desired "real life" is described as nearly *painless*: "And be sure that it is a matter of moments, which will then pass, God willing, so blessed are those who win the great reward of God." The passage between the two lives is *fearless* as well, for "the believers do not fear such things [as "their (the enemy's) equipment and gates and technology"]. It is only "the others" ("the allies of Satan") who experience fear. Painless and fearless, the passage between life and death is a fusion, a serene *Liebestod* (love-death)—and *Liebesmord* (love-murder).

Fear

Fear is conspicuously absent yet ubiquitously present in this letter. Fear is almost nonexistent in the state of mind described here, or, should we say, there is no visible anxiety (the terrorists' high performance level demonstrated in the use of planes and people (the passengers and the crew of the plane) in New York City and Washington, D.C., is obvious proof of that). The dynamics here form a process whereby all *anxieties*— past and present, and even those anticipating a realistically difficult future—all transmute into a *fear*, which is then narrowly directed toward God.[23] Such a process would have affinity with the paranoid process, in that anxiety, a more vague, complex, subjective affect, is exteriorized and simplified into concrete fear. Fear is a simpler affect that has a clear object, which is often magnified; it is a primitive reaction designed to ensure survival, but it can be most weakening and humiliating. The emancipation from fear and humiliation that have been transmuted into the fear of God can be tremendously liberating and empowering. Fearing a person means paying a kind of tribute to him that is humiliating, since it is an avowal of that person's power over the person fearing him. As the Quakers say, to fear a human is degrading. This important point is picked up in the text: Fear "is a great form of worship, and the only one worthy of it is God. He is the only one who deserves it." Fearlessness, while maintaining fear of God, can be attained through the feeling that humans are small and contemptible. Their smallness makes them not worthy of being feared. The possibility that one can achieve liberation from anxiety by transforming it into a unitary, homogenizing fear of God is translated in the religious-terrorist discourse into the notion that fear should not be wasted on trivial mundane matters. Elevated to a momentous role, fear creates a categorical difference in a person between himself as the one who fears and the one whom he fears, between those who fear and those who are feared.[24] Fear and idolization are not too far from each other, and fear becomes a form of worship.[25]

By instilling fear and terror in their enemies, the terrorists diminish them and strive to turn them into their own (the terrorists') potential worshipers, in a way analogous to how the terrorists themselves worship God. Feelings of helplessness and confusion—about the grisly act they are about to commit, about the identity they have chosen, all superimposed on fears from the earlier phase of their lives when they had presumably attempted to assimilate the "fearless," godless modern world—have been submerged. Under the auspices of a loved-feared God, any pang of conscience disappears.[26] A corrupt, disdainful, persecutory superego has been instantiated in the image of "the only God."[27] Projecting upon the figure of God their own corrupted (defeated and resurrected) wills, the terrorists acquire absolution from all moral constraints as well as permission to destroy human lives and to launch terror in the lives of those they do not destroy. As Robert Lifton says, "The sense of transcendence and infinity can be pursued all too easily by means of murder and terror, no less than by love and creative work."[28]

The act of legitimizing and condoning butchery by constructing a particular God, a feared and loved Father who does not command "Thou shalt not kill," who does not say "no" to dissoluteness and crime, who has (in Lacan's language) become the imaginary father,[29] has to be complemented by considering a large number of human beings as nonhuman. Before exploring this subject, however, let us first elaborate on the altered state of mind in which mesmerized fear is offered to God. We have mentioned the conspicuous element of body management and care in the letter. We know that harsh ascetic practices heighten religious (or political or sexual) fervor.[30] The letter speaks of the making the body into a clean, shaven, perfumed, aestheticized instrument that moves in a world whose immediate and human significance has become remote and inaudible through the terrorists' incessant incantations and repetitive bisyllables.

Psychic Numbing

Being immersed in a state of intense focus on God in word and thought, not ceasing to attend to His presence for one minute, sustaining a kind of numbed, awed adhesion, yet at the same time functioning with extraordinary vigilance and competence, may be likened to cold, psychotic paranoia at its height. The subject adheres to the idealized persecutory inner object, while the world, having become insignificant and contemptible, vanishes into derealization. We tend to stress the persecuted, self-referential, hostility-imputing quality of experience in paranoia, but we often forget another dimension that marks this state of mind: solemn reverence and grandiose adoration. Kohut apparently spoke about such a state of mind. Regarding it as a way station in the regression toward psychosis, he wrote about "disjointed mystical religious feelings; vague awe."[31]

The severance of the outer world from human meaning, made possible by a persistently cultivated contempt for that world (the descriptions of Atta's facial expression, body posture and emotional stance toward his hosts and costudents in Hamburg illustrate this well). Such contempt enables terrorists both to focus on monitoring the instrumental tasks at hand and to remain immersed in an intensely religious state of mind, which by its acuteness screens out all undesirable affects and thoughts. According to Lifton, it is "a numbing process . . . similar to that cultivated among Japanese soldiers during WWII in serving the Emperor," as well as among the Nazis, for whom "the soldier was to steel his mind against all compunctions or feelings of compassion, to achieve . . . a version of the *'diamond mind'* that contributes both to fanatical fighting and to grotesque acts of atrocity."[32] In addition to its capacity to enhance functioning, a mesmerized, mechanized mind likely feeds on hatred turned into dismissive contempt. It uses the power of contempt to chill any heated feeling, any affiliative, compassionate emotion. But for religious terrorists the mental process does not stop there. Another phase is ushered in when the loathing and despising, the building blocks of contempt, are transformed into a state of enthrallment and deep, total love for the superior divine power. The intriguing process whereby contempt becomes love and adoration challenges us to try to imagine the nature of such love.

The all-or-nothing nature of this love led Karl Abraham to call it "pre-ambivalent," and to place it in a pre-Oedipal stage of development.[33] We also get the sense that such love, rather than expressing itself on an "horizontal" axis of an imagined affiliation (compassion, nurturance, attachment, etc.), is located on the "vertical" axis of total self-(un)worth, superiority, and inferiority, which spans affects such as shame, humiliation, degradation, pity, awe, and veneration. A first step in understanding this affective grammar is to consider the blend of contempt and "love" found in the most blood-curdling phrase in the letter: *"you must not discomfort your animal during the slaughter."* This phrase is well beyond anger or hatred. It is the utmost in disparagement. What is it that is transformed into the magnanimous pity for animals, creatures that live and breathe but are devoid of a human soul and mind? Is it the basic human sense of solidarity, or is it contempt? One has some duty toward one's animals (the expression "your animals" resonates with an image of wild, lustful predators, which have been tamed and brought under one's control over life and death, but also with that of the sacrificial animal).[34] By having mercy on one's animals, one is imitating God, who rules over life and death and who takes pity on His creatures. One's moral righteousness is set in place. Although one's animals are one's possession, one's "nobleness" and "morality" will not let him hurt his animals unnecessarily, even at the moment they need to be slaughtered.

Concerning the Theme of Evil

Sitting at a window in a New York City restaurant a few days after 9/11, watching the human faces passing by, I found my mind straining to reconcile two opposing and impossibly jarring attitudes. We all seem to hold a basic assumption that these are faces of human beings, who, in the most taken-for-granted and unquestioning manner, command our respect, and who, we feel, though we are not aware of it all the time, are intrinsically dignified, even sacred. How can we put in this same place the sustained striving of the terrorists to erase and wreck these faces, to annihilate the bodies that carry them? I found myself making a huge mental effort to move from our deeply inculcated view of humans as absolute entities to the view of humans as tissues to be squashed. It is the latter view, I realized, that is absolutely necessary to reach the state where all sense of crime, sin, and evil is eliminated.

How does one legitimate hypercriminal behavior? How does one make the passage from the abhorrence to killing human life to the experience of killing as good and noble and therefore sanctified? Apparently a tremendously subversive process is at work, a process that culminates in a radically altered perception of human beings, who must be made to seem other than how they are normally perceived. As Paul Oppenheimer writes, the eyes of the evildoers and their followers must be "taught to see the ordinary as freakish and [subsequently] to consider the freakish as horrible and as worthy of extermination as insects and diseases. Any sort of violence . . . becomes intelligible and necessary when dealing with creatures, formerly considered human, who are suddenly shown to be poisonous."[35]

When we listen to the explanations of such authors as Roy Baumeister,[36] who speaks of evil as being the result of an incremental accumulation of pressures, rewards, the need for acceptance, and the process of losing one's identity to the group, we recognize that certain configurations of social, political, historical, and group circumstances indeed promote this kind of experience. Yet what interests us here is a particular register, to wit, the *psychic* process that builds a perverse killer-discourse, the discourse of evil that transgresses human bonding, self-existence, and death at the same moment. In a way, it can be described as the passage from the human to the superhuman. To experience humans as small dots, so to speak, to be cleaned from one's windshield, and thus to be gratified of having done the right thing can easily be visualized as the view from God's eye, to paraphrase Thomas Nagel. As must be clear by now, we are specifically interested in the process that leads from the human to the "superhuman."

In particular, I believe, we should try to get in touch with the experience of authentically accomplishing the highly religious task of sacrifice of the other and of oneself. It seems plausible to assume that Islamist terrorist acts are authentically religious;[37] they are performed with faith in the sanctity and rightness of the acts, even if other factors, such as social pressures and incentives and particular historical and cultural circumstances, play their role too. What psychodynamic issues are involved in a decision that caused, and in all probability will go on causing,[38] horrible suffering and grief to masses of people? We need to inquire about the themes that are linked with, and explanatory of, this kind of evil. Obviously, the present analysis in no way implies that evil is found only within Islamic fundamentalism, or even only within religious fundamentalism in general. Michel Foucault and Hanna Arendt, among others, have written illuminatingly about the nonpersonalized, noncentralized, and banal aspects of power (Foucault) or of evil (Arendt). Innumerable politico-economic situations and decisions of the West should be considered evil. Giving priority to economic and antiecological considerations over human lives and well-being, as well as environmental considerations, or using a military situation or religious narratives to oppress another people, are forms of evil, examples of which abound.

The term *evil* has been minimally dealt with in the psychoanalytic literature because of a justified wariness of using terms whose provenance is theology, terms that lend themselves to the reification and hypostatization of their *designatum*, such as seeing evil as a power incarnated in nature, Satan, or the Devil. Worse, such terms may be said, in addition, to lend themselves to the demonization of human beings whose psyches are the same as ours. Hence, by talking about human beings as evil, it is argued, we do to them precisely what they are doing to us. Most of us, I believe, would see evil as not existing in itself, but rather as a sequel to a multitude of factors, a process that is most often gradual, and that, in addition, requires complex judgments about the meaning of human acts. "Evil" may sound too allegorical or too concrete, too essentialist or too objective, too impassioned or too intimidating for psychoanalytic ways of thinking, which are oriented toward the study of individual subjectivity.

A case in point is Melanie Klein, a profound thinker on destructiveness, envy, hate, and violent impulses, who nevertheless does not use the term evil in her writings. Klein famously uses the term the *bad object* or *bad objects* to designate inner presences or presences in the psyche that are the result of the internalization of experiences with real others that have been colored by fantasy and inner structures. A bad object notably should not be confused with a human being, since it denotes an internalized figure, or rather, the subjective cluster of experiences and beliefs created out of certain affects lived in fantasized relations with an other.[39] The bad object is a cluster that is crystallized out of bad experiences and serves as a carrier and evoker of experiences of frustration, abandonment, persecution, or the projection of violent affect. The bad object is a human representation that is subjectively (and internally) experienced as "bad" but that objectively may not be bad at all. More precisely, it may not have intentionally done anything bad to the person who harbors it. When this event then plays itself out on the outside, between people, the ability to perceive the other as a whole object may be compromised, and the other becomes a "part object," a representation of a person that is distorted and compressed into a truncated, simplified part of a whole and complex representation of a human being. Seeing a person as wholly good or wholly evil, vilified or idealized, means slicing him or her into a wholly good and/or wholly bad part and ignoring the other parts that make for the complexity and ambiguity of a live human being with a subjecthood of his or her own.

The Kleinian notion of the bad object is individual and subjectivistic, whereas evil is, by definition, something objectively bad and blameworthy that has been perpetrated on another person (occasionally on one's own self). In contrast to the subjective experience of the bad object, only an objectified judgment can designate an act as evil. Judging acts as evil from an external vantage point parallels the repeated observation that, for the most part, evildoers do not themselves consider their acts to be evil but rather necessary; occasionally, they even feel they do what they do for the good of their victims, or for the glory of God, Nation, or Party.[40]

It is not surprising, then, that very few psychoanalysts have addressed the subject of evil. Fewer—in fact next to none—have written on the conjunction of religiosity and evil. Among the first group, two authors stand out: Christopher Bollas and Sue Grand. Bollas writes penetratingly about the serial killer as a "killed self," a child who has been robbed of the continuity of his being by abusive or murderously abandoning parents. This person goes on "living" "by transforming other selves into similarly killed ones, establishing a companionship of the dead."[41] Bollas also distinguishes between the passionate murderer who is driven by rage and the murderer who "lacks a logical emotional link to and is [emotionally, not necessarily physically] removed from his victim."[42] Sue Grand writes about traumatic experiences, which, for the perpetrator, are acts of "rape, incest, childhood beatings" that are often committed by close family members.[43] The evildoer here is a survivor of unspeakable trauma that has resulted in unformulated, incommunicable loneliness. Deadness and vacuity have become the defining characteristics of the perpetrator's identity, and evil is "an attempt to answer the riddle of catastrophic lone-liness."[44] Grand speaks of a vacuous no-self that is so derelict as to drain both perpetrator and bystander from the desire or the illusion of "under-standing" the "no-self"; on the contrary, "the no-self is in the presence of others who confirm the truth of catastrophic loneliness, even as these oth-ers do not know this loneliness."[45] Evil for Grand is thus an opportunity to be in the only context that makes it "possible to achieve radical contact with another at the pinnacle of loneliness and at the precipice of death."[46]

Both Bollas and Grand have given us illuminating studies of evil, evil done by one human being to another, but the species of evil that is com-mitted specifically in the name of religion has not received attention in psychoanalysis. Evil can be perpetrated with passion or with detachment, in the privacy of a twosome or in a group; evil can be done for self-serving purposes or out of belief in an ideal. Evil done for idealistic purposes (in-cluding nationalism, social utopias, and other not necessarily religious idealism), I will later suggest, possesses a dynamic of its own. It is time psychoanalysts began reflecting on the phenomenon of evil that is com-mitted in the name of idealism and specifically in the name of religion, and ponder the context for organized acts of terror executed by groups mostly of men in the name of God. At this point I am addressing the affec-tive transformations that enable one to do evil specifically out of love for an idealized object, deferring a more general analysis of evil to Chapter 3.

Thinking about evil requires a tremendous effort of the imagination and a willingness to incorporate this phenomenon into one's thinking. It is no easy task to enter deeply into what it feels like to be immersed in violently disinhibited, or superhumanly entitled, or radically contemptu-ous and hateful, or ecstatically numbed states of mind. Our attempts to immerse ourselves in such states meet with an instinctive pull to repudiate them and cut them off from consciousness, thereby alienating them into a foreign or inscrutable presence, or bloodless cerebral knowledge. But this sense of alienness can imminently change into a looming sense of dread and threat. The ruthlessness and intended severance of any compas-sion in acts of evil jar with professed ideals of human affinity. After all, it is precisely by its lack of compassion that perverted religiosity, socially expressed as coercive fundamentalism, distinguishes itself from more moderate forms of religious sensibility that preaches and commands com-passion. A psychoanalytic sensibility, the imperative that nothing human shall remain alien to us, compels us to uphold the effort to understand something that is meant precisely to annihilate understanding and replace it with mindless obeisance. Fundamentalist terrorism aims at fighting the very stance that opposes, or even tries to comprehend, fundamentalist terrorism, and in this sense, terrorism attempts to terrorize thought itself. Terrorism "aims to disrupt its targets' customary and trusting relation to perception."[47] It is against this impediment that psychoanalysts need to examine the phenomena encompassed by the term *evil*. Evil is a conspicuous manifestation in human life, a central dimension of existence.

Evil, as Paul Oppenheimer notes, has begun to appear again in the press because of the "growing awareness that it is the only word capable of bringing certain awesome events into our sphere of intellectual proxy, of diagnosis."[48]

Some Sources for the Killing

What we have read in the press about the life trajectory of Mohammed Atta tallies with Lifton's descriptions of the adherents of the Aum Shirinkyo cult, who were dominated by their leader, Shoko Asahara, to execute plans of mass murder.[49] Most of the cult followers were quite intelligent, though not brilliant. They were moderately successful in their education and career; for various reasons, they remained stuck in middle positions in the West where they did not enjoy great success (in Western terms),[50] and they found themselves outside their traditional lives and families, without, for the most part, having built families of their own. With time, their conflicts with identity, identification, and self-definition became unbearable, and their frustration, helplessness, sense of masculine failure, and self-loathing became massive. In many cases, the distress accompanying such an emotional stalemate goes on for years, until a magical solution comes along that offers the wonderful cessation of the conflict and an end to the need to continue toiling to achieve success and recognition. There is a significant structural similarity in both groups.

Manic Triumph

A solution that bypasses physical and psychic reality is by definition manic, as in turning to otherworldly, messianic means to accomplish one's ends. An activity is manic when it is carried out with the conviction that one has found the right and only answer to all problems, thereby experiencing tremendous power and extreme optimism. Such activity is colored by a sense of elation, and it feeds on grandiose ideas that come from the illusion of having attained one's ideal and mastered it. A manic state abolishes the need to obey rules. It exempts one from hard work and from dependency on others, who are treated dismissively or contemptuously, and it promises permanent relief from distressing conflicts, anxieties, and uncertainties. Manic solutions seek to evade the psychic pain and potential depression that accompany the realization that there is a distance between an actual state of affairs (or state of self) and an ideal one, which can never be totally bridged.[51]

The manic state is only half of the picture of the religious terrorist mindset. There is a polarization that occurs between the grandiose illusionary state just described and masochistic abjection. Recent psychoanalytic theory describes the son whose love for and wish to identify with the father, and his desire to be loved by the father, clash with his father's indifference or repulsion. Freud writes about how the son is hypnotized by the father's power and how in this enthralled state the idea is "awakened" "of a paramount and dangerous personality, toward whom only a passive-masochistic attitude is possible, to whom one's will has to be surrendered."[52] Drawing on Freud's model of the son's hypnotic love for the father-leader of the group, Jessica Benjamin suggests that when the son's identificatory love—the love for his father as the ideal with which he identifies in order to develop and achieve independence—is thwarted, it turns into servitude and masochistic submission.[53] When the son incurs his father's contempt by openly showing his adoration and need for him, the son reacts by identifying (himself) with the annihilating, contemptuous figure. As a consequence of his identification with a condemnatory figure, the son wants to externalize and get rid of this miserable and openly needy part of himself by externalizing it into his human surroundings, outside of himself.[54] The miserable, abject part of his self involves the boy's love for the mother, which becomes shameful and inferior in a culture in which women are marginalized and devalued. As we mentioned, the newspapers reported that Mohammed Atta was painfully shy with women. They also reported that Atta's mother was extremely close to him, which his father felt made him "soft." For the son, this mother-bound side of him becomes hateful and despised. The son cleans and purifies himself of all bodily odors and defilements; he shaves, puts on perfume, and with a determined coldness sets out to slaughter the "soft" and "feminine" parts of the world that do not believe in the father. Ironically, the terrorist assumes a feminine role in relation to the father as he undertakes a mission against the feminine in his surroundings. He becomes soft and smooth, hairless and perfumed, and assumes a submissive attitude toward God while despising the "soft," self-indulgent behaviors of his enemies. A rigid, stereotyped gender role is played out in these behaviors.

Killing the subversive, disturbing part of oneself that has been projected outward will forever silence, it is hoped, confusion and bad feelings about the self. The calm, confident tone of the letter echoes the peace of mind that has been achieved after the killing has been contemplated and carried out in fantasy.

Along with splitting and killing off the "weak" part of the psyche, another dissociation occurs. The design of the September 11 attacks transforms the meaning of death in a single act. We can visualize the scene of the attacks as an attempt to redefine the boundaries of death. One part in this deadly "performance" (a term used by Juergensmeyer to emphasize the theatrical, attention-seeking character of terrorist violence) is a reenactment of Western works of art that have depicted the damnation of sinners: bodies upside down, limbs spastically intertwined, burning in hell, a picture of what the human beings in the Twin Towers might have looked like as they burned in a blaze of molten steel.[55] Seen from the perspective of the perpetrators, the opposite part of the scene is their glorious ascent to heaven in a soaring chariot of fire. Although in reality the terrorists were obliterated together with and at the same moment as their victims, they did not entertain the possibility that they were not going upward, smiling,[56] toward their Good Father, but rather were heading toward the same end as their victims—the same, all-too-human, final fall into the darkness of death.

God the Father

I have suggested that the process whereby hatred is transformed into a certain kind of perverse love is at the same time a contrite and all too happy return to the father.[57] As mentioned, "God" here symbolically stands for that part of the psyche which sanctifies and assists in the killing of the impure, disturbing, "infidel" part—the part that is perceived to

have strayed from faithfulness to one's past and one's father. Psychoanalytically speaking, this is a "regression"—or rather a clinging—to an archaic
father. One of Laplanche and Pontalis's definitions of regression is "the
transition to modes of expression that are on a lower level as regards complexity, structure, and differentiation."[58] Instead of a rebellious, liberating
symbolic "killing" and separation from the father (whether the prehistoric
father of the primal horde or the primal father within) and identification
with his strength, this regression represents a retrograde conciliation with
him.[59] In *Totem and Taboo* Freud constructed a narrative of how killing
the greedy, envious father who takes everything (and every woman) for
himself allowed his sons to build civilizations and establish moral values
and prohibitions that would be held in historical memory.[60] Furthermore,
experiences of compassion and human care were born of the creative guilt
that the sons had to unavoidably experience in the aftermath of their
"killing."

The regression to the father, foregoing the step of "killing" tyranny and
instead "regressing" to it, does not look like a "regression to the mother."
Once we realize the distinctness of this kind of regression and its difference from regression to the archaic mother, a space for new reflection
opens up. And it goes beyond the primal-horde theory, which Janine
Chasseguet-Smirgel, for instance, uses in her portrayal of the inhabitants
of the enchanted Islands of Utopia.[61] Chasseguet-Smirgel describes these
islanders as a horde of brothers who have banished the father and taken
possession of the mother. But she equates utopia exclusively with a return to symbiosis with mother nature, and she describes utopian wishes
as cravings for immediate satisfaction by the child whose father is absent
and who therefore experiences a symbolic return to the uterus and a new
fusion with the mother. I suggest that the form and fantasy behind terrorist attacks has aspects of a regressive *return to the father and the banishment
of the mother*. The promise of fulfillment is not that of happy beatitude,
of sated envelopment and plenitude, but of ascetic overcoming of oneself,
transcendence of time and the body, and an assenting sacrifice of one's
will in the service of a higher will.[62] The regressive process of becoming
mentally subjugated is both intensely relational and has affinity with the
process whereby hate and fear (whether artificially induced or accumulating during one's life) are transformed into a perverted, enthralled "love."[63]

The transformation of hate and fear into love is undergone by a whole
group. The brotherhood that is emphasized and constantly encouraged

in the letter (and probably in other spaces where the group lived and met) suggests a cardinal contrast with Freud's mythical "primal horde." The fable of the horde of brothers narrates their gathering around their despotic, depriving father, whom the sons overthrow, kill, and devour. Following this murderous act, they develop toward their dead father a posthumous, ambivalent, dialectically complex relationship of guilt and love, hostility and remorse. It could be said that it is precisely this evolutionary process of overcoming an oppressive authority, while simultaneously transcending and safeguarding it (what Hegel called *Aufhebung*), that was bypassed by the terrorists. Instead of liberating themselves from unjust authority, whether divine or political, whether in the form of corrupt governments, calcified dogma, authoritarian patriarchal customs or fear-instilling authorities, the terrorists returned to "their father" to identify with him, seeing therein their strength, not oppression. The terrorists became an instrument of "the Father"; in retrograde conciliation with Him they carry out the slaughter in His name—not only on their victims but on themselves. "The Father" becomes an all-devouring entity who kills His sons who have regressively returned to Him, asking Him to kill parts of themselves through abdicating their own judgment and desire for life and abrogating to Him the total claim to knowledge of the True and the Right. The group collectively experiences the ecstasy of self-obliteration, performing an act of a double-faced love that is simultaneously submissive and murderous. Not only did they not "kill their father"; they spared themselves the awareness of having committed a crime against the other humans and themselves. They let "the Father" kill them.

The Sons

The mental state of these errant sons, masochistically returning to and fusing with a cruel, depraved Father—who, they "know," will be content when they serve his homicidal needs in identification with Him as their ego-ideal—is a homoerotic state of merger and abjection. The sons love their corrupt father *because* He allows them to get rid of the impure, "infidel," soft, "feminine," "godless" part of themselves and reach the certainty, entitlement, and self-righteousness that deliver them of painful confusion and guilt.[64]

Violence is necessary to build civilization; parricide, on this account, is primal sin in the same way as the Fall is the primal sin of disobedience, of eating from the Tree of Knowledge. But as Freud saw, putting the historically violent roots of nations, countries, and civilizations in mythopoetic terms, the primal sin of parricide (and the resultant guilt over this necessary killing) is required for building civilization by bringing people together in solidarity. "United, they had the courage to do and succeed in doing what would have been impossible for them individually. . . . The violent primal father had doubtlessly been the feared and envied model of each one of the company of brothers: and in the act of devouring him they accomplished their identification with him, and each one of them acquired a portion of his strength."[65]

Becoming subject while defying subjection is the subtext in Freud's narrative of paternal order and the subject.[66] Rather than rampant, disowned violence, civilization grew on some foundational violence that was followed, however, by remorse and guilt (Freud speaks of both "creative" guilt and "tragic" guilt), and by affection.[67] Consequently, the sons established socializing and civilizing regulations to "atone" for their "sin," to integrate their allegiance to old traditions with their transgression of them. The task of settling down, individuating, acknowledging the temptations of violence and using this acknowledgement to build culture, rather than denying the violence at the basis of human enterprise and waging excessive violence that is dissimulated or rationalized away, is arduous. Such a task flies in the face of the fantasy of an exclusive brotherhood of men whose tribal loyalty and collective closeness trumps closeness to women and their "weakening" effects. Such brotherhood is based on each "brother" being divested of his individuality, a sacrifice that enables him to become assimilated into a horde, or a training group, or a terrorist cell. This process of de-individuation and masculine group formation as we find it in Islamist terrorist organizations is a revival of ancient cultures, such as the Spartan one, that survive and conquer other cultures by training "alpha-boys," as Lee Harris ironically calls them, to be willing to die in order to kill.[68] Such a culture seeks to survive by maintaining a class of "heroes and warriors who, unlike normal people, do not fear violent death."[69] While violence can destroy civilizations, and religious parables and religious history are most often coupled with the theme of war, violence can also be sublimated. Complexly linked with a deepening of intersubjective consciousness, guilt, remorse, concern, and caring love, violence is a part of civilized life, and even helps to build it, for civilized life is a mixture of violence, envy, solidarity, and reparatory needs.

Going through some of the literature on religious traditions and symbolism, I am impressed with religion's preoccupation with a primordial, eternal, cosmic war between good and evil, and with how a religion depicts its own origins, vicissitudes, and promises of salvation via the language of war. When the fabled and symbolic epic of war becomes concretized—or, in psychoanalytic language, when the inner war between goodness and badness is split off, projected onto infidels and heretics, partitioned between God's children and God's enemies—then religion functions as a "splitter" of affect. Such a degenerative process of literalization allows religious men, such as the September 11 terrorists, to experience heights of exalted love for God simultaneously with the cold determination to destroy lives. Religious philosopher René Girard believes that violence is at the heart of the sacred: "The sacred consists of all those forces whose dominance over man increases or seems to increase in proportion to man's efforts to master them. . . . Violence is at the heart and secret soul of the sacred."[70]

Girard elaborates the idea that human violence, particularly violence that humans in ancient times could recognize only as alienated, unconquerable violence that comes from the outside, from the divine or from nature as God's creation, rather than from within themselves, radiates an aura of the sacred. The sacred, for its part, with its rituals, beliefs and myths, particularly those pertaining to sacrifice and scapegoating, is a device for dealing with violence. In other words, a system of sanctioned ("holy") violence can assure the prevention or cure of the violence that is inherent to life: that of nature, death, and other human beings. This conception explains sanctioned, sacralized violence as a kind of homeopathic device that collects the violent impulse and expresses it through sacrificial rituals, thereby drenching and immunizing the particular culture at large from having to deal with massive, indiscriminant violence, in the manner, Girard contends, that Christ carries our sins and absolves us from them—including the "need" to commit violence. Legitimized violence is introduced to contain rampant, uncontrolled violence. Concentration of legitimized violence is accomplished by *sacrifice*, a kind of token violence, which Girard, like other social thinkers,[71] views in a positive light as the religious act par excellence (in that it seeks to replace the violence of all against all by a focused, sanctioned violence). Girard warns us, however, that it may be extremely difficult to separate the ritualized, delimited, *pars pro toto* violence from human violence, itself a response to the fear instilled in humans by the overpowering forces of nature. The division between channeled, ritualistically regulated violence and rampant, overflowing, chaotic violence may be vital, based on the (psychoanalytic and realistic) assumption that human violence is unavoidable. Ultimately, however, there is the danger that the two kinds of violence may become indistinguishable and fuse into one.

Sacrifice is thus a regulatory mechanism against violence, yet sacrifice itself is violent. I am thinking of the biblical story of God asking Abraham to sacrifice his son, Isaac. In a deep sense, God did not ask Abraham to sacrifice Isaac, but to sacrifice himself, Isaac representing the most precious and desirable part of himself, the part that would revitalize him in his old age. Isaac is here a tool for God's demand-need for proof that He, God, is loved beyond life and beyond Abraham's love of himself. God needs Abraham to kill and immolate what is most precious to him, thereby killing a part of himself. This is a love of a special kind: *it asks God's worshiper to kill himself in the other*. Abraham "had to" prepare to kill Isaac, who was part of him; the terrorists "had to" kill "infidels," who represented aspects of the terrorists' selves, in order to empower God to make His dominion (His "kingdom") prevail. In the aftermath of their killing of arbitrary, authoritarian cruelty and deprivation, the mythical brothers of the primal horde learned and affectively understood the meaning of crime, and, concurrently, the binding power of moral precepts. Only by opposing archaic tyranny could they develop a sense of guilt and further civilized thinking. They could then achieve the necessary understanding of the double-edgedness of affect, or ambivalence, as Freud calls it—seeing it as paradigmatic to the father-son relationship.[72] This affective complexity in the act of revolt and regret is what may have saved mankind from blind idolizing enthrallment to Freud's mythical father, whom Freud called the *Führer*,[73] a figure who hypnotizes adherents into participating in a de-individuating cult, exploiting their fears and their pathetic craving for love.

§2 Fundamentalism as Vertical Mystical Homoeros

Was Abraham's readiness to liquidate any obstacle on his way to God by sacrificing his son to God a sublime act of faith? Or was it a terrible pact between the believer and his God, whereby Abraham was asked to return God's gift, Isaac—the promise He had made to Abraham as a reward for his faith—in exchange for eternal progeny, numerous as the stars in the sky and the grains of the sand? The violent erasure of human obstacles to a transcendent merging with ("love" of) the deity expresses the desire to return to "the fundamentals," to a state of pure, unrivaled oneness with the Creator. This desire, conjoined with cultural and group processes, leads to fundamentalist religious practice, and with further developments, to coercion and violence. The person possessed by this desire exudes a sense of certainty, of being in the right; he possesses a certain kind of assertiveness, self-confidence, and airtight cohesiveness; he tends to feel superior to the other and to devalue him. He simplifies complexities into binary oppositions (basically of good and bad), not only creating order out of ambiguity and chaos but also constituting a "vertical," homoerotic quest for God's love. Such processes of division and ordering are enacted by increasingly severe purification procedures, and are subtended by a sacrificial attitude, by masochism, and by coercion. It is usually assumed that the religious quest is a search for *meaning*, but what is often downplayed is the observable fact that this quest is at the same time a series of transformations of *fear*.

What is this fear? Actually, there are two: one is the fear of death, of human finitude, of personal annihilation;[1] and the other is the fear of the other's existence, of the force of the other's own intentions and aims.[2]

The desire to put an end to these threats leads to the search for radical solutions, such as fundamentalism. The fundamentalist mindset—and since it is a mindset, I essentially make no distinction between the Jewish, Christian, or Muslim variety of it—would then be the quest to rid oneself of one's fears of finitude and loss of identity and self-validation. Such a mindset aims at liquidating the necessity to surrender and depend on other human beings; it wants to destroy its own fears of dependency and the helplessness, humiliation, and rage they engender. The transcendence of fear and rage can be accomplished through processes of idealization and purification, which are meant to oppose destruction of the self even as they enact destruction on another level.

The World Is "Furiously Religious"

Since the late twentieth century, we have become more acutely aware of the dangers of global religious terrorism. The abruptness of this realization has been proportional to the strength of the assumption that we live in a secularized world, in which religious wars are mostly a thing of the past. That religion has been waning in the face of increasing secularization is a view that was developed by (among others) Max Weber, the father of modern sociology, who argued that a process of *disenchantment* (*Entzauberung*) is underway in all areas of human life, a process that has dispelled our experience of the world as enchanted, divinely conceived, and grace-dispensing. Yet, as Peter Berger, the sociologist of religion, claims, the disenchantment thesis, widely accepted throughout much of the twentieth century, is patently false: "The world today, with some exceptions . . . is as furiously religious as it ever was, and in some places more so than ever."[3] Berger, together with other students of religion, maintains that the world is becoming not only increasingly desecularized and religious, but increasingly fundamentalist. What hides this situation from view, he argues, is the high visibility of a small number of intellectuals in the West who project their own secularism on the world at large. Berger's notion of the radicalization of religion finds support in his and his colleagues' findings that the more reactionary and less adaptive to secular environments religious institutions are, the more they flourish, whereas the religious systems that are more "progressive" and accommodating to modernism succeed much less as judged by their scope and the number of their adherents. The more isolated an enclave of a religious culture is from its modern surroundings, the more likely it is to survive and expand.[4] The Islamic upsurge is conspicuous in most modern cities in the world, as the Latin American mass conversion to Catholicism has created a cultural transformation in this continent, and North American Christian fundamentalism is gaining in power. These authors emphasize that the Islamic revival in particular should be seen from a spiritual perspective and not only through a political lens (although it carries serious political ramifications), for it constitutes "an impressive revival of emphatically *religious* commitments."[5]

Is this religious upsurge, which is so often fundamentalist and prone to degenerate further into militant-coercive fundamentalism, a simple reaction to modernity, as many suggest? It is a prevalent view today that fundamentalism, and particularly violent fundamentalism (the difference between them will be discussed later), is a direct counterreaction to the combined elements in contemporary culture of individualism, despiritualization, and economical globalization.[6] More forcefully, Jürgen Habermas regards religious Islamic fundamentalism as "a uniquely modern disruption," a response to the challenges of modernity confronting the Arab world.[7] The West in its entirety, says Habermas, serves as a scapegoat for the real experience of loss suffered by Arab populations torn out of their cultural traditions during processes of accelerated modernization.[8] From this viewpoint, modernity and the frustrations that come with it breed contemporary fundamentalism.

My view is that the increasing religiosity of the world is linked with the inextinguishable human need, growing in proportion to the emergence of Enlightenment rationality,[9] for magic, for transcendence, for places where one is elevated above finitude and suffering. Religion, and in particular patriarchal monotheism,[10] has the power to draw our attention to much of the enchantment that still inheres in the world, even after technology, scientific advances, and the deconstruction of the numinous, say, in minimalist art have altered us irreversibly.[11] The project of the Enlightenment, it turns out, the systematic secularization of life and the world, that is, the view of life and the world as prosaic, unmagical, and identical to itself can thus never be an exclusive option; magical thinking is necessary and religion lives on. Christopher Dÿkema suggests that magical thinking never actually vanished; rather, it focused on a decreasing number of imagined objects, eventually limiting itself, as in later and contemporary monotheisms, to God the Father.[12] Thus, monotheistic religions, which are always patriarchal, may be no less (and possibly more) "enchanted" and "enchanting," no less magical and mystifying, than polytheism or paganism. Coercive fundamentalism is rooted in a kind of mind-paralyzing enchantment. Patriarchal monotheism is consistent and continuous with both coercive fundamentalism *and* "the liberal religion of loving-kindness and compassion most of us would prefer," writes Dÿkema.[13]

Patriarchal Monotheism: Abstractness, Oneness, Invisibility

The view of patriarchal monotheism as one of the last vestiges of enchantment contrasts with the notion of monotheism, held for example by the thinkers of the Frankfurt school, as the peak of religious disenchantment. Horkheimer and Adorno write approvingly on the "disenchanted world of Judaism," with its *Bildverbot*, the prohibition of pictorial representations of God.[14] In line with Freud,[15] for whom the monotheistic prohibition on images made Judaism into a religion of instinctual renunciation, Horkheimer and Adorno regard the Jews' prohibition on image making as allowing them to move from sensory imitation (mimesis) to abstract ideas, and from mythology to rationality, by enabling them to convert primitive, sensual images into a series of ritualistic duties.[16]

The idea that the peak of spirituality and moral development is synonymous with (or dependent upon) "instinctual renunciation" seems dubious. To give up on one's "instincts," that is, one's desires and pleasures, for the sake of spirituality is often a slippery affair. We know that what is split off or violently suppressed often returns through the back door. To put it in Freudian terms, the proximity of superego and id can generate easy reversals, in which the superego, or the ego-ideal, acts as ruthlessly and wantonly as the id, whereby ascetic renunciation of instinct and desire becomes the motive force for cathartic violence that is then justified and sanctified by the ego-ideal. Deception and self-deception, the return of what has been "renounced" under a different guise, are ever present.

The taboo on images and the idealization of abstraction and renunciation was an integral part of Judaism, the virtues of which Freud praised in *Moses and Monotheism*. This taboo has been further radicalized by Islam, which prohibits pictorial representations not only of God but of all creatures. The notion that one must not make God visible in any way led to the creation of the beautiful arabesques featured in Islamic art. These patterns are not only nonhumanly shaped, but are also tightly packed within their unyielding, repetitive outlines. To create an image of something, by contrast, is to imagine it. To think in images is to be enabled to imagine a different reality, many realities, pluralities. To think in images is to speculate, to make things specular, make them mirror new knowledge. This free play of the imagination, this making-visible, is, from a fundamentalist perspective, bound to create anarchy. Imagination threatens the fundamentalist with excessive individual choice, which harkens back, for him, to the pagan anarchy of pre-Islam, called *jahiliyya*. To overcome anarchic proliferation, Abrahamic (but not Christian) monotheism professes and wishes to be about the singularity and abstractness of God. Fatema Mernissi, a Moroccan religious feminist scholar, tells us that "Mohammed proposed to reduce the many to One, to abolish all idols and believe in one God. From the year he began to preach publicly, to the year of his conquest of Mecca, Mohammed succeeded in destroying the statues of gods and goddesses and in unifying the Arab world around *al-wahid*, 'the One.'"[17] This was revolutionary, and it began with the story of Av-raham shattering the idols of his father, Terach, thus establishing the basic Abrahamic fold, and its repetition in Islam reverberates with the power of this narrative. It was revolutionary, since from then on, "Opposition to the One would forever have a negative color. Submission to the One is paid by immortality and the vanquishing of death."[18]

Belief and Desire

Monotheism is about the One who is invisible.[19] It is usually patriarchal; that is, it has at its core the belief in a masculine and paternal deity. Regarding monotheism as masculinist and patriarchal, and as generating problematical forms of desire, poses a challenge to the cherished belief that monotheism is the most evolved form of religion. It is usually assumed that patriarchal monotheism represents an advance over polytheism (or matriarchal religions) by virtue of its sanctifying a single, integrative entity. Challenging these assumptions may offer new knowledge that extends feminist critique to the religious realm.

My approach to these issues foregrounds the libidinal and perverted relations between a certain kind of believer and his God, where the libidinal and the violent come together. As I have suggested, assuming that cultural forms reflect underlying motivations or structures of desire,[20] coercive fundamentalism is based on a violent, homoerotic, self-abnegating father-son relationship, as we so clearly see in Atta's letter, or in bin Laden's poetic discourse with his fatherly God (quoted in Chapter 4). Speaking in psychoanalytic terms, *this relationship ultimately obtains between the fundamentalist and himself,* but it is obvious that group processes and internal dynamics combine in the production of fundamentalist coercion.

In fundamentalist worldviews, as expressed in the Islamic revolution in Iran in 1979, or in the Taliban rule in Afghanistan, or in all the futuristic visions of Islamic rule, the regime represents the divine power that rules over men, while men in turn, rule over women. Fundamentalist groups and regimes are marked by an obsession with controlling female sexuality, shaping gender relations, and banning women from any public positions of power.[21] Ibn Warraq compiles sayings from the Quran to the effect that women are regarded as profoundly inferior to men, infested with guile, deceit, envy, and moral backwardness. Women cannot be trusted and under no circumstance are they equal to men before the law. A virtuous woman is an obedient woman who satisfies her husband's needs.[22] In Islamist regimes or extremist groups, women's legal rights are curtailed, and so, to varying degrees, is their freedom of movement. Women are relegated mostly to domestic life; their most significant role being to increase the number of believers by bearing many children.

Having acknowledged this dynamic in Islamic society, for now I would like to focus on the oppression and control of men rather than of women in fundamentalist cultures and to inquire about the way fundamentalist power and control of men produce distinct forms of desire and sexuality. In such a world, erotic arousal and excitement (except brief sexual encounters meant to discharge immediate bodily needs) are often only marginally directed toward women or toward other men. Real excitement and passion are invested instead in God, who is conceived and experienced as a superior male commander father-figure.

Of course all this does not do justice to the finer distinctions among different fundamentalist formations, or even among individual fundamentalist men, but I still wish to make the point that by turning away from individualism and doubt, the fundamentalist mind pursues altered forms of desire. The fundamentalist loves and fanatically believes in divine, preordained Truth. This kind of love is far from being simply a love of God; rather it is full of reverence and fear, of a desire for a God who manifests Himself through absolute, unconditional demands. This desire is a kind of love that is marked by its dissociated tone and its secret, alienated intimacy. The psychodynamics of such love determine and shape its typically opposed elements of abject submissiveness and ecstatic glow. I call it vertical mystical homoeros.

Vertical Homoerotic Desire

Let us begin with a general observation. Religious men, particularly Jewish orthodox men as well as some Christian clergymen, are sometimes viewed as soft or "feminine,"[23] antiphallic, "refusing to be a man."[24] These men present themselves as having qualities such as gentleness, marked sensitivity, often a desire to be *en phase* with others, coupled with an impressive capacity to integrate and to express their sensory impressions. I have described how these men respond to ambiguous, complex situations with a certain freedom of inner movement and imaginativeness.[25]

On a deeper, less overt level, however, such men give a distinct impression of entitlement and superiority. In other words, behind the softness, the frequently impeccable manners, and the delicacy, there is a certain kind of submission-with-arrogance. Some of these religious men could appropriately be described as possessing a "hidden," vicarious, divine phallus. These men, I imagine, are engaged with a "vertically phallic eros," or a phallicism-by-proxy. One feels that such men think, "God is my rock, my strength. Why should I think anybody can hurt me, or even reach me?" In other words, God is the phallus of these men. They bear it inside themselves with a covert feeling of tremendous confidence, a kind of manic triumph, as the Kleinians call it. This stance is comparable and contrastable with the militant fundamentalists, who, in their experience, have not yet attained the feeling of having acquired God's phallus in a manner that is satisfying to them. What is common to these orthodox men and to religious fundamentalists, however, is a basic "vertical" axis of unequal and nonmutual relations. Fundamentalists thrive on this vertical relation; they entertain a "vertical" striving, a palpable, real desire for God.

My use of *verticality* is different from Heinz Kohut's "vertical split," with which it might be confused.[26] Unlike Kohut, I am referring not to a split in the personality but rather to a particular relation to an elevated entity, a subject who is perceived as inhabiting a categorically different, higher plane than the plane on which the individual situates himself and his peers. In his study of the group, Freud strongly distinguished between the ties of group members to each other and the tie of each member to the leader.[27] Certain groups, which Freud calls "primary groups," "put one and the same object in the place of their ego-ideal and have consequently identified themselves with one another in their ego."[28] The concept of verticality, as I use it here, is consistent with and a product of the structure of fundamentalism, which gathers men together in a group in which each identifies with the other and all identify with their common, vertically placed, superior ideal, an ideal that holds one set of religious teachings that contain the foundational, infallible truth about humanity and divinity.

Discourses on fundamentalism ordinarily stress its black-and-white cognitive style and the absolute certainty and self-justification that shapes its mindset. It has been said that fundamentalists do not want understanding, negotiation, compromise, or even dialogue. People and phenomena outside the fundamentalist "enclave" are "shorn of context and historical circumstances"; they are seen as transparent and a priori knowable,[29] at the same time as they are uniformly perceived as "not one of us." For the fundamentalist lens, nothing is opaque and truly puzzling, nothing needs further interpretation beyond the preestablished frame of reference. Within this narrowed mindset, there is nothing genuinely new under the sun; everything is self-evident and self-identical. Such a mode of thinking finds order and certainty, and creates a patterned, predictable worldview that offers feelings of safety and freedom from potentially self-eroding doubt. Fundamentalism provides a sense of mastery and pellucidity in the face of powerlessness and existential anxiety, in the face of the will of the other, even in the face of one's own will and desire.

By strictly following religious fundamentals, separating the good from the bad into clear and ordered categories, fundamentalism acts as a kind of mind control, providing a kind of soothing iron belt,[30] a shielding carapace to keep away the confusion and fragmentation that come from a weakened, brittle self. The inner weakness which is overcome derives from a looming sense of futility and failure, and from various resentments at contemporary culture,[31] whether experienced as rejecting and unattainable, corrupt and hateful, or frightening and predatory. To uprooted, frustrated, lost, envious, sometimes degraded persons, the group's construction of such a carapace seems the most natural, sure way to strengthen the threatened sense of self. The enclave, the boundary, the wall that separates good and bad, the faithful inside and those outside it, are vital components of this elaborate defense.

Islam, the Occident, and the New Manicheism

In the face of the two fears, fear of death and fear of being overwhelmed by other persons, religion offers protection against the dread of death by endowing life (and death) with meaning, and it offers protection against the other human by dividing and distributing people between co-religionists and nonbelievers, thus charting a more reassuring map of who is a friend and who is a foe. These two functions of religion play themselves out in the politico-religious agendas of fundamentalist movements. As to protection against mortality, "Fundamentalism is a religious dream, and the Hereafter is taken very seriously," writes Islamic scholar Johannes Jansen.[32] At the same time, a divide is created between truth seekers and decadents. Contemporary Islamic thinker Shaykh Abdalqabir as-Sufi,[33] alias Ian Dallas, elaborates the point, made by many other extremist Muslim thinkers, that the decadent West is in the same situation as were the pre-Islamic societies of ignorance and depravity (*jahiliyya*). In as-Sufi's view, the basis for the moral depravity of the West lies in the "failure to recognize that we are finite and limited beings, and that our physical, biological, and psychological reality is without hope unless we can have recourse to a transcendent reality. Authentic reality means a form of awareness."[34] Abdalhaqq Bewley offers an interesting narrative of how Christianity became increasingly corrupted after the Renaissance and Luther's Reformation.[35] The only response to this decline of the world, he says, is Islam, with its divine legislation and its provision of answers to every troubled area of human life. If it is to halt its own degradation, the world must turn back to God, and particularly, since Allah is the only God, to Islam. In these and similar writings, the two great aims of religion, assuaging fear and giving meaning, come together. As-Sufi's views share key themes with the writings of other modern Muslim fundamentalists, such as the Shiite Shariati or the Sunni Qutb.[36] They all condemn Western lack of awareness of our mortal condition and our human fragility, comparing it negatively with the legacy of Allah, a legacy that removes the pain of mortality and fragility for those who follow His rules. These writers decry how modern society pursues corrupt and distracting ideals as a way to deceive itself about human finitude and death.[37]

Religious scholar Karen Armstrong's study of the history of monotheistic fundamentalisms also illustrates the two motives of religion and fundamentalism we have named—the search for meaning and the avoid-ance of fear.[38] In her historical account, Armstrong first explains funda-mentalism as a quest for transcendence in a world that has become devoid of spiritual values, but then she gradually switches to portraying the fun-damentalist mind as above all tormented by danger and angst that can-not be assuaged by purely rational arguments. This interesting shift from positive meaning-giving and spiritual enhancement to negative apotro-paic protection, is significant. The attempt to curb a sense of persecution, escalating anxiety, and revulsion at the present state of affairs, and a sense of dread of the unknown and of the enmity of the world at large, perhaps more than the effort to give spiritual meaning to life, is what helps create fundamentalism.[39]

Submission, Verticality

The danger that is being propagated in the writings and broadcasts of the jihadists is conceived in the fundamentalist world differently from how it is seen from an outsider's perspective.[40] From within fundamen-talism, there is a sense of urgency regarding the moral and social decline from better times to the present situation of corruption and license, even, or especially, in relation to the fundamentalists' co-religionists. The dan-ger fundamentalists fear and warn against is that God's truth and righ-teous values will become eroded or forgotten and the world will sink into sin and chaos. To psychoanalytically minded outsiders, however, the dan-ger the fundamentalist mind evades has to do with annihilation anxiet-ies, weakness, and shame, as well as with the personal confusion (Erik Erikson called it "identity diffusion") that comes with sociogeographical dislocation and the differences and contradictions among cultures.[41] For the fundamentalist, combating the danger is what deepens his religious faith and supports his pride; for the nonfundamentalist, by contrast, it is precisely the endangered, combative cast that turns the sense of the sa-cred, the sense that the world is suffused with invisible meaningfulness,[42] into a dangerous fuel that stokes fundamentalist passion.

The shift from religious devotion to fundamentalism parallels the dete-rioration of the sacred into an alien, persecutory presence.[43] Whereas the religious sense of the sacred is the facing of the numinous and the sub-lime by letting oneself go and being open and receptive to a sense of deep meaningfulness and benign presence, fundamentalism is a sense of being held tight, enveloped by a comforting straitjacket. Notably, the sense of the sacred can involve the deity of a particular religion or can engage a more generalized sense of the numinous as the experience of transcendence and of ethical and spiritual meaningfulness. The sense of the sacred and transcendent is precious, and many of us would agree that life is poorer without it. Fundamentalism, however, is the self-rejecting submission to an ideal authority, a submission that finally, on psychoanalytic accounts, turns out to be subjugation to an alienated (because projected outside of oneself), horrifying aspect of oneself. This kind of submission promises great benefits to those who submit, namely, achieving not only safety in life but attaining an ostensibly far greater reward. Fatema Mernissi summarizes her researches into the Islamic history of thought by holding that *Islam gave the faithful the promise of immortality in exchange for total submission* to God.

> The Arabs (in Mohammed's time) were to become immortal. A great Beyond opened to them the royal road to the conquest of time. They would no longer die. Paradise awaited them. Because the child born of the womb of the woman is mortal, however, the law of paternity was instituted to screen off the uterus and woman's will within the sexual domain. . . . The new code of immortality was to be inscribed on the body of woman. Henceforth the children born of the uterus of a woman would belong to their father, and he is certain of gaining Paradise if he submits to the divine will.[44]

Thus, men are promised security until the end of time, at the price of total repudiation of women and total submission to God. While woman is a repulsive reminder of mortality and the finitude of the flesh, God is the promise of paradise and eternal life. Life and death become highly symbolized. Temporality, earthliness, feminine desire are all linked in the fundamentalist mind and must be obliterated. Devaluation of the present and a forcefully sustained hope for a glorious future is a hallmark of cults and totalitarian movements. In the fundamentalist world, desire for anything that is not divine is a dangerous subversive force. Islam promises peace at the price of the sacrifice of desire (*hawa*), which is considered in the Muslim community as the source of dissension and war. "Desire, which is individual by definition, is the opposite of *rahma* [grace, mercy], which is an intense sensitivity for the other . . . for the group."[45]

Nonearthly Vertical Desire

What Mernissi does not attend to, however, is the desire that grows and luxuriates on the stump of lopped off "earthly" desire. As Altmeyer and Hunsberger point out, "Those who espouse this ideology have a special relationship with the deities."[46]

It is this "special relationship" that is of interest to me here, since I assume that fundamentalism is not just strictness, rigidity, and literal adherence, but is suffused with a libidinal dimension of desire. For the fundamentalist, keeping the laws is a practice with a fourfold advantage: it is the Truth; it protects him; it gives him a special relationship; and it "marries" him vertically with superior perfection.[47] Verticalization of difference engenders vertical desire. On this view, the starkly opposing terms, the polarizations which suffuse fundamentalist thinking, come to assume higher and lower positions on a vertical axis. Such binary oppositions, which deconstructionism has shown to be characteristic of Western modernism, always strongly privilege one term of the binary opposition, which then dominates and controls the other term. Binarism, whether in feminism, race theory, or colonial theory, always results in creating a hierarchy of power. This applies to fundamentalism too. Inscribing inequality, *fundamentalism is not only a psychic mode of separation; it is also a psychic mode of inequality.*[48]

Within this mode, the black-and-white division creates a vertical ladder, on which the nonbeliever is profoundly unequal to the believer, man is eternally unequal to God, and woman is unquestionably unequal to man. When we think about fundamentalism, we tend to be aware of woman's inequality to man and the nonbeliever's inequality to the believer, but we tend to forget *the believer's inequality to God.* In fundamentalist regimes, God rules over men, while men rule over women. Being oppressed by God, oppressing women, *fundamentalism is an oppressed oppression.* Although so persistently present as to be invisible, so totalistically embraced as to be sacralized, this inequality generates a desire aimed at overcoming both the distinctions and the verticality. The striving to overcome verticality through mystical reunion and kill all obstacles to this trajectory can generate deep faith and powerful hope.

Certainty and fundamentalistic knowledge are linked to a desire that springs from the so-called verticalization of difference, whereby difference is scaled and graded perpendicularly. Whereas heterogeneity spreads and sprawls "horizontally," encompassing different kinds and species, difference in the fundamentalist order is sharply circumscribed. Cognitive simplification is the underside of archaic emotional intensity. In this vertical mode, there are purified, triumphant, superior believers, and puny, defiled, noxious nonbelievers. The exorbitant, absolute distance between the two, the extremes of exaltation and degradation, mark this verticality. It is the distance between self-loathing and adoration. Rather than the rebellious son fearing castration by the father and overcoming it,[49] what is at stake here is the subjection to a lethal ideal, a regression to the archaic phallic father. Such subjection involves more than a "castration," if by castration we mean the curtailment of vital assertion and individuation, immobilizing the fighting of "the father," the interrogating of ossified tradition, and overcoming the anxiety of transcending it. In other words, submission to the father involves more than a castration, since such submission effects wholesale investment of all of one's (and one's group's) energies in fighting *for* the father's sake, rather than fighting *the* father.[50] Such submission leads to a vicious circle whereby more weakness follows capitulation and capitulation becomes more desirable as the weakness and self-rejection increase. Eric Hoffer writes that "the revulsion from an unwanted self, and the impulse to forget it, mask it, slough it off and lose it, produce both a readiness to sacrifice the self and a willingness to dissolve it by losing one's individual distinctness in a compact collective whole."[51]

The transformation of abject self-hatred into exalted love occurs through a vertical mystical homoeros. It is an adoration, a "looking up to" an absolutely superior Being, who represents everything that is desirable. It is the striving to make oneself continuous with Him in a spiritual union that has all the ecstatic desire of sexuality. The woman below the fundamentalist is treated as a physical necessity while the God above us is transfigured into an infinity of longing. Desire can only be understood spiritually, between male substance (man) and male essence (God).

"Whereas the ego submits to the superego out of fear of punishment, it submits to the ego-ideal out of love," writes Freud.[52] Thus, at the core of variously structured fundamentalist groups, we find psychodynamic processes involving transformations of fear, hatred, and (notably) self-rejection into idealizing love. These projections and transformations of hate, and the idealization of a religious persecutory object, temporarily purchase respite from fears of destructiveness and inner persecution. Since what is involved is a thorough transformation of a persecutory object into a loving one, this process cannot but be profoundly paranoid and destructive.

The Fierce Struggle with Self-Hatred

Erez, my patient of long ago, a tempted but warring antifundamentalist, whose story will be told later, hated himself so much that he often felt he wanted to leap out of his skin, his body, his shape. He wanted to become a woman, or just "somebody else," at the same time as he was also terrified of being transformed by God into a "something else," a different creature, maybe a small animal. Erez's case was that of an extended act of liberation from his individual fundamentalism, so to speak. Erez's liberal cultural background (he did not grow up in a fundamentalist or even religious home), his prolific fantasy life, and his trust in the analytic process allowed him to liberate himself from the terrible inner tyrant by whom he was dominated. Erez's analysis provided a rare glimpse at "fundamentalism" as a process that begins with self-hatred and abjection, with the perception of oneself as being victimized and hence weak and ineffectual. Harsh rules and minute rituals are erected in an effort to steel oneself against the weakness and in order to get rid of one's sense of being bad in some way. At the same time, the obsessive rituals are not sufficient to ward off these affects, and an inner war is ignited between the feeling of being bad, a sinner, and the feeling of being wronged and humiliated, including the hate and compensatory aggression this arouses. As these struggles are going on, one's Inner Protector is still at work, assuaging miserable feelings of loneliness and the constant fear of predatory attacks. Coming to realize that the source of one's greatest fear is the very same entity that is supposed to be one's protector and sponsor is sometimes terribly difficult to achieve. I was fascinated and sometimes in awe of Erez's battle to become aware of this fact. Analysis enabled this person, who had entered analysis as an isolated, fantasy-ridden youth to gain a sense of being part of the human community through coming to enjoy "horizontal" human acceptance. Concomitantly, Erez became able to modulate his characterological violence, since our work made it possible for him to gain a sense that he was redeemable, that is, that his sins, including his violence, were not bad enough to weigh him down and rob him of his powers to challenge his persecutory inner self.

Walter Davis contributes to our understanding of the internal object—basically one's own creation—whose condemnation can demolish the person within whose psyche it dwells: "In depth destructiveness is what happens when a subjectivity defined by self-loathing finds in cruelty the only release through the free projection of all the hatred one feels toward oneself in one's inner world upon a host of objects. . . . Elation then beckons with the discovery of new targets, richer occasions, with but one proviso—the feast of aggression must never end."[53]

Davis sees humans' core anxiety as *the inability to reverse inner destructiveness*. From an opposite angle, Michael Eigen touches on the same central configuration by suggesting that self-hatred should be transformed and made psychically useful by our directing aggression against the self: "We keep ripping at what pains us. We take inner baths, try to clear away barriers. . . . Soul rubs and shines itself by immolation-demolition. . . . We must learn to kill ourselves without end without doing ourselves real injury. We may discover ways of 'killing' ourselves that make us better people."[54] Eigen talks about purification through ascetic self-castigation, which, he believes, can relieve the torturing experience of one's destructiveness and self-loathing. By beating oneself, one cleanses oneself of one's torturer; by flagellation of self-body, one becomes pure, one shines. The similarity between religious ascesis and fundamentalist purification rites is unmistakable; there is a continuity, though not an equivalence, between self-denial for the purpose of spiritual purification and destructive acts that are paradoxically aimed at crushing destructiveness, in those moments when, as Eigen says, "good deeds can no longer deflect destruction from oneself."[55] One then has to purify oneself in order to destroy the destroying other within oneself. Eigen equates cleansing parts of oneself with "killing" those parts. One kills those parts in order not to feel that one is bad, or weak, or despicable, or irredeemably fallible. The fantasy circulates that one is being purified as a way of dying in order to be reborn ("A new heart create for me, O God" prays the Psalmist). Such dying/killing preempts a more fantastic, terrible death, death as a final verdict on one's worthlessness. Although the dividing line between religious devotion and religious fundamentalism is crucial, the continuity between them becomes more visible the closer we look at them. There is a certain structural resemblance between the intimate, loving discourse a believer holds with God while praying and supplicating, and the intimacy that is acted out in fundamentalist desire.

In my clinical experience, I have witnessed many painful moments that I came to realize can be seen as the core, or at least one of the kernels, of the gravest human ills, namely self-loathing, or self-hatred, the disguised or direct searing, amplified recognition of the destructiveness within. A profound rejection of oneself, of one's very being, is synonymous with deep shame that is internalized and affirmed. After all, we internalize the ways we are treated by others and we treat ourselves in accordance with how we are being treated. Usually it is well into an analytic process before one encounters the inner sense of worthlessness, of self-condemnation and revulsion, and realizes the extent to which this sense impacts behaviors and feelings. Shame and self-rejection can be disguised by rage, by a compensatory sense of entitlement, by seductive charm, or by aggression and bravado. Intense shame is most often repressed, or dissociated, or denied in many other ways so as to protect self-esteem and prevent psychic catastrophe.[56] Sometimes the analyst gets a strong glimpse of these feelings at moments when she senses the patient's overt or hidden vulnerability, or recognizes the confused mixture of self-aggrandizement and self-deprecation. Some great narratives of protracted analyses with very damaged people wind up reaching the pit of self-hatred and self-persecution, which is where trauma worked to create the original wound and illness, and which is the site where work must be done for the person to heal.[57]

In clinical work, we see how states of self-loathing breed the worst kinds of illness and paralysis, eventuating in wasted lives and damaged bonds. The "self" in self-loathing refers to the self as that which is hated, hating all selves as selves and avidly seeking to submit to a transcendent collective that will swallow it and make it into a no-self, a fungible unit that has at last found peace of mind.

To further clarify these processes of purification and self-absolution, let me delineate their progression toward increasing destructiveness. In the next chapter, I wish to spell out stages of purification as the growing efforts at eliminating bad feelings about oneself, and to elaborate how religion can provide potent means toward accomplishing this procedure.

§3 Purification as Violence

There is a paradox at the center of religion. While it functions as a source of meaningfulness and spiritual inspiration, while it represents an institution that bases salvation on the doing of good, it can also be a notorious breeding ground for fundamentalist intransigence and may further deteriorate into coercive militant homicidal and suicidal violence. How are we to understand this paradoxical inclusion of goodness and murderousness? Why is religion so often associated with violence? Furthermore, why is sacrifice, a form of sacralized violence, accorded such a central role in religious traditions? After all, sacrifice, considered by many scholars as the foundational religious gesture, is killing that is surrounded by an aura of the holy. It is a destruction of life, whether of a human or an animal, that is meant to please God, to bring peace, or, in the case of Christ, to redeem humankind.

Most religions are permeated with images of cosmic war as the ongoing and perennial situation of the world, a war that is often believed to endure as long as the world does. The theme of a cosmic mythical war waged between two forces, good and evil, light and darkness, points to an irreconcilable conflict that has to be battled to the end. Battle, or conflict, is a crucial part of the human condition, whether the conflict obtains between groups of people, within a person's inner world, or between the joys and sorrow of life, its pleasures and its finitude. Since religion deals with the meaning of human existence, the conflicting aspects of life and the need to protect it, religion provides a powerful means of visually dramatizing these conflicts and of indicating courses of action to resolve them in a manner that seems clear and promises simplicity.

But all this is a general conception of how religion functions in relation to the human condition. I wish to focus on one conspicuous dimension of the relationship between religious faith and behavior, specifically behavior that becomes increasingly violent, and examine it in more detail. Psychoanalytic thinking characteristically highlights the continuities that underlie ostensible opposites by tracing the root similarities of these opposites. Thus it can inquire whether there is continuity between good and evil and what the nature of this continuity is. Inversely, a psychoanalytic way of thinking seeks to expose how apparently identical or similar phenomena can have different meanings. Differences in significance of overtly similar phenomena depend on the motives that are served by each particular event or circumstance—such as, for instance, the amount of psychic destruction or repair intended. What makes for differences is also the quality of the human relations involved, for example, if there is compassionate relating or narcissistic use of the other. To continue our specific example, how good is "good"? Are there qualitative differences between different kinds of "goodness"? Often the difference is not obvious to the doer: people who perpetrate evil, particularly on a large scale, are convinced that they are doing good deeds and usually act out of a deep, often loving sense of devotion to a "noble" cause. Collective evildoers often believe that they are accomplishing benevolent acts: they are saving Germany from the lethal parasites breeding on its body, they are bringing about the revolution that will liberate mankind, they are redeeming the Promised Land from its heathen inhabitants, they are helping God's Kingdom to reign on earth, or they make mankind submit to Allah's will. It seems that the differences between "good" and "evil" cannot be unanimously and transhistorically adjudicated. To make things clearer, I propose we trace a trajectory where good can turn into evil. Key here will be the concept of purification.

Purification and Its Progression

The Good occupies a central position in religion, since religion guarantees salvation through the doing of good as decreed by God. Doing Allah's will and thereby satisfying Him, is the thread running through the utterances of Islamic extremists. We know that doing good, in religious parlance, is often synonymous with fighting the bad, which can have different faces. The bad can be seen as equivalent to diabolic temptation, it can appear as human hubris that seeks to appropriate godly power, as heretical skepticism about benevolent divine intentions, or as the loss of one's connection to God. The conflict between adherence to religious precepts and giving in to temptation to disobey, but also to pursue rageful, hateful feelings and actions, is portrayed in religious language as the war between good and evil. Most religions encompass elaborate foundational myths of war between Good and Evil, Light and Darkness. Religious lore is laced with narratives of temptations, hardships and battles saintly heroes have withstood that serve as inspiration and sources for emulation.

In the history of Islamic thought, there have been some serious attempts to articulate and explain jihad as an inner struggle against the baser elements of the self. The jihad (struggle) on a personal, ethical level, is conceived as the constant war with oneself against an internal enemy in the effort to shape and improve oneself, somewhat as Michael Eigen describes in the last chapter. This is *jihad-al-nafs*, the war with the self (*nafs*), which involves cultivating virtue, refining one's character, even creating oneself, in the sense of developing strength and courage and taming and moderating one's natural dispositions and character traits. These conceptions are found, for example, in the teachings of Abu Hamid Muhammad al-Ghazali (1058–1111), an Islamic theologian, philosopher, and Sufi mystic. Al-Ghazali wrote about the self (or character), the reasons for its fulfillment and suffering, and about taming and domesticating it through the will and through spiritual exercise so as to channel it toward a more balanced psyche. Some of the phrases in Atta's letter regarding the taming of the self and calling it to obey bear strong resonances with the al-Ghazalian tradition of striving to cultivate a positive character.

The all-too-human, impressionable soul (*nafs*) is softly spoken to, in an attempt to "convince it."[1] As Atta wrote, "Remind your soul [*nafs*] to listen and obey [all divine orders] and remember that you will face decisive situations that might prevent you from 100 percent obedience, so tame your soul, purify it, convince it, make it understand, and incite it." It is plausible to assume that the war between good and evil is an externalized expression of the psychic conflict between a sense of inner badness that causes a sense of inadequacy, guilt, shame, even self-loathing, and the wish to be good and to have a good internal object (a good inner representation of another being) for the sake of whom one is doing the right thing. The sense of goodness can be attained through the erasure of inner badness by purifying oneself from defilement and sin. In group terms, the community is purged of evil through the aid of certain practices and rituals. Practically every religion, whether pagan or monotheistic, is replete with motifs of spiritual purification, modeled after the cleansing of bodily dirt. The purificatory endeavor to exclude the profane and, more broadly, to effect "a new beginning on a loftier spiritual level,"[2] often translates into a sequence of increasing efforts to prevent the degradation of cherished ideals into sinful thoughts and acts.[3]

But what actually occurs in the course of these efforts can often be the degradation of these spiritual states of mind into acts of violence. Why this degradation? How does the intention to do good and to act righteously turn into bloody violence? And more specifically, how do transitions occur from religious faith to fundamentalist adherence and from quietist fundamentalism to its violent aspect, militant, religious terrorism?

Assuming the continuity between religious faith and fundamentalism and between fundamentalism and religious terrorism, we can track the degradation of good intentions into violence and evil by following the path of escalating processes of *purification*. Let us begin with two simple assumptions. Behind the procedures that bring about the transformation of the good into the murderous, lies the basic human belief that it is good to fight evil, and further, that doing the good means eliminating the bad. However, under certain circumstances, the action of protecting the good may become monstrously proliferative and perverted, extending concentrically into ever greater spheres of violence, which, however, will be perceived as being in the service of the good; it will be seen as "holy violence" as opposed to "forbidden violence."[4] When this happens, stages of escalating violence succeed each other, always with the idea that it is good to fight evil and hence to eliminate everything and everyone who represents evil. When such belief is seen as ratified by a divine command and when it is supported by processes of group dynamics and mind control ("brainwashing"), the ground is ready for massive carnage.

Rituals and Taboos

Rituals and spiritual practices are prescribed routines that characteristically involve scripted gestures or phrases, or certain objects or movements, designed to influence the deity on behalf of the performer's interests and beliefs. In order for rituals to have power, the performer must believe and participate. Belief transforms the ritual from an empty, gratuitous behavior to a highly meaningful event, and participation adds a layer of personal meaning to that event. Ernst Cassirer describes how in "primitive" times, the sense of danger and dread coming from unfathomable outer forces produced taboos as demarcations against these impersonal powers so as not to be controlled and contaminated by them.[5] He describes how more advanced religions could not rid themselves of these primordial taboos, but instead incorporated them into their systems by superimposing on them a positive sense of inspiration and adoration for a sympathetic, positive deity. Rituals are ways of establishing contact between the human and the superhuman: "a strict and elaborate ritual regulates this cooperation," writes Cassirer.[6] On a different level, rituals are ways to shape and channel human wishes, fantasies, and conflicts in such a way that relief and psychic integration are provided by the learning and internalization of the child of his culture's rituals, and later, by the social participation of the adult. The emotional experience provided by the rituals lends vividness and conviction to the feelings and fantasies stirring within. Laws of purity and impurity are legislated in all societies and religions to impose order and to keep things within their proper bounds. Under the aegis of such laws, the group maintains its cohesion and thereby its survival, protecting human life from rampant violence and social chaos. At the same time, it offers each individual in the society a sense of closure and relief at having their personal tensions responded to through the language and shaping power of the ritual. Religious and cultural rituals customarily use concrete materials, tools, and places to express and validate symbolic meanings and events. Religious purificatory rituals make use of *concrete* cleansing materials, such as water or fire, in the service of *symbolic* purification. Cicero ruled that "the means of getting rid of the evil effects of contagion . . . are usually by water or fire."[7] Islamic scholar Annemarie Schimmel details the different means by which purification can be attained in Islam. Ablutions are indicated as a frequent practice, as we can see in Atta's letter. When water is absent (as in desert regions), sand replaces it. Fire, however, is an even more radical and formidable cleansing agent than water. Because of its consuming power, fire in its various ritual manifestations is considered as bringing about the elevated status that is attained when the baseness of the soul is burned away. The biblical burning of sacrifices, the Christian purgatory, the Holy Inquisition, the burning of "witches," and Muslim fire-walking for women suspected of adultery, all testify to the extraordinary power accorded to fire as a cleanser. "Purification," writes Schimmel, "is a central Islamic tradition, based essentially on the Divine order of the Prophet: 'And your garments, purify them.'"[8]

The 9/11 terrorists were instructed to perform numerous ablutions in preparation for the attacks, only to reach the endgame in which they launched a fiery "new beginning on a loftier spiritual level," as Schimmel puts it, by burning. Notably, impurity is not equal to dirt. In *Purity and Danger*, Mary Douglas analyzes the anthropological dimensions of purification and defilement, contextualizing purity and impurity in terms of the body and society.[9] She regards the body and what is tabooed or permitted in it as symbolizing society and its parts, by way of analogical, magical thought, whereby one system represents or corresponds to another. Purification ostensibly refers to the cleansing of dirt, but there is no absolute dirt, since dirt is always dirt within a system or a specific context. What qualifies as dirt within one system will not be dirt in another (body excretions are a prime example of substances that are dirt the moment they leave the body); dirt exists in the eye of the beholder. For Douglas dirt means disorder and offence against order, and rituals of purity and impurity "create unity in experience."[10] Obviously *dirt* in the context of spiritual purity is symbolic, and uncleanliness within religious or cultural systems is "that which must not be included if a pattern is to be maintained."[11] When a group is threatened, or when an individual is decreed impure, a set of purificatory processes is set in motion that is designed to reestablish order and safety. As we learn in the Book of Numbers in the Old Testament, the Israelites were organized in different concentric "camps" that separated the central, purest segment of the tribes from the less pure, and further, from the impure—the lepers and the otherwise maimed.[12] As was the case with the plague in Thebes, it was believed that separation of the pure from the impure, or the removal of the offensive unclean element will restore cohesiveness and inner peace.

Protecting Goodness: Self-Maintenance

There is a profound psychological necessity in human affairs of safeguarding a sense of a viable and valuable self-identity, whether group or individual identity. More specifically, there is a need to deal with notions of death and the annihilation of self-identity and self-esteem that are involved in facing death's inevitability. These necessities create the need to make use of culturally and religiously sanctioned apotropaic rituals to exert control over these fears. Thus, seen from the vantage point of the practitioners, purification is the quest for purity and impeccability; seen from a psychological-structural perspective, however, purification constitutes an elemental process of separation and splitting into external and internal, good and bad, pure and polluted. Psychoanalysis studies processes of separation and splitting of segments of the psyche as ways to keep psychic balance, including one's relation to reality and to others, while protecting one's basic optimism and self-esteem. As I have written elsewhere,[13] in psychic life we function in a dialectical relationship between contacting and articulating our emotions and sparing ourselves from their harmful potential. We strive to feel good about ourselves, about who we are and what we do, and we use various ideals, defenses, and compensatory rituals to transform experiences such as shame, loss, helplessness, hatred, and self-hatred (that is, the sense of inner badness) into ideas through which we explain to ourselves why we did not intend to do bad, that it was the other who was wrong, that our mistakes were actually beneficial—in short, that we are good after all. We constantly parley a balance between a lucid assessment of the situation we are in and turning a blind eye to this assessment when we have reached the limits of our capacity to take in reality. Such negotiation means a constant balancing, a weighing operation, a gyroscopic steering between what can be described as inner goodness, that which must be cherished and protected, and inner badness that needs to be expelled so that it may be declared as outer badness. The war between good and evil is thus an externalization of the inner struggle between taking oneself to be good, and deeming oneself bad or undeserving. On a more integrated level, the struggle is waged between embracing flawed life and our faulty self in tandem with maintaining a sense of goodness of self and world, and, alternatively, remaining obsessively and bitterly preoccupied with insult and self-loathing, and with despair over death and finitude.[14]

The religious realm has powerful and simplifying means of expressing these conflicts, since religion dispenses a colorful narrative vocabulary that is designed to express human conflict and suffering in terms of good and bad. Religion also incorporates a profound capacity for symbolic ways of dealing with limitations and of transcending the dread and insult such limitations incur. Most poignant, religion promises to deliver spiritual redemption as a way to leave behind abjection and terror. But religion does not only function symbolically; rather, it is two-directional: material concerns become symbolic and symbolic sublimations may again become all-too-concrete. En route to symbolic transformations, the war between feeling good and feeling bad about oneself is expressed in mythical terms—the War between Good and Evil. Since, however, religious notions move between the literal and the metaphoric, this inner struggle, a jihad in the sense of a personal spiritual struggle, is liable to become concretized again.[15] Within a group of like-minded believers who have become religious activists, spiritual jihad becomes concrete, coalescing into a bellicose religious dogma.[16] When finally the jihad is waged against nonbelievers, it explodes into a full-fledged holy war that aims at purging the world, in God's name, of humans who have different beliefs.

The foregoing process is a fascinating and enormous theme that can only be touched upon here. A sustained study is needed of these transformations, possibly to be undertaken by cultural and psychoanalytic scholars. In any case, what seems to have gone unrecognized in the understanding of these processes of reification is the crucial part played by *purification*, the striving to triumph over and destroy disorder and earthliness as a means to attain perfection and infallibility, rephrased in this context as "purity." An analysis of the basic actions of purification reveals a process that can be broken down into three schematic stages:

1. Cleansing oneself of impurity, becoming pure through separation of goodness and badness and through reinforcing one's good deeds.

2. Assuring purity by the elimination of badness through bolstering inerrancy and the giving up choice.

3. Assuring purity through vehement action. Achievement of the good through death.

Religious rituals are attempts to separate good and evil to ensure God's protection of the righteous and the good within a stable sanctum, unassaulted and uncontaminated by evil and impurity. In this sense, religious rituals are an expression of the normal necessity of safeguarding goodness, love, and whatever is most cherished against harm and corruption. Rituals create meaning and order. They are creative, symbolic, meaning-conferring and unity-offering acts that help express, symbolize, and memorialize a common cultural heritage and central life events of the group, as well as love for ideals and commitment to future visions. Purificatory rituals help attain a peaceful state of mind. Acts such as ritual bathing and ablutions, water sprinkling and sweeping, prayer and fasting, removal of excremental symbols (body secretions such as blood, semen, urine, and feces), circumcision, and the like all function to symbolically segregate the good from the bad so as to safeguard the former.

When these practices fail to offer a sense of security and protection, proving inadequate against defilement and danger, when the sense of alarm and peril lingers, and particularly when the social context provides a fitting framework, a second stage is entered.[17] This is the stage of fundamentalism, that is, of a more strenuous effort to protect oneself against doubt and danger. This stage involves increasingly rigid rituals and more determined actions, resorted to in an effort to more forcefully and irrevocably eliminate badness in oneself or in one's community. Now the concretization of symbolic, metaphorical ideas is further developed. At this point, some device has to be established that will permanently (or at least more powerfully) prevent the return of the Bad and its infiltration into the realm of the Good. Warranties are sought against uncertainty, ambiguity, and inner ambivalence, that is, against all liabilities that can make the boundaries between right and wrong, good and bad more porous. Badness is now actively and meticulously distanced from and polarized with Goodness.

Although there is a world of difference between the quietist, isolationist forms of fundamentalism and its coercive, militant varieties, psychoanalytically speaking they are both motivated by the need to simplify the relation between goodness and badness and by the need to eliminate badness—realized in errancy, betrayal of the divine, faintness of heart, loss of faith in God's goodness—through fighting the bad outside of oneself. Fundamentalists, as empirical research has shown,[18] carry deep discontent regarding the present state of the world as it compares to a pure, golden, idealized past. They resort to this good past, in an attempt to recapture it, by adhering to fundamentalist, archaic ways of life, as do the Mormons or some quietist Jewish Haredim.[19]

But sometimes this utopian past is sought not by ritual but by brute force. The more force that is employed for the purification of the world (and by implication for the purification of the self), the more violent the fundamentalist mindset. What is felt to be required now is to take action to eliminate the heretical, impure, inimical elements. The symbolic, culturally mediated practices that aim at differentiating collective good from badness and corruption is now de-metaphorized and concretized. Eliminating the bad means attacking its ostensible manifestations, such as corrupt non-Islamic governments, or non-Muslims who are regarded as attacking Islam, or critics of radical Islam who are considered apostates. Eliminating the bad is now expressed by eliminating—or killing—the infidels who do not believe in Allah. Launching into holy (cleansing) wars is as a rule preceded by preparations in which one purifies oneself ahead of the battle.[20] Further down the line, body ablutions and baths are joined by cleansing through fire. Thus, in Atta's letter the terrorists are instructed to wash and shave their bodies since as long as they perform the ablutions the angels will ask for forgiveness on their behalf and pray for them. But the bodily ablutions prescribed in the letter were famously followed by fire. As we have seen, fire is considered by most religions as a cleansing agent that removes all "dirt." The Inquisition offered death on the stake for repented heretics as an act of mercy that constituted an improvement over hanging or killing by the sword, since fire was regarded as a purifying means to forgiveness. Suicidal terrorism produces flames in which sinner and martyr are consumed together. Violence by fire is conceived by many religious leaders (whether Islamic extremist, Christian militant, or Jewish fanatical) not only as a means of purification but also as a way to heal humiliation and restore dignity and masculinity. The act of burning brings about the merging with God, consummating the eliminatory cleansing stages of religious purification.

With this fusion in fire, we have reached the third stage in the process of purification-as-separation-of-good-and-bad. This third and ultimate stage of increasingly violent purification is instantiated in suicide killings, and it is this stage that may be, psychoanalytically speaking, the most intriguing. Here the killing of oneself creates a self-destructive counterpart to the killing of "God's enemies." We are now no longer in the realm of the simple splitting of good and bad; instead we witness the mechanism of purification as the effort to oust repudiated, unwanted, hated parts of oneself. *The longing to repair oneself through killing oneself* is one of the deeper meanings of martyrdom and self-annihilation. When the repressed feelings of badness cannot be entirely redeemed through the purifying killing of others who projectively harbor one's own badness, the badness returns to haunt the subject's experience anew. This is the famous "return of the repressed": what has been repressed and suppressed, namely, self-hatred and the so-called death drive, reenters the psychic scene. The total failure—or total grim success—of purification is brought about when the self becomes annihilated in the process of purification. One purifies oneself to death, out of existence, and one purifies the world through massive elimination of its impure human elements.[21]

Tracing the sequence of escalating purification, we make the startling discovery that both the evacuation of the bad and the attainment of the good conclude, if taken to extremes, in death. Death is a final solution and an arch-answer to the refusal to embrace life and its limits. Finding themselves estranged in their host countries, no longer in their native lands, the 9/11 terrorists were called upon to form a special unit of superior holy warriors behind deceptive secular appearances. This appellation gave them a powerful means for refusing their existential situation and for exiting their devalued present into a purgatorial procedure that promised them a pure future by immolating themselves and their enemies on the altar of the superhuman. Rather than the end of existence and sentience, death became the threshold to a new, purer, worthier life.

At this extreme stage of the religious process of purification, the attempt to magically terminate suffering and feelings of badness about oneself, to exterminate defilement and infidelity, leads to one's annihilation together with the killing of others, as if the boundary between life and death, self and other, has been obliterated by the destruction of all materiality. Notable is the experiential quality of such mastery over death: a jubilation that is supported by cultural enticements and pressures, such as the encouragement and valorization of friends, leaders, and (in the case of Palestinian suicide bombers, but not Islamic suicide bombers who live in Western countries) family. Purification often comes with a sense of the loss of one's individual boundaries. Whereas Islamic extremism luxuriates on intense religious preaching of hatred of the West, the empowerment this hatred affords is different from the power that comes with the dazed exhilaration and joy that accompanies the dissolution of one's individual boundaries in self-purification.[22] The perennial desire many persons feel to rise above the body, through spiritual, mental, or artistic means, enriches life and gives it deeper meaning. But in the psychological process of projecting the bad parts of the self on the infidels and the idealized parts of the self on God, nothing is left. The splitting of sublime immateriality and base badness is complete, and the remaining body of the terrorist has thereby ceased to exist. Unconsciously, the terrorist's physical body has already ceased to exist earlier, since his body with its needs and desires has become superfluous.

Like a pencil that is reduced to nothing by continual sharpening, the terrorist's body will find its redemption by becoming a pure instrument of God's will, eventually merging with God in a cataclysm of purifying fire. Becoming ashes—passing from the organic to the inorganic in the quest for passing from the human to the superhuman—is the ultimate act of purification and spiritualization. There is no more flesh and no more desire of the flesh to defile one's self-image. The desire for God has been given its most extreme and loving due.

The link between purification and violence is complex and double-edged. The purity of Dostoyevsky's Alyosha in *The Brothers Karamazov*, the purity of some true saints, is a generosity and goodness that is the opposite of violence. Overcoming baseness and meanness in oneself is a serious and splendid matter (and occasionally a by-product of a good analysis, or of some spiritual practices). But the power of purificatory practices to lessen violence while enhancing compassion and goodness can obscure their application as tools for promoting violence. Religion, often a response to fear and dread, subdues violence that is the result of fear,[23] fear of death, fear of finite existence, fear of the body whose inexorable decay makes us mortal, and fear of the mortification, humiliation, and dependency that our fellow humans arouse in us. Fear breeds violence. Panic makes human beings contract and hide, or it makes them strike back. Through ritual sacrifice and other means, religion helps regulate violence by attempting to magically and ceremoniously expel it. But religion can become perverted—showing its other face—once the sacred sacrificial violence it preaches (against animals or other humans) can no longer contain and avert indiscriminate violence. The more perverted the use of religion, the harsher and more violent the means it seizes to control violence. By spiritualizing violence, religious practices serve as powerful mediators in the links between human destructiveness and the awareness of the violence of finitude. In other words, religion is a formidable attempt to help humans come to terms with their finitude through enacting it and denying it at the same time. René Girard conceives of religion as "that obscurity that surrounds man's efforts to defend himself by curative or preventative means against his own violence. . . . This obscurity coincides with the transcendent effectiveness of a violence that is holy, legal, and legitimate, as opposed to a violence that is unjust, illegal, and illegitimate."[24] The obscurity that Girard points to, the secret hidden since the dawn of human history, as he puts it, involves the recognition that there are ways to make violence holy, legal, and legitimate, to use "holy" violence to ostensibly oppose a violence that is unjust, illegal, and criminal. This type of (primitive) thinking uses controllable and divinely sanctioned violence as a weapon for fighting the "natural"—intentional and nonintentional—forms of violence with which we are surrounded. Subtending this magical thinking is a primitive "homeopathic" theorem which postulates that only violence can cure violence—on the condition that this violence be sanctified. According to this logic, if one applies "good" or "preventive" or "sacred" violence—in the form of sacrifice, scapegoating, symbolic or focused violence—one can preempt uncontrollable, proliferating violence within one's community and within oneself. Only by opting for a sanctified, legitimate form of violence and preventing it from itself becoming an object of disputes and recriminations, can a society save itself from the vicious circle of violence avenged by further violence, which is then in its turn avenged, in an endless spiral of violence, which is the ineluctable lot of primitive man and some modern societies and countries.[25] This magical homeopathic device can be said to constitute the means through which religion protects us from "big" violence by violently ejecting its negative agent outside itself, even as it keeps hosting violence right in its midst. Alas, this attempt often fails miserably.

Satisfying God: God's Orgasms

God's satisfaction may be pursued with devoted excitement to an extent that it may invoke the unconscious fantasy of procuring orgasmic satisfaction for the deity, where the explosions and deaths phantasmatically stand for God's orgasms of pleasurable destruction. The planners and executioners of the destruction of the World Trade Center must have visualized and revisualized the scene that was going to erupt. Did it occur to them that the grandiose shattering, the infernos that were to spring up from the Twin Towers would be a most satisfying godly cataclysm? Or did they consciously think only of their dedication to God and their triumph over their enemies? Could the spectacular prevision in the mind of an enthralled God's son-servant imaginatively represent and stage God's fiery orgasms, God's "satisfaction," a kind of divine *jouissance* materialized? Is this scenic turmoil a staging of imagined pleasure for the divine father that is procured by his son(s)? What is the context and backdrop of such a relation between father and son?

§4 Regression to the Father

Clinical Narratives and Theoretical Reflections

Notions of a phallic, "primal" father have curiously not received much attention in psychoanalysis in comparison to the figure of the phallic mother. The figure of the father who withholds himself condescendingly from his son's plea for closeness, or of the father who looms threateningly over his intimidated son, has been invariably displaced onto explanations that put the onus on a seductive, invasive, engulfing, phallic-narcissistic mother—never on the father himself. Could it be that the notion of father-fusion as the desire to merge with the archaic father imago arouses too deep a dread to contemplate? The tendency to equate any regressive phenomenon, in fact the equation of regression *tout court*, with a "return" to the mother, but never a "return" to the maternal father, speaks to this possibility. The fact that there is hardly a vocabulary for this father-son constellation likewise indicates the existence of a gap in thinking about it. It seems that Freud remained unanswered to in his singular obsession with a primal, archaic father; and this theme has not been adequately picked up by later thinkers, so that it gradually faded into the margins. Is it possible that the avoidance of thinking this figure is linked with where this line of thinking would lead us, namely that male aggression is at bottom masochistic?

Many and diverse psychic phenomena cohere around father-son relations. Important work has been done by analysts such as Abelin, Burlingham, Bloss, Herzog, and Pruett concerning the role and the importance of the father in the child's development.[1] Most psychoanalytic thinking about the father focuses on the importance of the father's *presence* and on the his provision of developmental needs for the child, as well as the traumatogenic impact of the father's *absence*. A good and vital early father is posited, who is loved by his son. Several psychoanalytic writers,[2] making a strong case for the need to study the child's pre-Oedipal dyadic father, focus on notions of a loving, needed, enlivening, and empowering father, emphasizing his facilitative, identification-enhancing role. One could say that this benevolent fatherly figure is a developmentally normative, downsized, "secular" version of the internalized archaic object I am discussing here. Contemporary psychoanalysis addresses a domestic attachment-father, rather than the mythopoetic figure that is bestowed with sacred or quasi-divine qualities, and that looms large not only in the individual's inner world but also in social and cultural domains.

Compared to the mother as an internal object and a major figure with her own specific characteristics and modes of relating, little has been written about the father as an internal object. The "phallic mother" is a mainstay of many psychoanalytic theories,[3] in which this fantasy serves as an anchor for archaic fears (e.g., castration anxiety), as well as for purposes of defense and as the basis of perversion. In contrast, the figure of the archaic, primal, or "phallic" father has scarcely been touched upon. The prevalent trend in psychoanalysis has been, on the contrary, to attenuate the father's authoritarianism and ferocity. Thus, Peter Blos criticizes the accounts of the Oedipal father as one who threatens and punishes the boy's competitive strivings and his patricidal and incestuous passions. Blos stresses the importance of "the early experience of being protected by a strong father and caringly loved by him."[4]

On the cultural level, the father has been conceived as a lawgiver,[5] as well as a liberator and facilitator of desire and ambition.[6] The father's role is widely and traditionally conceptualized as that of creating an escape from the mother-infant orbit (sometimes called "merger," "symbiosis," "the Imaginary," or "regression") into the outer world, reality, language, the symbolic order, and the law. We note that even this cultural, symbolic role tends to be regarded as overwhelmingly positive, exemplary, respectable, embellished with a majestic tinge. Again, aside from Freud, very few (and very disparate) writers such as Lacan, Kohut, and Benjamin, address the themes of the father's power and threat, and the corresponding needs on the son's part for submission to authority as a means of both securing power for himself and escaping the father's (fantasized or real) destructiveness, occasionally through violence.[7] That these aspects of the fatherly figure and the corresponding aspects in the son have been ignored should give us pause. Looking more closely at them may contribute toward resolving the puzzle by tying together seemingly disparate phenomena that reveal themselves to possess similar underlying structures.

In Freud's essay "The Ego and the Id,"[8] where he postulates the structural theory, he recognizes the subversive power of unconscious guilt that subtends the ego. With time and with analytic experience, it became patently visible to Freud that the ego is not the transparent and all-conscious, self-same, and integrative structure it was taken to be, a psychic kernel progressing linearly through paternal identification into symbolic internalizations, accompanied by identification with the law, making it one's own. On the contrary, Freud became convinced that the ego itself harbors parts that make it deeply (unconsciously) guilty, occasionally even abject, craving its ideal's affirmation, or its "superego's" love.[9]

How "Father Regression" Was Conceived

In Chapter 1 I described my surprise on reading the letter that was found in Mohammad Atta's luggage after the 9/11 attacks, and seeing that far from being a manifesto of hate speech, vociferously inciting its addressees to kill, it was a love letter. The tone was that of serenity and exalted adoration, suffused with a joyous expectation of an imminent sublime event. The dawning understanding that behind the most horrific suicidal terrorism lies a desire for sacrifice and self-sacrifice to a fatherly figure was unsettling. When I began writing and speaking about Atta's letter and its implications, I further realized that the elemental posture of the believer supplicating God is applicable to an equal degree to the Psalmist murmuring his trust in God who protects him against his hunters,[10] to Jesus on the Cross melting into his Father—and to bin Laden in his complaint to his fatherly God.

Following this discovery, Erez, the patient I discussed in Chapter 2, came to mind, now wrapped with a new and sudden understanding of the meaning of one of his transferences onto me, a transference that I had found persistently enigmatic during the years of his analysis. Later, other patients of mine, with much less severe pathology than this young man, joined the picture. With all the differences between them there was still, I could see now, an unmistakable common theme, a thread which ran through these different cases and those of the terrorists. To the religious terrorist and the biblical/liturgical son who submit to their divine father,

I now added another pair: the patient who had wanted to be a woman in order to submit to his persecutor and the powerful men who had accepted their fathers' frailty with love, bonding with them in a role-reversal of power, but still adoring their fathers. New understandings of patterns of submission to and enthrallment with paternal authority presented themselves across different personality profiles. The devout believer who appeals to God while immersed in profound spirituality; my patients—sons who trusted and loved their fathers and dismissed women; my other patient, who had to kill the ghost of his physically dead father so as not to be afraid to be a man; and the religious terrorist who seeks to merge with God through cataclysms of murder—all had something in common. As disparate and even contradictory as all these different "sons" truly are, they all share (to a greater or lesser degree) a certain psychodynamic constellation. The profiles of these people are as different as can be, and there are vast differences in personality levels, qualities of identification, and states of psychic cohesion between men who are excessively attached to their nurturing fathers and reject closeness with mother, and religious terrorists who are paranoically fused with an exalted tyrannical inner presence and regard women as irredeemably impure, and there is a difference between these two cases and a man's deep filial faith in God. But the similarities between them are illuminating.

The Archaic Father

Rather than the concrete biological and personal father,[11] this inner fatherly presence is an entity which I choose not to define sharply, so as to be better able to illuminate its thrust and shape. We could call it, with Lacan,[12] the "imaginary" father, the prototype of God-figures in religion, who is the terrifying father of the primal horde and an agent of privation at the same time as he can be an omnipotent protector; or we could speak of a father "imago," in Jung's terminology. We can discern the outline of this father in Freud's group leader, the *Urvater* of the primal horde, in the patriarchal (monotheistic, fundamentalist) version of the Judeo-Christian-Islamic God; or in Lacan's Big Other. All of these are diverse psychoanalytic conceptions of a powerful, idolized, impervious entity who promises protection and metes out punishment. Such an archaic figure has unmistakable affinities with the archaic perverse superego, which comes to resemble the id. As we know, id and superego are dialectically

related terms.[13] Primitive superego and id can be metaphors for unbri-
dled, ruthless impulses (whether of cruel purity or of lust and greed). The
cruelty and righteousness of the superego resonates with the unscrupu-
lousness of unreined id appetites.[14] Literary and artistic versions of this
persecutory "paternal" figure can be found outside of psychoanalysis as
well: in the mythically cruel, arbitrary, blood-thirsty Creator in Lautréamont's *Chants de Maldoror*, where a cannibalistic God eats his created
human beings, who swim in a pond of blood;[15] or in Chronos, who can-
nibalized his sons, portrayed in Goya's mural *Saturn Devouring His Son*.
This imago inheres also in the father who calls his sons to kill and sacrifice
themselves and others.

As mentioned, I am talking about a certain, mostly unconscious, paternal representation, which immediately calls for explanation about the
presence of the "father" in the son's unconscious (without having recourse
to the obsolete idea of phylogenetic legacy). To Jürgen Reeder, as to David
Lee Miller, the "Father" is a male figure conceived as residing outside of
any symbolic order, and "to whom all is allowed, since his only law is his
own desire . . . and his pleasure is limitless." This is a father imago "who
brings dread and chaos to all and everyone he comes near, for he is not
touched by the requirement that we show care toward our fellow beings
and the world we have created. Uncastrated, he is . . . not encompassed
by oedipal guilt, with its imperatives concerning love, creative work, and
procreation."[16] The "uncastrated man," writes Reeder, is the relative of the
primal father in Freud's *Totem and Taboo*.[17]

There is a brilliant psychoanalytic logic in Freud's *Totem and Taboo*.[18]
One day, the sons of the archaic father, a cruel tyrant who possessed all
the women and harshly oppressed his sons, bonded against him and
killed him. So goes Freud's narrative. When the pseudohistorical cast of
this story is read as a myth and acquires symbolic value, it translates into
a deep insight. Recognizing that one has to "kill the father" in the sense
of individuating and growing away from a tyrannical, totalizing ur-force,
from the allure that slavery holds for humans, is equivalent to achieving
a lucid perception of this kind of "father" that is won by tempering one's
need to idealize such a figure. Furthermore, recognizing the pain and even
damage inflicted on a parental figure is akin to Melanie Klein's depressive position (that is, in Kleinian language, "depressive" rather than "paranoid-schizoid guilt"), with the added poignancy that accrues from the
knowledge that the pain and damage that comes with separation *had* to

be inflicted. A complex dialectic ensues, that of killing yet keeping alive, preserving yet changing tradition, respecting time-honored values yet straining to free oneself from tutelage and subjugation to entrenched customs. The guilt that is thereby produced calls for some creative resolution.

The guilt over the killing of the father, says Lacan, has to be understood as symbolic, rather than as a personal feeling, conscious or unconscious. In Hebrew, "guilt" means both culpability and being indebted. Lacanian symbolic guilt is indebtedness. Being guilty is to stand in a position of obligation and indebted duty. Therefore "inherited guilt," to be repeated by each generation through the son's wish to have his father out of the way, is a considerably more effective force for regulating human transactions than the violence exerted by the primal father: 'men have always known . . . that they once possessed a primal father and killed him.'"[19] After the brothers realized they had killed their father, Freud tells us in this legend, the loving side of their ambivalence came to the fore and reasserted itself. The brothers felt remorse, they reflected, they atoned, and out of their guilt they sought justice, created law, crafted civilization, and coined codes of compassion for the other. These human edifices were an outgrowth of and tribute to the processes unleashed by the "murder of the father." Guilt, in its reparative and creative manifestations, brings one into contact with oneself and leads to compassion and industriousness. In the service of the positive side of his ambivalence, the son will now guarantee the continued existence, or shall we call it resurrection, of his father in the son's inner world by establishing therein an enduring, authoritative paternal image. There are, however, cases where this mental work is bypassed.

Patients Who Did Not Separate from Their Fathers

The men I have in mind all had a loving and strikingly nonambivalent relation to their fathers, whom they wanted to protect and spare, and with whom they never felt any competition or hostility. All these patients were highly motivated, successful, powerful, controlling, and quite aloof. Interestingly, while they appeared "hypermasculine," they all had warm, often nostalgic, solicitous relations with their fathers. These patients were neither afraid of their fathers, nor defiant of them, but were rather benevolently attached to them. They did not manifest "Oedipal" affects (e.g., hostility, competitiveness, or power struggles with male authority figures). On the contrary, their "hearts belonged to Daddy" rather than to any woman, for the sake of whom they would never betray their fathers.[20] They were notably creative in their careers, which they regarded as the real center of their lives; they all shunned strong emotions, and were aversive to any emotional display except when talking about their fathers, whom they all invariably described as good men. At such moments they became visibly moved, and two of them became tearful. These were the occasions where they revealed their greatest emotional depths.

H—— perceived his father as weak but extremely kind and wise in his own way, and would follow his father's councils with religious devotion. F—— remembered his father as powerful and as having protected him against his childhood fears. At the same time, F—— regularly served as a buffer between his bitterly quarreling parents, absorbing the shocks of their mutual hostility and rage and, especially, the effects of the histrionic and scorching emotions of his mother. When F—— grew up, he lost his awe for his father, replacing it with the affectionate feeling of wanting to protect any man who resembled his father. Meanwhile, H—— harbored a deep and genuine admiration for powerful men of action. As a child, G—— idealized his scholarly father, and when he grew up his under-standing that this father was far from being the genius he had taken him to be generated more love and protectiveness, rather than leading to a typical adolescent revolt and disparagement.

While these men deeply loved, idealized, and protected their fathers, their relations to women were highly problematical (though only some of them were conscious of this). In each case women played a marginal role in their lives and were treated with overt or subtle dismissiveness, and occasionally, with contempt. Two of the older men, who were married, were superficially gallant with their wives, yet they subtly devalued them and were unable or unwilling to treat them as genuinely equal partners. Their wives were "good wives": social, elegant, practical, and supportive of their husbands. These women never ventured beyond the traditional roles of housekeeper and mother. The other, younger patient had polite, casual but basically contemptuous, phobic-paranoid relations with women. He went through an endless series of short-lived, enthusiastically embraced, but ultimately vacant and boring sexual episodes. All these men were priggish, stiff, and "proper"; they all had preconscious or unconscious anxieties that made them defensive about their masculinity; and all were considerably homophobic.

Regarding the parents of these patients, there was either no real connection between father and mother (H—— and G——), or a chronic, embittered struggle raging between them (F——). In the analysis of these patients, we came to realize that their fathers needed them for their emotional completion, as compensation for their fathers' absence of meaningful relations with women. As the mother played no significant role in the emotional life of the father (either because she was unable or unwilling to, or because her husband would not let her), she became extraneous and apparently superfluous to both father and son. The mother could not serve as a "third" in relation to the father-son dyad; she could not function as the necessary element that intersects the imaginary, merged, regressive aspect of the father-son bond. The sons' tenderness, protectiveness, and emotional surrender were wholly given to their fathers. Such sons do not need their mothers, for on a manifest level, they get all their emotional, "motherly" needs from their fathers. On another level, there is a perverse contract between father and son, whereby the son serves as his father's "mother" by being deeply empathic, nurturant, and sparing toward his father. Son and father are ensconced and locked in a mutually nurturing and gratifying relation that enables them to dispense with the woman-mother. This is an altogether different perspective than one whereby the child learns about father through sensing and knowing him to be connected to mother in ways that are beyond question and not even fully understood by the son, and as the one who occupies mother's desires and fantasies, and with whom she has the real relation, or through learning that the parents are a strong couple that in some ways does not include him.[21]

These men loved their fathers and would never surrender the exclusivity of a totally devoted, nonambivalent relationship with them. On the contrary: they felt that their relationship with their fathers was the only place where true love and human trust were possible. The dyadic relationship between father and son empowered their sons to such a degree that they were free to pursue their careers with no inhibition or waste of energy. Their success was not truncated by any (Oedipal) guilt over hostile feelings or competitive experiences with their father. Was their attitude expressive of their expectation that their fathers would be destroyed if they attempted to revolt against them? Indeed, why should they destroy the authority of such a beloved father? Possessing power and success, cherishing a loving relationship in which they served as each other's "mother," they seemed to feel they did not need anything else. Yet they were seeking analysis. One man asked for a consultation regarding his disturbed son who, after a violent clash with his father (my patient), made a serious suicide attempt. The other patient came because he felt maniacally restless and overstimulated by his professional ambitions, which, he felt, were getting out of control after his father died. The third man came to analysis when his wife left him, making him feel deeply uprooted and disoriented. Clearly, this ostensibly "pure," unambivalent father-son relationship exacted a steep cost.

The men I am discussing here experienced their fathers as granting them unconditional love, trust, and the free pursuit of their goals, but at the price of abdicating their "souls" and being barred from meaningful relationships with women. Functioning as their fathers' delegates, his emissaries in this world, these men incorporated an ever-present, never-mourned, unabandoned father imago. While treating these successful men, I came to think of the theme of the "pact with the Devil," where a man, in exchange for having his greatest ambitions fulfilled, sells his soul to the Devil. Freud interprets this literary theme as the symbolic contract of a person, usually an ambitious man, with a father-figure.

Selling One's Soul to the Devil

In a paper entitled "The Devil as Father Substitute," Freud recounts the story of the painter Christoph Haizman, who could not reconcile himself to his father's death. Falling into depression and losing his capacity for work, Haizman signed a bond with the Devil, in which he agreed to be the Devil's son for nine years, his hope being that by obtaining a father substitute, he might "regain what he had lost." "At the end of nine years," said the contract, "the painter becomes the property, body and soul, of the Devil."[22] Shortly afterward, Haizman was found, stricken with convulsions and pains, by the Merciful Brothers. After a long period of repentance and prayer, the Devil appeared to Haizman and relented the pact; Haizman became well again. But after a while he was assaulted by a second round of visions, apparitions, convulsions, and painful sensations. Now he had to confess to the order of the Brothers Hospitaliers that he had had an earlier pact with the Devil. This time, the struggle to overcome the temptations of the evil spirit was greater and fiercer. Haizman succeeded in repelling all the Devil's renewed attempts, and "Brother

Chrysostomus (alias Christoph Haizmann) died peacefully and of good comfort in 1700," writes Freud.

Freud was not the only one to entertain the hypothesis that God and the Devil are two mythologized representatives, two sides of the figure of a man's father who were originally one. The "Devil" here is a twilight figure, a demon nether-father, who replaces the dead father and strikes a pact with the son to help the latter deny his loss and limits, to sidestep the need to deal with reality's hazards and calamities. The upshot of this fable is clear. In order to work creatively and strive to accomplish one's ambitions, there comes a time when one has to surrender living on the borrowed, that is, "paternal" or "devilish," strengths that kidnap one's soul and make it sick and convulsed. "The son," that is everyone, is called upon to own and spend his own energy and preserve the freedom to pursue professional and creative goals, with all their risks and uncertainty, and to love and desire through developing the ability to stand apart and tolerate difference and alienation from one's beloved (or hated) predecessors, including one's "paternal" tradition and the beliefs it inculcates.

My patients had fathers who needed, and, to put it metaphorically, had signed a pact with them. The neediness of the fathers was partly the result of their repudiation and hatred of their wives, who were seen as heartless, emotionally exploitative, and false. Faust in Goethe's play, and Elliot (John Cassavetes) in *Rosemary's Baby*,[23] are two such figures. Faust's wisdom is humanly limited; Elliot's talent is small and his success meager. Both Faust and Elliot trade their humanity for superhuman knowledge or undeserved success, and both betray their women and sacrifice their sons or let them perish: while Faust hurts and abandons pregnant Gretchen (who in her despair kills her "illegitimate" child), Elliot delivers Rosemary to copulate with and be impregnated by Satan. Faust and Elliot represent more sinister and corrupt versions of selling one's soul to the father-figure than do my three patients. But these patients in a sense also "sold" their souls to their fathers by remaining deeply (and exclusively) faithful to them, attaining success, but betraying their women by devaluing them at the same time as they deprived themselves of fulfilling and loving relationships.

The Need to Idealize the Father

According to Heinz Kohut, abrupt, potentially traumatic disappointments in the "idealized paternal imago," that is, in the paternal self-object's

perfection and omnipotence, abort the idealization on which the superego depends so as to raise the person's self-esteem. Such a narcissistically
disturbed person becomes fixated on what Kohut calls a "prestructural
ideal figure." Reduced to the constant search for an external idealized parent imago,[24] he is barred from gradually and wholesomely discovering
his father's realistic limitations, and cannot channel his need for idealization (which is a developmentally sound need, the need to endow certain things with an elevated value and significance) toward internalized,
denarcissized, reliable ideals and values. When the archaic fantasy of an
omnipotent father cannot be modified by processes that modulate and
integrate limitless idealization, it becomes repressed or split off and goes
on living forever, internally demanding constant proofs for its grandeur
by means of the son's servitude.

The traumatic cessation of an organic relation with a benevolent, idealized but still human father can come in many forms. There can be an
unbearably abrupt disillusionment with the father's perfection through
a certain event, or through the father's death, and there can be a rejecting, dismissive response from a contemptuous or indifferent father to
the son's open show of affection. In such cases, the son will be overcome
with shame and self-rejection; in order not to drown in these affects, he
will feel contempt for his own needy, loving, and love-seeking part. These
people may sometimes undergo what psychiatrist Harry Stack Sullivan
called "malevolent transformation," where consistent expectation of re-
buff and humiliation makes such a person show hateful behavior whenever he feels the need for tenderness.[25] Or the son may, like Ferenczi's
tongue-confused child, become a compliant automaton to his parents'
will, an attentive servant who has lost his identity.[26] The process is sealed
when the son is censured from loving his mother (which is typically the
case in cultures where women are marginalized). The son is then taught
to be dismissive, even contemptuous, toward his mother, sister, and wife,
which further restricts his chance of identifying with tender intentions
and relations. Deprived of identification with his mother as well, the son's
shameful parts are projected onto others who are now treated with contempt, even violence.[27] The son's quest for the father's approval and love
does not cease, however, but acquires increasingly desperate and abject
tones, which are suffused with shame and self-loathing.

The state of being unresponded to and unrecognized creates an enthralled, helpless, ideal-seeking attitude, which in turn generates a peren-

nial desire to submit. In clinical analyses we hear about patients' *fear* of yielding to the male analyst, often called "homosexual" because of the affection and tenderness involved. We hear more about the fear, and less about the *desire* and temptation to submit. The desire to totally yield and erase one's self can be a formidable psychic motive, no less ominous and destructive than wanting to have others submit to one's powers. I have called such a desire to yield to a superior entity "vertical desire," or "vertical mystical homoeros."[28] The enthrallment to power and the willing submission such vertical desire carries, its liability to lead to the renunciation of self, agency, and personal responsibility, can be most powerful. Such desires are radically different from and possibly opposed to what can be regarded as "horizontal desires"—affiliative needs, peer-bonding, or romantic longings. We know that under the press of a group controlled by a leader, people tend to abdicate judgment, moral inhibitions, even a sense of reality, and incur impairments with catastrophic results to the individual, to the group, and to those outside the group.

Rather than a Kohutian *superego that is insufficiently idealized* and cannot confer worth on one's self, and similarly to Benjamin's son's scorned love, Stanley Cath describes *the cruel, persecutory superego* of cult followers. Cath's research of these individuals led him to observe the pervasive search of these anxiety-ridden and hollow-feeling people for a charismatic group leader to fill the void of the father's absence. Lack of an internalized secure and soothingly mirroring parental (paternal and maternal) presence not only impairs the ability of cult followers to deal with the excitement and aggression that are involved in the thrust toward intimacy and self-realization, but in addition leaves them at the mercy of an implacable, unforgiving, and cruel ("egocidal") superego. The only way these people feel that they can withstand the onslaughts of such a superego is by seeking a leader who can be related to as a self-object, yet who would be safely distant and nonthreatening, at the same time as he would wield absolute control over all aspects of their lives. Under the impact of this kind of impersonal intimacy that is provided by an idealized father figure, the original (faulty, nondifferentiated) self and family self-representations dissolve "in the solvent of cultic frenzied activity, as helpless insignificance is transformed into an acceptable cosmic narcissism."[29]

Submission and obedience, enthrallment and compliance—these attitudes have been underrepresented in psychoanalytic thinking for a long time. Perhaps the pendulum of theory has swung too far to the side of mother; or perhaps the democratic, "horizontal" sensibility has come to reign in psychoanalytic thinking. But there is no doubt that in light of contemporary history, plagued by fundamentalist, terrorist violence, we need to deepen our understanding of the internalized father and his impact on personal and cultural events. The mythopoetic forms of tyrannical structure call forth rebellion and submission. And, paradoxically, the ability to dismantle paternal authoritarianism strengthens the positive side of the son's ambivalence and allows the continued existence of the father in his son's inner world by establishing a benevolent, authoritative guiding image. In Winnicott's terms, if the father survives the son's attacks without retaliating and without being destroyed, the son becomes a man who "knows how" and can therefore love women.[30] The "murder" of the father can be bypassed through pity or guilt over aggression or through striking pacts with the "devil"-father, as did my father-bound patients. The "murder" itself can be symbolic and virtual, as was the case with Erez, or it may become literal and psychotic, homicidal and self-sacrificial, as is the case with suicidal religious terrorists.

Killing the Father

Hans Loewald observes that Freud describes the resolution of the Oedipus complex with terms like "destruction," or "demolition," words that reverberate with what takes place in the Oedipal conflict—*parricide*, "the [symbolic, poetic] destruction of the parent by the child." The distinction between symbolic "killing" and concrete murder finds expression in Loewald in the differentiation of *parricide*, "the murder of a person to whom one stands in a specially sacred relation," from *patricide*, the murder of the biological father. While parricide is the murder of parental authority, *patricide is a crime against the sanctity of such a bond*. Loewald elaborates on how, "by evolving our own autonomy, our own superego, and by engaging in non-incestuous object relations, we are killing our parents. We are usurping their power, their competence, their responsibility for us, and we are abrogating, rejecting them as libidinal objects. In short, we destroy them in regard to some of their qualities hitherto most vital to us."[31] The process is circular: it is not only the case that by becoming autonomous, we "kill" our parents: the aftermath of the "murder," with its guilt and repentance, and the "expiatory" costs exacted by the dynamic processes of individuation, self-responsibility, and emergent subjectivity, enable the emergence of moral values and "independent energies of the self," as Loewald put it.

Loewald's ideas are penetrating and astute, but I suggest we look beyond (and earlier than) the Oedipal father. Interestingly, Freud himself in his writings shifts to an increasingly primitive father figure. Not content with the concept of the Oedipal father,[32] Freud elaborated the figure of the prehistoric archaic father in *Totem and Taboo*.[33] Freud made the crucial shift from the Oedipus complex to the totemic father when he realized that in the Oedipus complex, parricide (and incest with the mother) has the status of unconscious desire. All (male) subjects (unconsciously) wish to kill their fathers, since the paternal figure prevents our access to the maternal object. In *Totem and Taboo*, on the contrary, parricide is not the goal of our unconscious wish—it is, as Freud repeatedly stresses, a prehistoric fact which "really had to happen": the murder of the father is an event which had to take place in reality in order for civilization to begin. In other words, in the standard Oedipus myth, Oedipus is the exception who did what we all merely dream about (kill his father, etc.); while in *Totem and Taboo* "we all actually did it, and this universally shared crime grounded human community." It has been said that nothing binds a group together more than a shared crime.[34]

A Case of Successful "Deicide"

In the analysis of my patient Erez, I found myself squarely facing the image of such an archaic "father," whom Erez occasionally experienced as benign, but more often as implacably (and stupidly) cruel and harsh. Erez came to analysis before acting on his wish to undergo a sex-change operation. He was in his early twenties, brilliant, deeply schizoid, big and manly looking but awkward and disheveled. He spoke in a slow, monotonous slur, swallowing his words or spitting them out with great speed, while carefully avoiding looking at me. Erez told me that he intensely desired to be a woman, but also that he was getting into arguments, disputations, insults, and even physical fights with everyone around him. His wish to be(come) a woman and his transsexual conflicts, fantasies, even ways of dressing, were dramatic enough to occupy almost all my attention, at the cost of understanding another prolific part of his inner world, which, however amazing and forceful, always remained a mystery to me. This part had to do with his relation with God. With no

background of religious upbringing and with no immediate social influence, Erez entertained a personal, terrorized, loving-and-hating, needy-
and-contemptuous relation with "God." Erez's God was terrifying and
constantly brandishing horrific punishment; He was omniscient, yet, to
my surprise, He was also stupid, corruptible, and petty, attributes which,
however, did not prevent Erez from venerating Him. Eventually, when
parts of this analysis fell into place for me, I realized that the insights that
Erez reached regarding this particular relation, and his ultimate dramatic
ritual of killing God, both of which enabled him to calm his terror, were
in an important sense what freed him from his terror of becoming a man
and led him to an impressive personal evolution. Erez himself linked his
strong wish to become a woman with his fear of becoming a man lest he
be punished and killed by a despotic God-like father. At the same time, as
Erez told me, and in the multidetermined way psychic phenomena take
place, Erez's wish to become a woman also meant giving in to his desire to
totally submit to an imaginary, cruel despot.

Quite early in his analysis, Erez realized with a shock that the tyrannical God who had ruled his life since his early childhood and with
whom he was constantly preoccupied, the reigning figure in his savage
fantasy world, was none other than his father, who had died when Erez
was five. This shocking insight, however, lasted only briefly, and was
covered over by a torrent of memories of his horror of being punished
with castration, against which Erez frenetically created elaborate rituals,
which he performed compulsively to appease God. Laboring to erase
items from his ever-lengthening Sisyphean list of sins and misdemean-
ors,[35] Erez gradually came to the conclusion that he would not be able
to eliminate the list, shorten it, or, at least, maintain it at a stable length.
He then decided he "needed to crush the image of God." Erez also no
longer wanted to be "father's girl," a role he had desired for many years.
Recruiting me into the conspiracy, he "plotted," as he put it, to liberate
himself from God's hold. At the same time, he was filled with terror
and guilt, and kept imagining with hallucinatory clarity God standing
behind his shoulder and looking down at him. As he felt stronger, he
began to experience bouts of "love" for me, a "love" that had the quality
of worship and adoration. I was now his god in the transference; I had
replaced the Father God.[36]

In this process of emerging from a merger with God to separate from
Him, Erez gave up part of his delusional world for a quasi-psychotic

deification of me in the transference. Now he was less afraid of me-God, but nonetheless careful not to incur my wrath. His relations with me became extremely ritualized. He now began performing again the rituals he had devised in his childhood, which he addressed to God in the past, performing them now for me in the hope of securing my protection against his dread of the world, and making me take responsibility for his life. At the same time, in his typically secretive and indirect way, he reinforced his compulsive battling with me lest I wreak vengeance on him. He once explained to me why I had become God to him. *I became God because he felt I did not love him*, he said, which he figured out from the fact that whatever I said "was bad and hurtful because it was not words of love." I understood him to mean (and interpreted to him) that the pain he felt every time I was not completely in tune with him left him but a single recourse: to deify me, that is, to hold me in veneration, fear, hatred, in an electrifyingly ecstatic and dangerous merger. It was not easy to grasp how his experience of being deeply humiliated by me (he was exquisitely vulnerable) created such thralldom and subdued excitement simultaneously with a wish to annihilate me. "Not feeling loved" meant to him feeling rejected and humiliated. Masochistically identifying with my "rejection" of him as proof of my absolute ("vertical") superiority over him, what was left for him to do under these circumstances was to deify me, or, to put it differently, to "verticalize" our difference: to move from the horizontal plane which proved too painful, to the vertical one.

Erez's liberation from subjugation to the divine figure I incorporated came in stages. A landmark in this process was a chance encounter in a grocery store. Seeing me shopping started the gradual loss of his perception of me as perfect. This change helped to supplant his idolization with violent sexualization. Following these developments, Erez conjured a hallucinatory scene in which he found himself in a Roman temple which was filled with statues of gods whom he tried to shake and shatter, dreading all the time that one of them would recover and annihilate him before he had finished demolishing them.

In the analysis, I was such an idol for him that to fortify himself he put much energy into destroying, or at least reducing, my powers. He was haunted by horrifying animistic images, yet he kept fighting me from within a state of determination and cold hatred. Whenever he felt he had beaten me, he experienced enormous satisfaction. Now he could really grasp that I was a human being who had weaknesses. At the same time, he dreaded that, should he defeat and destroy me, analysis would end. He feared that the moment he realized that I was weak and stupid, and that he should leave me, I would take a most cruel revenge on him. Following cycles of hatred, fear, and neediness, he could, with great effort, describe in detail his extremely elaborate fantasies of assault and destruction of my body, of which he did not leave one part intact after he had burned it, strangled it, torn everything off it, and sealed its apertures. He now felt tremendous relief, and his self-confidence strengthened.

The third stage of his "killing of God" came when Erez began to mourn his father, whose death he had denied for years by clinging to a haunting, ritualized, ubiquitous relationship with him. He now realized that the fear he felt of his father as a rival protected him against accepting his father's final, irreversible death. For the first time in his life, Erez could acknowledge his father's irrevocable absence and yield the intricate plots and narratives of gods, ghosts, and skeletons, which fantastically enlivened his paternal object. In his conscious fantasy, his father's death was a slow, tortuous, voodoo murder that Erez himself committed. After difficult analytic work, the avenging phantom of his father, the living skeleton he often used to visualize, vanished. Analysis was a process of "rebirth" from psychic deadness, violence, and fearful thralldom to a protective cruel God.

Erez's life shows how a relationship of deprivation such as he had with a depressed mother,[37] an ongoing relatedness to an absent, idealized "father," and chronic feelings of helplessness and inferiority toward constantly taunting older siblings (a basic configuration that is found in the Islamic terrorists as well), can breed an assumedly protective but wrathful and castrating God. Absent parents and attacking, humiliating siblings create in a person a desperate need to erect an omnipotent figure against helplessness. Erez created a God who was punitive at the same time as He bestowed upon Erez a sense of superiority and entitlement to attack and violate people ("simple mortals"). Erez identified with God's omnipotence, at the same time as he was obsessed with his debts to God and worked hard to produce offerings to calm God's wrath. Erez felt the need for sacrifices to assure the legitimacy and continuity of his aggressive attacks on people, which were attempts on his part to harm and kill the soft, nonmilitant parts of himself. Becoming a woman was hence the attempt to reintroject the alienated soft parts he had projected to the outside.

Erez used to repeatedly ask, in a tone of exhaustion, "How much killing can I take upon myself?" This question encompassed many meanings. At that time, I understood it to express his guilt about his murderous rage and attacks on people. The "killings" (the attacks) were an aggressive attempt to resolve the conflict between his aggressiveness and his guilt by ridding himself of all badness and projecting it into the outer world, to other persons. These persons became to him persecutory and malevolent, and had to be fought against in endless, exhausting spirals of violence, which then nourished new guilt. But Erez's violence was not only the expression of narcissistic rage at the abandonment and failure of his primary objects. His aggressiveness was also the manifestation of a pressing need to "kill" his persecutory paternal object. The compulsive aggressiveness, which he called "killing," was thus a double project, aimed at evacuating his rage and "badness" and at offering resistance to despotic oppression. To complicate matters, Erez also had to fight his fear of dying like the males around him (father, brother, unit commander), all of whom, by unfortunate coincidence, died or were killed. Erez either had to become a woman, or to combat God and Fate (his words) to save himself from the doom that had befallen those men, who, in his fantasy, had all been sentenced to death and killed by a cruel, malevolent, fanatical Godhead.[38]

Daniel Paul Schreber

In contrast to belligerent Erez, Daniel Paul Schreber relinquished all opposition to a tyrannical father figure and plunged into a psychosis. Freud uses Judge Schreber's memoirs to launch his theories of the "father complex," homosexuality, and paranoia.[39] Freud traces Schreber's successive deification of paternal, authoritarian figures in the asylum to which Schreber was committed. Similarly to my patient Erez, Schreber elaborated a system of delusions through which he was to become a woman and unite with his powerful father. In a series of papers, William Niederland shows that Schreber fell ill when he had to take the place of a (his/the) father, an eventuality he dreaded so much that he psychotically turned himself into a woman.[40] His psychosis emerged when he had the "ominous fantasy that 'after all, it must be very nice to be a woman submitting to the act of copulation.'"[41]

Schreber's psychotic elaborations were regressive versions of the ways his father, Dr. Daniel Gottlieb Moritz Schreber, a well known and popular

German educator, related to his son and recommended to children in general. The various tortures consisting of orthopedic straightening, disciplining, and punishing infants and children were formulated as "educational" measures. They were specifically used by the father to psychically batter his sons.[42] Schreber introjected these experiences early in life and later released them in his psychotic delusions. Having been coerced, tortured, and humiliated by his sadistic father, lacking a mother who was strong enough to protect her son against the crushing "influencing machine" of a father, the torture and soul-murder committed on his self reappeared in Schreber's inner world as delusional or hallucinatory entities. More specifically, Schreber turned the sadistic manipulations of his body and mind into excruciatingly intense experiences, centering on the father, who was psychotically transformed into the superior figure of God and who stood at the center of his prolific delusional system. Schreber sexualized what must have been felt by him as attacks on his body's integrity, at the same time as he sacralized the loss of subjectivity and agency he had suffered (he experienced miracles that were performed on his body; he heard divine instructions to close or open his eyes; and so on). These processes of sexualization and sanctification were means for Schreber to make sense of what was happening to him at the same time as they were meant to help him with his pain and humiliation by turning them into an excited, paranoid gullibility regarding his father's benevolent intentions. The similarity with Erez's inner processes is unmistakable. Both Schreber and Erez let their father *as such* disappear from their fantasy lives, only to reappear as manipulative, terrorizing divine entities. This transformation was a function of these sons' desperate attempts to restore their libidinal ties to their fathers.

The Primal Father: Regression and Perversion

The son's maintaining a libidinal tie to the father and being incapable of "killing" him is a further stage in the process I am discussing. If, as Erez put it, "everything . . . [the father] say[s] is not words of love,"[43] father's love has to be purchased with utmost urgency, through complying with his every supposed wish and commandment. Furthermore, on having internalized the idealized persecutor into one's inner world, the other parts of the psyche have to be eliminated. The son will now seek to evacuate and annihilate the pathetically miserable and openly needy part of himself. Part of this self is the boy's love for the mother, which becomes shameful and unacceptable.

What I have called *regression* (to the father) can also be called a *perversion*. While the son regresses to his father, the father perverts his son, or, differently put, the son's identificatory love for his father, so vital for the son's gaining access to a liberating space—the symbolic space, if we stress Lacan's law, or the space of play, if we think of Winnicott—is annihilated. The submissive relation to the father is a perversion of sublimation and growth. What under one description appears as a regression to an archaic, primal aspect that precedes the mother-child bond,[44] can be seen from another perspective as a perverse structure, subversive of the mother-child bond that runs parallel to it rather than integrating with it.[45] The father in his subversive role perversely sets up the son against the son's longing for his mother and positions him against the principle of life and maternal desire, replacing them with his own ostensibly "sacred values," an ersatz version and a caricature of what are normally peaks of human ethics and compassion. Such a "perverse love" is denuded of earthly, incarnate existence; it is a wombless love, a love that denies bodily birth as the product of sexual intercourse. The father presumes to birth his son out of his phallus instead of his penis. What may apparently look like an alliance with an Oedipal father is a relationship in which the father himself is regressive, in the sense that the father himself is so scared of his own needs and of his bonding with any feminine element, that he bars his son from bonding with the feminine. This is a father who destroys life, a perverse father, not the primal father who enables existence (coming into life), who generates a tribe. It is a father who exists (who supports himself) through hostility rather than through real power.

The Archaic Father: Propitiation, Resuscitation

Curiously enough, as much as Erez held God in thrall, he also perceived Him as stupid and in need of support. In other words, Erez was also feeding and propping up his God-father in his anguish not to be left totally alone in the world. In his transference to me as God, but also in his earlier transference to "God" Himself, Erez feared that God might become exposed as weak and might tumble down with a devastating crash. Marvin Osman expands the Loewaldian idea that "birth, growth, and self-realization are inextricably correlated in the human psyche . . . with a diminution of the powers of one's procreators."[46] Osman adduces anthropological resources that highlight the cultural belief that humankind and the gods share common blood, or in psychoanalytic terms, the fantasy that self and object are psychically fused, sharing a communal fund of vigor and fiber. Consequently, in this imagined zero-sum game, any autonomous functioning and self-expression is liable to rob the father (the parent, the "progenitor") of his resources (his blood and potency). This psychodynamic is a universal experience whereby "persons of each generation . . . are likely to regard their development and accretion of powers as being accompanied by a corresponding diminishment of their predecessors."[47] Growing up means draining the parent, which in turn arouses archaic guilt and necessitates the reinstatement of vitality of a God who needs to be propitiated and bribed to look aside and not take revenge on his son's young strengths, but also needs to be kept alive and continue to function as a protector against life's dreadful contingencies. Erez's analysis provided unusual glimpses into such a world. First, Erez was convinced that in living he was offending God; second, in the psychotic part of his mind Erez believed, as he told me, that he had magically killed his father; third, before setting out to "crush God", Erez had to arm himself against his fear of being left without God by anointing me to be his substitute God; and finally, when Erez did "destroy" God, he was haunted with the dread of God's vengeance. The weak, puppetlike father who needs to be resuscitated by sacrifices in order to function as a protector is the other side of the terrifying father. This is where the believer comes close to exposing the bootstrap operation that subtends such religious activities.

What becomes immediately apparent is that without sacrifices a zero-sum conflict would establish itself, in which it would be *either* the father *or* the son who would be the one to have the resources and means to survive. Needless to say, such a cruel struggle to the death is the hallmark of disturbed relations within any family. We know from psychoanalytic reconstructions, as well as from research on parent-child relations, that pathological, harmful, or insecure attachments tend to become "aggressivized": love becomes hatred, peaceful coexistence becomes a ferocious or compliant battle for survival, and sibling affection becomes murderous war. In particular, toxic humiliation becomes agglutinated (pseudointegrated) through mechanisms of incorporation, identification, and guilt-exploitation. Notably, Erez described the atmosphere in his family in these terms. On the mythological level, the belief that the god demanded the periodic shedding of blood suggests that primitive tribes assumed responsibility for impairing or diminishing that god, and felt the obligation to make restitution for this "crime" through various bloodletting sacrifices.[48]

Today, the most extreme cases of offering life substance to the gods, that is, offering God glory through killing of humans, are those of religious suicidal terrorists. These uprooted "sons," embittered by their sad situation, seeking to flee despair,[49] envious of the entitlement to comfort and pleasure of others, and doubting or contemptuous of the efforts of secular cultures to create real individuality, stay enthralled by the archaic fatherly figure. Their experience and affect have become lethally, explosively destructive. Tragic guilt—or "creative guilt," as Freud calls it—is antimanic. Its message is not, "I've finally killed the monster," but, "I have 'killed' whom it was necessary to 'kill,' yet at the same time I have not lost my human feelings; my hatred is suffused with remorse, even love. I do not deny my badness; it cannot be split off and projected into others." Freud put it in mythopoetic language when he said that after his death, the father does not pass away and disappear; he returns stronger than ever, for *once he is dead, he can no longer be killed*. I read this idea as pointing to the fact that once a person, a state, a culture, has liberated itself from its oppressor-"father" it has to find new and original ways to rebuild itself, to turn to new possibilities and resources. Once the tyrannical power of old authority is overcome, old frames no longer hold their inhibitive threat. New impulses can be pursued to create freer social institutions and ethical cultures. The way is open to new possibilities and different modes of acting.

No Deicide

Religious terrorist mentality represents the acme of lovingly selling one's soul to the Devil-father, the height of thralldom to a lethal paternal presence. Religious terrorist mentality is essentially a perversion. Characteristic for such perverse relationship is a pact with someone against the world, against reality, against truth.[50] The incestuous, archaic, homoerotic relation to the father is mystical and "vertical," playing itself out as two poles on a vertical plane of abject worship and sublime superiority, which unite only in the common act of annihilating mother and woman. Father and son maintain a vertical relationship, and lessening the steep vertical distance between them becomes possible only in merging. The moment when Erez began to deify me was the moment he felt rejected and humiliated. This was also precisely the moment when a horizontal relationship became transformed into a vertical one.

Trying and failing to contend with the contradictory demands posed by a bicultural life and the dissonant family structure it produces, the terrorists seem to have found a solution. They opted for a retrograde psychic movement, a withdrawal from the labor of achieving autonomous masculine identity and "earthly" (mature) love relations. The narcissistic distress and identity diffusion they must have experienced in their troubled life circumstances, where they were not poor enough to drown in labor nor sufficiently content and gratified to lead a "normal" loving and working life, became transmuted into a vast, collective, projective, and projective-identificatory process.[51] The combination of their individual discontent and the hybrid-cultural upheavals they had undergone seems to have truncated their capacity, in the face of an alien, puzzling, and competing culture, to integrate the complexity and plurality of their lives.[52]

Resorting to fundamentalism, with its cognitive simplification of right and wrong, true and false, black and white, and its emotions that find release in such simplification, creates a particular state of mind. One detaches from one's self and becomes insulated against reality, and one acquires a new identity and a secure sense of righteousness and moral superiority. At this stage, the link tightens between "moral superiority" and a primitive father imago, one who is outside the law, who seizes, robs, usurps. It is this lawlessness upheld by sheer force, and the lure of such force by virtue of its being a force, which are not combated. Human love and striving is renounced in favor of father-worship. A potentially loving and equal relationship between man and woman (or between man and man) becomes hyperbolized, idealized and demonized into a perverse love relationship with a God who demands endless sacrifice and self-sacrifice in return for His satisfaction—which, for those who love this God, culminates in murderous religious ecstasy.

The God of the terrorists is a monstrous transformation of the liberating father. Rather than releasing and encouraging his son into exploration of the world, this God releases the son from his attachment to life, from his individuality, from his body. What is monstrous is the conjunction of his murderous cruelty and the ecstatic joy he supplies. It clearly attests to the tremendous power of religious ecstasy to overcome negative affects and moral inhibitions. Religious ecstasy, I suggest, has the capacity to effect the transformation of self-hatred and envy (such as that experienced by those who become Islamic militant extremists) into love of God, a love-of-God that promotes the obliteration of those parts of the self which are antagonistic to the sense of compulsory purity, which affirm life and the pursuing of one's desires. Here the choice is to strengthen God while killing the "impure," messy, ambivalent, but autonomy-seeking parts. Obviously, what subtends this love of God is fear and hatred, a kind of loving paranoia that is generated by the craving part in the son's psyche that cannot be fully eradicated but has to overcome a terrible knowledge, the knowledge of paternal cruelty. Although the fear and hatred are split off from the "father" to others (infidels, women, moderate co-religionists), these emotions nonetheless cast their shadow on the son's pining for the father.

I have suggested that the process whereby hatred is transformed into a certain kind of perverse love is at the same time a contrite and all too happy return to the father. As mentioned, "God" here represents the part that sanctifies and assists in the killing of the impure, disturbing, "infidel" sector of the psyche. Such a reunion can be usefully conceptualized as a "regression" to an archaic father—whether the prehistoric father of the primal horde or the primal father within.[53] It is a retrograde conciliation with him rather than an identification with his strength, drawing on his strength in order to seek paths to new forms of life.

The regression to the father, exchanging the step of "killing" tyranny in order to regress back to it, does not resemble regression to the mother. It certainly cannot be communicated through the metaphor of returning to the womb, which has become our generic term for regression, in which the father is a perennial antiregressive force, conceived as the one who offers himself as protectively preventing the child from returning to the mother's lap. As we have seen, the form and fantasy behind the terrorist attack has aspects of a regressive return to the father, and the accompanying banishment of the mother. Our habitual images of mother-regression are of boundless plenitude and fulfillment of all our needs, enticing and dangerous self-indulgence, an ebullience and a weakening of character (with the dark underside of the terrifying phallic mother). By contrast, the images of a father-regression include extreme, ecstatic asceticism, martyrdom, sacrifice, and renunciation of sexuality—an enticing refusal of any indulgence, which would lead, in later stages, to serene martyrdom or explosive self-destruction.[54]

Atta and Bin Laden

Religious terrorists like Mohammad Atta and most of his "brothers" function in this regressive mental mode (which does not mean that their level of instrumental functioning cannot be highly efficient). We read in the journals that Atta's father was worried lest his son become weak in the pampering lap of his mother. The father was contemptuous of the lack of masculinity and toughness of his shy, delicate son. Perhaps as a response, or as part of his overall reaction to his existential situation, Atta developed a solemn seriousness and a no-nonsense loyalty to his cause. Atta was stern, humorless, literal, seclusive, secretive, "shy." Perhaps he was trying to prove his mettle and excel in one area in which his father could not disapprove of him, namely religion. Defying his earthly father, perhaps following a failed quest for recognition of his manly worth, Atta turns to an idealized, spiritualized version of his father. An intense turning toward a father who is remote and intransigent becomes a posture of appeasement through self-erasure. The same inner strategy is dramatically revealed in a poem written by bin Laden. David Rohde, who writes about the poem in an April 7, 2002, *New York Times* article entitled "Verses from bin Laden's War," introduces it as follows: "The poem is a tale of betrayal, exile and siege, cast as a mournful conversation between father and son."

> Why, Father, have they sent
> These missiles, thick as rain,
> Showing mercy neither to a child
> Nor to a man shattered by old age?
> Father, what has happened
> So we are pursued by perils?
> Father, what has happened
> So your likenesses are depicted?
> Is your redeeming of an ancient house
> A crime that cannot be forgiven?
> Here are we, [locked] in tragedy:
> All safety gone—it does not show itself . . . [55]

We note the conspicuous absence of any woman in this text of a dyadic intimacy bonding against a hostile world, a world in which Americans are bombing Afghanistan mercilessly. Seen through a psychoanalytic lens, elements of a regressive father-son bonding cohere into a bloody destructiveness that is paradoxically sponsored by love—abject, masochistic, idolizing. In other words, the murderousness is not simply a direct expression of hatred (toward the infidels in America and the West, or toward heretics in Muslim countries, or toward Jews in Israel and elsewhere), but is concomitant with the spirit of devotion and loving intimacy.

The deified father and the sacrificial son are central motifs in Western culture, claims literary critic David Lee Miller.[56] He suggests that the theme of filial sacrifice is the most striking feature shared by the canonical, biblical, and classical texts of English literature. The son in these traditions acts as a complement to the father at the same time as the son points to the contradiction at the heart of fatherhood under patriarchy. Whereas the son is indispensable "proof" of fatherhood (only the male heir can extend the patriline), at the same time the son's existence provokes the crisis of fatherhood's uncertainty (there is no way to see and there was no way to prove that any particular boy springs from this man rather than that one, or indeed from any man at all). In a sense, there is no stronger evidence of embodiment than blood, and blood sacrifice has been chosen to substantiate patriline. At the same time, however, the father who sacrifices a son, especially if it is an only son, or a firstborn son,[57] would seem to be destroying along with that son the very paternity the ritual is supposed to create. There is a growing body of writing around the notion that patriarchal, patrilineal cultures recruit sacrificial victims as visible stand-ins for the fatherly body.[58] The growing prominence in psychoanalysis of the Laius complex—the father who abandons his son to death because of his fear of being replaced ("killed")—to supplement the Oedipus complex, is one such example. Sending soldiers to war as a sacrificial gesture of the father and the group is another horrific instance.

Indeed, Richard Koenigsberg adduces massive evidence that reveals a chilling face of war as a sacrificial ritual on a huge scale, going so far as to suggest that this may even be war's ultimate function.[59] General John Hackett, former commander, NATO Northern Army Group, states that "the whole essence of being a soldier is not to slay but to be slain."[60] Joanne Bourke argues that the most important point about the male body during the war is that it was "intended to be slain."[61] War from this perspective is an institution whereby sons give over their bodies to fathers in the name of validating or valorizing the sacred ideal. When the sons die for their fathers (as in war or in religious martyrdom), a reversal is effected in the "natural" order of things, in which the father loses power to the son: here the son loses his life for the father's will.

Obviously I am casting my net widely here, for I believe that the well-springs of a most central phenomenon originate in some as yet unmined yet deeply human psychodynamics. There is considerable support for the thesis that the terrorist wants (unconsciously) *to change the father from persecutor into an idealized love object*, to reverse the rage and discontent (and the pain and suffering) into glory and narcissistic enhancement. In this sense, when we use the concept of "regression to the father" to explain terrorist behavior and experience, we not only denote regression from a loving, supporting father to a primitive, malevolent one, but also, in a deep sense, the further regression from a more realistic experience of a father who has good and bad sides, and toward whom one has ambivalent feelings, to an abjectly idealized version of the "persecutor" (what I call "loving paranoia," a complex state of mind of love toward the persecutory bad object and the splitting off of suspicion and hate). This paternal persecutor is the target of the son's desire to remain a son forever. Very few religious suicidal terrorists become fathers themselves. They remain eternal sons. They do not have to clash with the father, and thus their masculinity is devoid of fatherhood.

What Is a Father?

Although psychoanalytic thinking has enormously deepened our understanding of the importance of the father in the child's life, the question of the father has always seemed to me a puzzling enigma. What exactly is "a father?" Father's love is neither mother's love nor an adoptive parent's love. Being generated in the flesh, from the father's body, yet invisibly so, being a tiny drop of the father's flesh, issued forth in a fleeting moment, one among a million projectiles: is father-child love of the same order as that of mother-child love, where the infant dwells inside the mother for a long period?[62] And if it is not "the same love," what is it? The invisibility of the bodily link between father and child makes for a mystifying and unfathomable bond—simultaneously abstract and concrete, close yet mediated, and ultimately ungraspable. Is "father" a basically elusive entity, engendering his son yet not containing him in his own body? Is the father someone who is connected through a procreative act in the (in)conceivable past and therefore through a law—abstract, but powerfully binding? Is the ejection of the son from his father's penis a token of separateness and thrownness? Must not symbiosis with the primal, archaic father be no less, although differently, terrifying than symbiosis with the primal, archaic, so-called "phallic" mother? Is the relationship to the father not forever a mystery, having to do with narcissism and with idealization and the quest for transformation and hence with awe, the sublime, paranoia, impersonal Law and Justice—all measuring one's self-worth in the face of an other, one's Last Judgment meted out by an idealized object?

§5 The Triadic Structure of Evil

The terrorist attacks of September 11, 2001, enacted the collective fantasy of radical Islam. A collective fantasy taps the multiple sources of a group ethos and, eventually, translates into an ideology. Ideology is a discursive, rationalized, objectified version of feelings and longings that become shaped and narrativized through culture and history but are rooted in unconscious fantasies. Acts such as September 11 are subtended by collective fantasies that express strivings to regain past glory and redress present injustices, whether fantasized, real, or, as is most probable, a mixture of the two. The belief—the golden fantasy—that it is possible to reestablish a long-lost reality, becomes prominent in societies that feel bypassed by historical events, or in peoples who witness the defeat of the rights and aspirations that they perceive as just, or in those who have failed to thrive and have become dysfunctional. The Jacobin fantasy of reviving the French (or Roman) republic, Mussolini's fantasy of rebuilding the Roman empire, Hitler's fantasy of reestablishing German paganism, the Sunni fantasy of restoring the caliphate, or the Iranian nuclear apocalyptic preparing for the coming of Mahdi, the Twelfth Imam,[1] are all fantasies supported by active beliefs that become transformative as they seek to change—to save or purify—the world. These fantasies use time differently, and move from the dreams and visualization to the actual and concrete plane of action, fueled by an enormous sense of power and conviction. They of course come closer and closer to the likelihood of massive, or even total, human self-destruction, a cataclysm which, according to Svetozar Stojanović, is now humanity's most likely fate.[2]

These fantastic, utopian, ultimately counterreal scenarios are not only destructive but apocalyptic,[3] even "auto-apocalyptic."[4] Theatrical acts of terror, though premeditated and carefully planned, are not merely spectacular and symbolic. They are, as well, performances from within enraptured, devotional states of mind that have been trained to imagine the overcoming of daily injustice and drudgery, and the apotheosis that comes with breaking away from the present to the near-redemptive future made present. These states of mind are elaborated from within certain social relationships, historical circumstances, and cultural conjunctions. When the appropriate time comes, the people who embody these states of mind are ready to act.[5] The acts perpetrated involve massive destruction and human death and suffering. Evil is usually linked to cruelty inflicted, often (but not always) on a massive scale. Cruelty and suffering that are inflicted on others, and hence unjustified (since they are not voluntarily chosen, such as the suffering that can accompany one's striving to achieve some end), are evil. The infliction of unjustified or gratuitous suffering on others is evil.[6] Massive, collective evil, I propose, is generated by a structure that differs from that of individual evil. Traditional psychoanalytic attempts to explain the individual evil that is committed between family members in domestic situations or toward strangers regard evil as psychic cruelty, abuse, or hostile malevolence inflicted on one person by another who himself has suffered psychic cruelty, abuse, or hostile malevolence. The person who has been abused then identifies with the perpetrator, and seeks to abuse, rape, or otherwise victimize the abused, raped victim within himself or herself by victimizing someone else who is equated with his or her victim-self. Victim thus becomes perpetrator. Such a perpetrator, identifying with the aggressor from his or her past, achieves psychic control over a traumatic situation by recreating his victim as his own annihilated self. Murdering the other, the perpetrator frees himself or herself from the victim's role. Of course there are also cases where the victim remains in the victimized, traumatized role, and unconsciously but tragically seeks to validate the suffering, injured role into which he or she has been violently cast.

Dyadic Evil

The few psychoanalytic thinkers who tackle the problem of evil conceive of it as a damaging physical or emotional attack on the other, an active repetition of a traumatic experience of "soul murder" or "killing the self,"[7] or of other kinds of humiliation that actually deprive the victim of his or her humanity or physical life. The massive evidence that violent criminals mostly come from broken families, and that those who become serial killers grow up in conditions of cruelty and extreme neglect, attests to the basic repetitive, enactive structure of trauma-caused victimization whereby cruelty is transmitted from one pair of victim and victimized to the next. In this history, people internalize their attackers as inner persecutors. The traumatic installment of an inner enemy into the psyche has been variously described by terms such as Fairbairn's "tantalizing object" or "inner saboteur"; Melanie Klein's internalized persecutory object; Franco Fornari's "terrifier"; or Peter Fonagy's "alien self."[8] The simultaneous internalization of the persecutor *and* the identification with him leads to reenactments of soul murder and abuse on an external victim, who has to be attacked and often eliminated as an effigy of the internalized enemy, or as oneself, in a compulsive repetition. The former victim who has now become the perpetrator inflicts trauma on a new victim who will then become a perpetrator to another victim. In the throes of identifying with the aggressor and internalizing the hatred and hostility of his caretakers, the victim turns into perpetrator, compelled by the project of announcing and transforming the scenario of cruelty and infliction of suffering by staging it on others. The abuse that has been suffered is now evacuated onto an Other, with whom the new perpetrator instinctually, malevolently empathizes but whom he also totally shuts out.

Kleinian analysts, while not referring directly to evil, write about so-called personality structures that are shaped by the moral choices that are caused by and cause perversity of character. In their view, one part of the personality of a victimizing individual takes another part hostage. "Terrorist" or perverse "gangs" are parts of the personality, not just in average neurotic patients, but in people who choose to become terrorists in their lives, treating themselves or others with open or covert mental violence and contempt.[9] The "good" and "bad" object (the representation of the other) in Kleinian theory is subjectivistic and colored by the experience it procures for each individual through his uniquely personal prism. The object therefore is to a great extent created by the subject's feelings.[10] This attention to the subjective, emotional, and fantastic factor, a great strength of Kleinian theory, underlines the fact that our perception and experience are most powerfully impacted by our feelings, anxieties, and desires. Our feelings and wishes may be utterly idiosyncratic, yet they always point to personal truths that touch on our deepest concerns about ourselves and what is vital to us. While attending to the crucial role of subjective feelings in human experience, Klein's and Bion's theories posit a hatred of external and internal reality in the face of its intolerable aspects, aspects that are too painful, envy-inducing, or enraging to accept with equanimity.[11] It is assumed within this framework that these inner realizations or realities are projected "onto" others, who suffer in turn. Kleinian theory also acknowledges the inner pain that, when it becomes unbearable, leads to horrific mental destructiveness as a means of release. Kleinian analysts vividly portray situations in the inner world where a bad, ganglike part of the psyche seizes power and comes to colonize and dominate other parts of the person. These personality constellations are definitely recognizable in the experience one has of certain patients, and they also insightfully delineate psychic events in large groups of people.

The psychoanalytic literature is replete with descriptions of the dissociative states that lead to and accrue from violent and cruel perpetration of suffering on another person, who then transmits that suffering to others. I shall call this kind of evil *dyadic evil*. Dyadic evil is essentially a chain of binary relations, in which a victim becomes the perpetrator on another victim, who in turn perpetrates evil on other victims—who are often themselves individuals who are sadly susceptible and masochistically prepared for being abused. Ferenczi's "traumatized child," rape victims who have been shown to have higher chances of being raped again, cases of the so-called horrific temptation to harm oneself, or fascination with being abused are all instances or consequences of dyadic evil.

Collective Evil

But dyadic evil in itself is insufficient to account for large-scale, collective, ideologically inspired acts of evil and cruelty. The conception of evil as psychic cruelty that inflicts one's suffered trauma and soul-murder upon the other can be applied only metaphorically, filtered and amplified in an ideology fitting a corresponding group identity, in the case of fundamentalists, as when the trauma suffered by a society is kept alive as a vivid memory of victimization. Vamik Volkan has compellingly documented such cases. Volkan writes about the sense fundamentalist groups have that those outside their borders do not understand them and threaten their existence. Shared feelings of victimization then become an essential component of the collective identity of such groups, inflaming retaliatory and revengeful fantasies and acts purported to redress the humiliation and injustice. Paradoxically, because such groups anticipate threats from those without, they in fact play a role in inducing persecutory attitudes in others.[12]

I believe, though, that the metaphor of individual trauma is insufficient to account for lynch mobs, military massacres, ethnic genocidal governments, or a totalistic ideology of which religious terrorism is but one manifestation. These phenomena produce killings and tortures that are quantitatively and qualitatively different from individual acts of evil.[13] The existence of numerous historical and actual, endlessly reverberating cycles of victimization and retribution is undeniable,[14] yet there are, in my view, important additional elements in the configuration of collective evil. The psychoanalytic conception of evil as psychic cruelty that inflicts one's suffered trauma and soul-murder upon the other omits the necessary element that could account for large-scale, ideologically inspired collective violence. For we need to recognize that what is prohibited for the individual is regularly practiced, condoned, even sanctified, by the group. In other words, the same laws or rules do not apply equally, or, rather apply inversely, to the individual and the group; the group emerges as an altogether different, and at this stage, more enigmatic, entity. What is it in groups that overturns moral laws and ethical rules? Is the violence perpetrated by collectivities only a matter of emotional amplification and group contagion, or is it also, or primarily, something inherent to the group, something structural, that is responsible for this inversion? It seems that cruel violence on a large scale has similarities with but also differences from individual cruelty. Indeed, we use a specific term to denote cruelty inflicted on large masses of people: *atrocity*.[15] Gil Baillie gives us a hint regarding this question: "Far from being a bizarre aberration in human affairs, collective violence with its mesmerizing and socially galvanizing power was the context in which human culture first formed."[16]

Triadic Evil

Collective violence has a formative and socially galvanizing power. We shall return to it later, but first let me describe its structure, which I see as triadic. Collective violence, that is, violence that is produced by a group, is perpetrated as a rule in the name of some ideal that binds the group together and enables it to persist. Systematic collective violence, I suggest, can be explained in terms of a triadic structure, consisting of the perpetrator, the victim, and the ideal. The ideal mediates, ratifies, even sanctifies the action of the (collective) perpetrator on the (collective) victim.[17] The triadic structure of evil in the case of religious terrorism encompasses an idealized but persecutory object that sponsors the control of passions and anxieties in a collective mode and that legitimizes the use of violence against other humans. Such a legitimizing object is loved and venerated,[18] and the readiness to die in its name attests to this love. Acts of collective violence are always undertaken in the name of some ideal that has become a moral precept. Without the mediation of this third element, violence cannot attain massive and public proportions, and cannot mobilize masses of humans for action. With no ideology to buttress the violence, violence remains within the domain of personal, tabooed crimes. Ideology enables one to jettison guilt and self-condemnation, legitimizing the desire to kill and destroy by reformulating it as God's, the State's, or the Revolution's will to action against "our" enemies.

In referring to collective evil such as terrorism, I do not include "loner terrorists" who are featured in history and literature. These are the resentful and disgruntled individuals, such as the Professor in Conrad's *Secret Agent* (even if he is part of a group of anarchists, he is a loner), or the cab driver in *Taxi Driver*, who set out to destroy society. Such isolated cases have more to do with individual psychopathology than with ideologically sponsored violence. My point is that evil occurs not just when a person engages in hateful action toward another person, and evil on a systematic basis is done not just when a person is involved in hateful action toward a collective of people. When a group of people begins to endorse and support hateful action such as cruelty and other forms of dehumanization that consist in the refusal to honor the humanity that connects all human beings, they adopt a collective ideal object with which they—their selves, their core values—identify. This ideal is safeguarded and protected from any threat. Large-scale violence proceeds with the aid of *a corresponding ideology that articulates an ideal object*. The ideal object carries the group's collective identity, that is, the group's most precious aspect, and can therefore become a venue for justifying and implementing the most variegated actions, among them, depending on the ideology, acts of occasional or systematic cruelty. Thus, the ideal that binds a group of people together can be constructive or destructive. It can dynamize people toward acts of compassion, helpfulness, and courage, or it can move the group to kill others and even sacrifice themselves for the narcissistic whims or the paranoid visions of their leaders. Since it is supreme and exclusive, the ideal object has the power to decree the liquidation of anything that challenges its validity and superiority. Postulating a triadic structure to collective evil goes a long way toward answering the question of why individually committed acts that are deemed evil and criminal are condoned and encouraged when perpetrated collectively, and why what is taboo and punishable on an individual level changes its valence and becomes a heroic feat, or a sacred duty, when it is done in a collective. Looking at the horrific ravages of the World War I, Freud wrote: "Two things in this war have aroused our sense of disillusionment: the low morality shown externally by states which in their internal relations pose as the guardians of moral standards, and the brutality shown by individuals whom, as participants in the highest human civilization one would not have thought capable of such behavior."[19]

There is today a type of religious violence that has evolved against a background of particular historical and geopolitical circumstances. This religious violence threatens to destroy the world. The implacable summons to war issued by religious leaders are not confabulations of a single deranged mind, and neither can they be regarded as purely political or materialistic. Attacks launched for religious reasons mostly (though not always) lack real political aims.[20] These acts are symbolic and demonstrative, and, as Scott Atran has demonstrated, are definitely not perpetrated for local or practical gains.[21] In his analyses of his own interviews with religious terrorists, Atran found support for the notion that suicide bombers—"self-martyrs," in Martin Kramer's phrase—are not significantly more traumatized or abused than other people, and further, that explanations of individual psychopathology are resoundingly irrelevant here.[22] Somewhat analogously, explanations in terms of poverty and exploitation—although these may be contributing factors—do not satisfactorily account for terrorist violence. After all, other regions in the world that suffer poverty, exploitation, and painful conditions of abjection do not resort to morally sanctioned violence on such a scale. It is a well-known finding that psychological tests did not disclose any particular psychopathology in the Nazis who were tried in Nuremberg, and that no particular personality profiles characterized the SS security service personnel. On the contrary, Nazi planners made a systematic effort to evict those members who might derive pleasure from what had to be done, lest their impulses would jeopardize the dependability and efficiency of their functioning on these special operations. Ordinary and sane people, loyal to a worthy cause, were thought to be preferable candidates. An absence of overt individual psychopathology seems to be the case as well among Rwandan, Serbian, or Islamist killers. Zygmunt Bauman goes so far as to say that "cruelty correlates with certain patterns of social interaction much more closely than it does with personality features or other individual idiosyncrasies of the perpetrators. Cruelty is social in its origin much more than it is characterological."[23]

Religious Justification of Evil

There have been historical attempts by religious leaders to prevent wars,[24] and of course there are moderate Muslim leaders who condemn terror attacks, but their voices are not overwhelmingly prominent. In contrast, holy wars are a historically constant phenomenon. It is undeniable that a combined sense of historical victimization, loss of honor, and humiliation, intensified by a collective recollection of trauma, creates a fertile ground for vengeful acts of collective violence. But collective evildoing goes beyond that. It has the capacity to generate a self-camouflaging aura of mythic, religious, or ethnic justification which provides the victimizing community with social solidarity while cementing its righteousness and its ritualistic practices. "For millennia, evil perpetuated itself by enveloping its perpetrators in an intoxicating moral fog which made it possible for them to regard their viciousness and brutality as virtue itself," writes Gil Baillie.[25] In a rather obvious sense, religious suicidal violence is a pernicious solution to the kind of cognitive dissonance that arises from conflictedness about modernity and its temptations. Such violence is not only a bid for making an impression and showing one's power; it is also an attempt to convert the other to one's side, to see one's own point of view as the truth, and if this is not possible, to make the other cease to exist so that the Truth can finally be liberated from its shadows and shine forth with no obstacles. Liquidating others who do not believe in one's own God establishes in fantasy a purer field of unadulterated belief in that God.

While these acts are meant for external consumption, designed to make a grand impact on the infidel world, they are likewise of great use among the community of religious zealots, demonstrating the viability and valid-ity of the faith.[26] Bringing forth the glory of God in an explosion of fire and blood is an act of evil. Terrorist suicide bombings kill masses of in-nocent people and are therefore atrocities. Plans for chemical, biological, and nuclear attacks are atrocities. Their justification is derived from the invention of what I have been calling triadic evil. Triadic evil is a kind of supermorality that supersedes and cancels ordinary morality, declaring it insignificant in comparison with the grand scheme of things. As men-tioned, triadic evil consists of a triangular relationship between an ideal-ized totalistic object, its adherents, and the adherents' enemies. In the case of Islamic terrorism, the triadic evil consists of Allah, Allah's adherents, and unbelievers, those who are considered a challenge and a defiance of the holy alliance between believers and their God. The devout adherent of Allah who believes that becoming God's purifying instrument through martyrdom is a way of pleasing God and reaching paradise strives to sup-press an enemy terminally tainted with God-denying sin and hubris. The believer will make great sacrifices, including sacrificing his life, to please God, an idealized object who in fact persecutes the believer by command-ing the latter to persecute others. This God incites the believer to elimi-nate his enemies at any cost, even at the cost of the believer's life.

René Girard's theory of the regulation of violence regards the ritual of sacrifice (and scapegoating) as a beneficial use of ritualized violence. Sacrifice in Girard's view is a powerful means of symbolically enacting violent impulses so that they do not have to be discharged against other humans. Islam minimizes the place of blood sacrifice (being absolved of one's sins by the blood of another) and prefers one's personal sacrifice, the willingness to submit one's ego and individuality to Allah.[27] Like the Old Testament prophets, Islamic scholars decried the cult of sacrifice that sheds blood and multiplies corpses but does not necessarily bring people closer to God. At the same time, as Mark Anspach, a Girardian, observed, Islam's lack of the developed sacrificial ritual structure that exists in many other religious traditions may have effected a merging and "confusion of ritual and history."[28] Lack of ritual in this case carries the risk of promot-ing the literalness of sacrifice and equating history with ritual and ritual with history, "resulting in ritualized—albeit real—violence against its sa-cred enemies."[29] Instead of localized, circumscribed sacrifice, the whole world becomes a scene of a grand priest, the radical believer, performing sacrifice of the world for the sake of God.

"God" in this context is essentially an organizing principle that effectively enables the perpetrator to project badness and abjection to the victim (the infidel, the woman, the defective co-religionist). The notion of God helps to obfuscate the direct hateful meaning of the violent act by signaling to believers that the sinners who indulge themselves are enemies and defamers of God, heretics who by definition are evil and hence should be punished with death, so that their expiry in a holy war serves as a lesson to believers and unbelievers alike. The human mind, as we know, creates conscious and unconscious fantasies that reflexively represent, not only external reality and relations to other people, but internal fantasies that reflect relations between parts of the psyche. Such relations are then enacted in (external) reality between people, or between people and things, or people and ideas, who then become internalized, and again externalized, in an ever-revolving circle. The creation of fantasies to represent parts of one's inner world is shaped by the religious violence of its bearer. Fantasies, which represent feelings and parts of one's inner world that correspond to those feelings, are blueprints for action, by virtue of their representative power. The action can take the form of internal transformation (mental acts) or of action in the world. Thus fantasies (that can be conscious or unconscious) of religiously toned fear and violence undergo a process of radicalization. Religious terrorism—or coercive fundamentalism—is a process in which fear and mental conflict are dealt with by depositing idealized parts of the personality in God, to protect these parts against the raging and enfeebling parts within. These idealized aspects now "work for" the believer, rationalizing and sanctifying violence—as a way to overcome misery and to feel effective and powerful—by renaming it as good and sacred. God is thus a construction, an abstract factor that mediates the murderous desire of fanatical perpetrators. God serves as a barrier between two human groups, zealots and "heretics," a barrier that blocks direct human contact, suppresses communication, and annuls any chance for negotiation since it replaces any possibility of collaboration with a lofty set of commands. Horizontal, affiliative, or negotiable relations between two groups of people are blocked, while the believer's capacity for connection transmutes into a vertical, exclusive relation with God.[30]

The religious frame of mind that commands evil acts is restless. It does not allow for a divinity that is peaceful and benevolent, as in other religious or spiritual states. Rather, God insists on His believers' duty to purge the world of His enemies, a purgatory for which He seems to be dependent on his adherents. In Chapter 1 I mentioned psalms and poems in which the son-believer laments to his Father God that he is being persecuted by enemies, and in Chapter 4 we read bin Laden's intimate poem addressed to God. But religious holy texts such as the Old and New Testaments and the Quran boast of God's "complaints" to His believer. In contrast to Jesus' and his apostles' message of love and redemption, and in contrast to the Old Testament prophets' warnings to cease sinning and the Quran's assertion that God is said to have mercy toward all monotheistic believers,[31] God often makes it known that His Name needs to be redeemed by the hands of His believers. God needs vindication, as in "trying" Abraham as to whether he will renounce his son Isaac for Him. God needs recognition and acknowledgment, as when He demands of his adherents to launch war to save His name from profanation. Dark processes take place at these junctures. At the same time as God provides his believers with justification for the discharge of their violent impulses, we note that He also becomes the persecutor, requiring ever-escalating dangerous violence and the risk of self-destruction.[32] This is no longer a God of benevolence and mercy, but a deity suffused with bloodthirst that is idealized and given omnipotent status. Omnipotence in psychoanalysis is the delusion of occupying a position of unquestionable superiority and the right to implement an unencumbered, morally simplistic, relentless desire to abolish any hurdle that stands in the way of achieving a final good, or, in religious terms, a lasting redemption.

Heinz Kohut, a psychoanalyst with penetrating insight into idealization, describes an intriguing process of psychic deterioration that can take place in narcissistic personality disturbances. Narcissistic personality disturbances are personality structures that strongly revolve around issues of self-esteem. The narcissistic personality has trouble regulating self-esteem and so tends to be either inflated or deflated. We all have narcissistic issues, since self-esteem is a crucial personal issue for everyone. But the self-loathing and self-rejection mentioned earlier in the discussion of purification are the flipside of the narcissist's apparent self-aggrandizement. The progressive deterioration Kohut describes involves the "healthy elaboration of a narcissistically cathected, omnipotent and omniscient, admired and idealized, emotionally sustaining parent imago," that gradually or abruptly turns into an "all-powerful persecutor . . . and manipulator of the self." The idealized figure (called self-object in psychoanalytic parlance) that is needed to empower and emulate the person becomes the notorious "influencing machine," a paranoid contraption that has the face of a diabolical enemy, "whose omnipotence and omniscience have become cold, unempathic, and nonhumanly evil."[33] There are two possible antecedents to the transformation of God from a benevolent enveloping presence to a malicious persecutory entity. One is regression from a "better" state, and the other is prior existence of that state. *Regression* is the term that Kohut uses to denote a psychopathological process in an individual patient. Since the latter is not my topic here, I employ the term *regression* to signify a process of corruption that takes place when God initially appears to his believers as a kind and compassionate entity but, due to processes of degradation—mind control,[34] the instilling of fear, the indoctrination of hatred, and the need for retribution—"becomes" a vengeful tyrant, an "influencing machine." This terrifying idealized inner presence is recognizable as a metamorphosis of the demon-gods with their terrible faces who adumbrate malevolence and have to be propitiated. On this conception, the third apex of the triangle of collective evil, the ideal, is an avatar, a manifestation, of the primordial father: for the love of the father, collectives are occasionally ready to do evil. According to another view, there is no degradation from a former idyllic loving phase, no "regression," no transvaluation of values in the Nietzschean sense. Here God embodies precisely the highest value in the culture in which He is worshiped. Historically, in the Abrahamic religions,[35] such value has been mostly, if not exclusively, that of the pursuit of vengeance aimed at redressing grievances (usually phrased as "restoring justice"). Be that as it may, whether the God-image becomes corrupted, or just substantiates its generic constitution, it exerts pressure on the worshiping subject to deny any badness the Godhead might harbor by rephrasing it as goodness, so as to hide the naked hatred deposited in the deity lest it become exposed.

False Religious Love

This denial of evil, or rather, this rephrasing of hatred as love, is essentially what perversion is about: namely, the falsification of evil and hatred through defensively reconceiving them as love. Perversion is false love; terrorism is false religious love. The recasting of hatred as love enables the believer to hold on to the passivity of being God's instrument and devotedly serving in a higher divine mission, at the same time as enjoying the immunity that accompanies the disavowal of one's will as one's own.[36] This process of disavowed desire that is executed through and for an Other (while claiming the opposite, i.e., that one is but the guardian and steward of that Other), is a way in which perversion reverses the active-passive voice. It also points to the notion that humans created God by imaginatively realigning, not only what they conceived as good and perceiving it in God, but by making contact with their intrinsic imperfection, their lack of being,[37] their nothingness. This nothingness is then projected outward, not as weakness or badness, but as sublime will, as godly inexorability and superiority, as God.

Reflecting on the way one's inner aspects succumb to one's hatred and self-hatred and crystallize into a persecutory God raises questions that go beyond the classical psychoanalytic theory of God as the projection of an ideal. Kleinian theory applied shows that we not only unconsciously project parts of ourselves that we deem sublime onto idealized structures, but that we also deposit unacceptable, even repellant fantasies, wishes, and acts into an externalized structure such as God.[38] Humans not only create God as an idealized being, a lofty but benign presence that gives meaning, succor, and a sense of purpose; they also project violence onto God and then idealize it as divine and good. What may happen during this process is that the human desire to relate to a benevolent sublime deity who radiates goodness succumbs to human fear, hatred, and self-hatred, whereupon a cruel God is born. This happens when a person's murderous, hostile parts, currently dwelling within the (imaginary) figure of the deity, are renamed and justified as good. Within this cast of mind, God's wrathful aspects can be experienced as burning love and be embraced with devotion.[39] This hostile, menacing element in the God structure is highlighted in Rudolph Otto's studies on religious experience that vividly describe the ambiguous transition from burning love to a destructive blaze. Otto writes about a quality of the holy called "energy" or "urgency," that is considered in mysticism as the "consuming fire" of love, whose blazing strength "the mystic can hardly bear, but begs that the heat that has scorched him may be mitigated, lest he himself be destroyed by it. And in this urgency and pressure the mystic's 'love' claims a perceptible kinship with . . . the scorching and consuming wrath of God; it is the same 'energy', only differently directed. 'Love', says one of the mystics, 'is nothing else than quenched wrath.'"[40]

This enthrallment to God's wrath—a wrath that is inherent to the godly nature and is not merely present when God punishes sinners—enhances

His exaltedness and is a crucial and poignant aspect of religious fervor. The believer, far from repudiating the wrath, jealousy, and terror of God, far even from resigning to and accepting them, is awestruck and rejoices in their harsh glow. In the most exalted waves of religious experience, God's ire and rage can be related to as part of His grandeur and even His love for us. Revelation of this overpowering—even if potentially evil!— capacity is adulated. Phallic wrath is worshiped and valorized as a kind of divine grace, as pure justice and the potency to protect. The affects of dread and awe, terror and trembling are the foundation, says Otto, for the subsequent rationalizing, moralizing, religious formulations that describe the doing of good.

The Hindu Vision

Hindu worship as described in the writings of Wendy Doniger-O'Flaherty seem pertinent to my concern with the interface between the knowledge and the nonknowledge of what goes into God making, the awareness of its constructedness and the will to ignore it so as to believe.[41] Hindu worship deals with these essentially self-deluding, potentially perverse practices in an interesting way. In a sense, Hindu conceptions forgo the self-deception and its disavowal that are involved in considering God, particularly in his violent form, as an impeccable ideal to be emulated. In fact, in Hindu thinking, God's badness is openly recognized and accepted, at the same time as this badness is willingly taken on by the believer as his own. Within Hindu faith it is believed and accepted that the deity projects its evil parts onto us, so that the deity can maintain its goodness.[42] But the Hindu believer knows that he is sustaining his deity in order to continue to enjoy the emanation of the deity's power on him, and that this is the reason he is prepared to acknowledge the deity's badness and assume it himself. The Hindu believes that "evil afflicts man because it is 'not' present in God. He [God] must make us evil in order that he may remain good."[43]

Within this framework, in contrast to Western thinking, human evil does not reflect problematically on God's benevolence, and does not clash with the latter. On the contrary, human evil here is rather a reassuring proof that God has become good and shows goodwill to his believers, since He is "drained" of evil (which is now deposited in, or introjected by, the worshiper). Hindu culture seems to have constructed an ingenious device for protecting oneself against "divine evil" and accounting for God's goodness in the face of the undeniable evil that fills the world. In this way, Hindu religion seems not to need to rename evil as goodness or to split it off as Satan. At the same time, the need to believe in the perfect and unalienable goodness of the divinity is renounced. Here God is not exclusively good, and evil is not split off into the Devil. Since the Hindu believer needs God as protector, God is allowed to be "sinful" and evil, and the Hindu believer is willing to take upon himself God's sins in an act Doniger-O'Flaherty calls the "transfer of sin." This mechanism creates a situation in which the belief in divine *benevolence* is given up (since God is seen as potentially and originally sinful), while the belief in divine *omnipotence* is maintained for the purpose of protecting humankind. Hindu theodicy (if it can still be called theodicy) lays bare the traffic between parts of the self. In this system it is within the person's own power to create a god who will suit his needs, at the same time as one can still acknowledge this power as one's own. On this view, divine omnipotence is constricted by some awareness of the bootstrapping of oneself that is involved in upholding it.[44] In this sense, the Hindu religious system is an example of an unconscious owning of one's true motives. On the face of it, this bargain between God and the believer grants that if the believer will behave righteously God will reward him with his benevolent care. But between the lines of this manifest contract lies another deal, to wit, *I, the believer, am the one* who allows God to appear as infinitely benevolent and omnipotent. The relationship between God and humans in Hinduism is reciprocal; there is no monolithic, commanding deity that overpowers an abject believer. Rather, there is an exchange between the deity and the human that implies that their relationship is, in psychoanalytic terms, introjective and projective, involving mutual exchanges so as to accommodate both deity and worshiper. Within this liberatory arrangement there is an owning, even if unconsciously, of self-seeking motives.[45]

Needless to say, the way in which Hindu belief is represented here is a great simplification of this intricate and historically varied ancient Eastern religion. It remains to be seen whether this different conception of the relation between humans and divinity has been prone to less violence.[46] But observing this core mechanism of Hindu religion makes transparent an important aspect that is occluded in monotheistic religions, namely that it is man who needs to sustain God with his human goodness—or blood, or soul; that the Son needs to be sacrificed to the Father. From the Hindu perspective as presented here, the suicidal terrorist operates like the archaic priest who performs the sacrifice of his victims for the deprived god, whereby he himself is that very sacrifice. He dies deprived of any awareness of the reciprocity and self-production that is manifest in Hindu religion.[47]

Emotional Balancing and Its Relation to Evil

The question now poses itself as to why all these interior dissociations, why all this idealization, demonization, and projection are necessary? To understand these inner activities, it is important to keep in mind the vital imperative of maintaining psychic equilibrium and protecting emotional well-being. The idea is that there is a primal psychic activity in humans that is presumed to work incessantly to maintain basic well-being, manifested as the prevalence of good feelings over bad feelings. Through complex cognitive-emotional and fantasy processes, feelings that are agreeable—those that elevate self-love, self-esteem, and self-power—are augmented, while the opposite feelings—those of self- and other-hatred, fear, suspicion, and pain—are diminished or shunted aside. The idea is that we humans want and need to feel good—to feel, at least in the long run, more good than bad. We want to feel good, whatever form that good may take. We cannot afford, however, to totally ignore the limits and constraints that reality imposes on us. Even as we are busy maintaining our self-love and self-esteem, we have to take reality into account in order to survive.[48] These two basic exigencies, the need for not feeling too much pain and the need to take in reality so as to adapt to it, are in tension; we all engage in the conflicts of balancing the two. The constant flow of psychic activity that goes into mental self-equilibration is normative; it fulfills the function of psychic self-maintenance and is not necessarily psychopathological. But when it is carried out as an excessively externalized, unacknowledged (disavowed), and disguised process, one in which a person unconsciously exports his or her inner dissention and lets it play itself out on the outside, human interreality is sacrificed for the benefit of psychic power and comfort. In such cases, the balancing activity becomes increasingly violent and self-mutilating; the processes of splitting and bifurcated projection (goodness toward God and badness toward God's enemies) remove and externalize both the abject and the grandiose-idealized parts of the psyche. This process of double splitting leaves the fundamentalist psyche denuded of diverse and complex parts, and licensed to act on a simplified, impoverished version of oneself. The terrorist thus is no longer a self but an instrument; he is no longer a center of being but a projectile aimed against nonbeing which is incarnated in the sacrificial object ("God's enemies," the "infidels"). God is both the launch pad of this missile and its final aim. In this enterprise, God is not just the high commander in whose service the terrorist operates; God is also, or rather primarily, an entity the terrorist aims at merging with precisely by obliterating the barrier to Him, namely God's enemies.

Since we assume here that "God" is the projected, idealized part of oneself, the believer basically strives to merge with his own idealized part that had been projected outward but is now transmuted into a demonic, alienated, cruel version of himself. *Evil* is thus *a merger with an object that is both idealized and persecutory*, omnipotent and contemptuous of human vulnerability. It is an object whose "enemies" need to be liquidated in the service of this persecutoriness. It is for the sake of such liquidation that like-minded believers come together in terrorist organizations. They gather in training camps, mosques, and private homes; they are invited to join the prayer, or to sign in on the Internet; then they often go on to prepare for a holy mission in the service of redeeming faith and aggrandizing God. This process is bidirectional: because the terrorist is merged and identifies with this idealized object, every instance of disregard or indifference toward this object is acutely felt as a dismissal or an attack on the self, and every attack on the self deserves cruel retribution since it is at the same time an attack on God.

Furthermore, since the object that is idealized is a persecutor, or, more precisely, has been idealized because it is persecutory (and therefore, according to this logic, powerful), the fantasy of a tight link with such a persecutory-idealized object creates a perverse structure. To say it again, the structure is perverse because the evil of religious totalitarianism is cloaked in false goodness, and because the mindset within this structure idealizes a negative, wicked human aspect. Robert Stoller defined perversion as the erotic (or eroticized, "loving") form of hatred, while I have written about "false love" as characterizing perverse relationships.[49] Perverse modes of experience and relations misuse and distort love to disguise more genuine feelings toward the other. These two characteristics, the reversal of good and bad and the dehumanization or "superhumanization" of the object of desire,[50] are hallmarks of perversity.

We know that both projection and idealization are normal and universal processes that help integrate the psyche and resolve divisions in it. We all need to externalize (project) parts of ourselves, which we have internalized at an earlier stage, and which we now need to idealize outside of us, onto external objects—persons, deities, belief systems—in whose power or sublimity we wish to bask. We also normally need to project some badness away from ourselves, be able to tolerate ourselves, but these projections need to remain within certain limits of reality. We might speculate that whereas *projection* is universally unavoidable for all religious experience and religious modes to function, there is more variability among different religious systems regarding *idealization*. It seems likely that processes of idealization operate more powerfully in monotheistic (that is, exclusionary) religions than in others (e.g., Greek, Hindu), differing across monotheistic cultures only regarding what values are idealized, what attributes are held in highest regard in a particular culture (e.g., love and self-sacrifice in Christianity, justice and charity in Islam, etc.). Since idealization and perhaps with it the "superhumanization" (a kind of dehumanization) of the deity are more pronounced in monotheistic religions, a greater vertical distance is posited between the elevated, remote, abstract deity and the worshiping human person. We could speculate further that the monotheistic fundamentalist believer holds in mind an image that is more omnipotent, perfectionist, and exclusive, more woman- and world-denying, than the image to which a nonfundamentalist worshiper relates.

God

The idea of "God" is useful and necessary for religious terrorist actions. It gathers them around itself and absorbs their love and devotion; thus they are acting on God's behest and on His behalf. The God representation under these conditions functions to transform ostensibly loving beliefs into violent hateful actions. From a certain psychoanalytic perspective, God is the unconsciously projected idealized self—greedy with narcissistic needs, avid to feed on sacrifice and to receive glorification and recognition, eager to eliminate resistance. But on a conscious level, the triadic structure of God, believer, and nonbeliever assigns God the part of the idealized object and one's own enemies are (re)conceived as God's enemies. In the unconscious layers of the psyche the triadic structure is unstable enough, however, to lead the believer to revert back to God as the enemy and persecutor, while the believer and his enemy perish together—as is the case with the suicide killers who destroy themselves while destroying others, all of them going up in flames together.

Imaginary Ideology

We have said that the idealized "bad object" functions as a "third" in the implementation of group evil. Reliance on an omnipotent object offers enormous aid to the psyche's economy and anchors it in the outer world. Such a superior object functions as a container of projections and as a purveyor of meaning at the same time as it is the unconscious expression of an idealized extension of the self, proclaiming itself through the discourse of its ideology. What is ideology? Like language, ideology is a structure or system which we inhabit, which speaks us, and which gives us the illusion that we freely choose to believe the things we believe. It supplies us, furthermore, with plausible reasons as to why we believe those things.[51] While ideology can be compelling for the individual person, on a social level, it is, as Louis Althusser puts it, a "representation" of the "Imaginary Relationship of Individuals to their Real conditions of existence."[52] While one's own ideology or the ideology of one's group is deemed obvious and true, everybody else's beliefs are recognizable as illusory or imaginary—that is, "ideological." Althusser and others have pointed to the specular structure of ideology; the fact that it reflects back the wishes and fantasies of its believers. Like Lacan's imaginary, ideology is locked in a self-referential recursiveness; ideology is by definition a closed, incorrigible construct. This is why the terrorist "God" is a structure that mirrors the terrorist's values, fantasies, and wishes. "God" as represented by the terrorists is their mirror image. The veil that dresses the mirror and hides the fact that it is but a mirror is the terrorists' ideological discourse of social justice and divine redemption.

In tracing bin Laden's biographical history leading to global terrorism,[53] one is struck with his search, in his younger years, for a missing ideology to help him freely express and rationalize his feelings of animosity and his ambition for power and fame, as well as his use of self-denying asceticism to aggrandize himself. Bin Laden uses Islamist scholars—Sayyid Qutb, Abdullah Azzam, Sheikh Omar Abdel Rachman—to provide him with ideological texts, to serve his rationalizing needs, to shape them, express them, and, finally, to justify violence as a legitimate, not to say sacred, response to having such feelings. Some see ideology as analogous to the manifest content of a dream, or rather, as I would suggest, the "secondary revision" of a dream, normalizing of some awful mad contents by giving them a seemingly coherent and plausible shape that hides their disturbing import. On this view, which is clearly psychoanalytic in its presuppositions, ideologies can normalize the most blatantly unacceptable wishes by justifying them as lawful and beneficial for the group. Ideologies can function as "Superlaw."

Superlaw

Superhuman law (Superlaw) allows for a "state of exception,"[54] an outlawed state that is accepted as necessary because extraordinary conditions justify it. Such "a state of exception" enables the transgression of the law, solidarity, and human rights. The transmutation of killing into sacred ritual is effected with the help of perverse mechanisms. One of the paradoxes of Atta's letter pertains to the way murderous, cruel acts can correlate with an experience of oneself as a good person who submits to a just and superior law. Contrary to first impressions, a perverse person does not place himself outside the law, and the pervert's challenge to the law does not entail the will to abolish it. Speaking in the context of social and political group dynamics, perversion will express itself within a political formation as the attempt to impose a preferred, "superior" law to the conventional, ordinary one. Such a Superlaw may reveal itself as the "higher" morality even as it culminates (as it has) in a horrifying vision of a genocidal utopia, where the law becomes more absolute and nonnegotiable than the ordinary, all-too-human law.[55] Its absoluteness allows for no compromises or forgiveness.

It is to Hannah Arendt that we owe the conception of totalitarianism as a superhuman cult operating under the aegis of a superhuman law, itself understood as the dictum of an inexorable and transcendent force, accompanied by disdain for the contingencies of individual existence and a sense that humans are essentially dispensable. Arendt gives two examples of such a force: History in the case of Stalinist Marxism and Nature in the case of Nazism. To these two we should now add, in the case of extremist Islamism, "Allah" (one version of this deity, of course not applicable to all interpretations of the Islamic God). The force behind the Superlaw is elevated above all human concerns, acclaimed as universal, since it is conceived as linked with the heavenly, the paradisiacal, the utopian. Extremist Islamic terrorism is not about comfort, pleasure seeking, or even a quest for ordinary political power. Extreme Islamism is an existential position, part of a war of ideas, and does not so much have an interest in worldly gains or benefits as it does a devotion to a cause linked to a supernatural force and law. Using a Freudian scheme to speak of totalitarianism and fascism, Adorno writes of such perversion of the moral law as "the superego acting in the service of the id."[56] This is a state of mind that brooks no opposition, calling for war as a collective action allowing the individual (who in this context is precisely the one who cannot bear the responsibility of individuality) to evade the personal struggle with doubt.

We remember that evil is dehumanized and dehumanizing cruelty that causes unjustified suffering. On the way to unpacking what this evil consists of, we arrive at the idea that "love" for the inhuman Superlaw is a form of evil, a grandiose and informed legislation of malevolence, loved for its monolithic destructive bequest. Even as committing evil acts is experienced as an act of love, this is "evil as love." We said earlier that to be able to attain a state of devotion, and more specifically devotion to a male deity, one needs to dissociate a part of oneself and expel it from the domain of one's mind and knowledge. The part that needs to be expelled in this mental state is the part that recognizes human dignity, vulnerability, and the connection between human beings even across cultures and religious allegiances. Another part from which one needs to dissociate in order to maintain one's devotion to the Superlaw is one's moral deliberation, one's unique individual judgment—the connection with oneself. Both kinds of connection, those with other humans and those with oneself, are the linking, affiliative aspects of our human existence, and are the parts that resist the extirpation of the inhibitions of states of mind that offer a license to kill and to degrade, a license that procures a manic sense of breaking free from the constraints of having to know oneself and from the constraints of feeling compassion for those condemned to die. This is "evil as liberation"—liberation from the fetters of individual ethical responsibility and from the moral imperatives of human solidarity. This particular state of mind combines the triumph of overcoming limits with the *jouissance* of a willed pain of submission.

Evil as liberation is joined by evil as (false) love, blending into a peculiar affective state that is marked by the pleasure of self-abandonment and the elimination of one's subjecthood by relinquishing it to a higher instance that has the power to dispense death.[57] Evil-as-love points to the contradiction between a state of mind of devotion and "love" and the hateful acts committed while in this state. This duplicity of love and hate is a hallmark of perversion. Perversion is the disjunction between professed intention and the significance of an act as evil.

Claiming moral values for oneself while committing acts that are considered evil by others is a most common event. This poses the challenge of distinguishing between evil done with the awareness of its undesirability and expediency (such as protecting threatened human rights or human life), and evil that is committed from within a genocidal, cultish, or theocentric fanatical frame of reference. Sometimes the difference between the two, although most visible, is hard to conceptualize, since a moral system of values always underlies acts of collective evil. After all, even Nazi ideology was based on a moral theory and a set of values. This realization led James Bernauer to attempt to reconstruct Nazi ethics, that is, to articulate the Nazi conception of the good.[58] Nazi ethics is not the oxymoron it appears to be, since what was done in Auschwitz was done in the name of the good, or, more precisely, a certain conception of the good for a certain community. It was done not as a deliberate denial of the moral law but as an intended affirmation of it.[59] The difficulty here resembles the occasional difficulty, in a clinical setting, of distinguishing between a relatively normal person and a well-reasoning paranoiac, or between a charming person and a perverse charmer.

Terrorism as Perversion

I use *perversion* in a more encompassing way than the sense of deviant sexual practices that are habitually associated in one's mind with the word. It seems to me that perversion remains through all its manifold manifestations, whether sexual or nonsexual, as that which alters and overturns the meaning of reality and basic "agreements" between humans, pretending to uphold and honor them while attempting to strip them of their meaning and value. When perversion involves two people, it usually begins with the perverse person skillfully and attentively catering to the other's needs and gratifying that other's most embarrassing wishes and shameful secret desires, conveying to the other, "I'll fulfill your wishes, I'll guess your desires, I'll be your servant, your instrument, I'll be your 'phallus'; I exist only for you, to gratify and pleasure you."[60] Analogous to the perverse seducer—who, while essentially corrupting and hurting the other, believes, or partially believes, that she or he is exquisitely pleasuring them—collective perversion enables a group to evade the guilt that might arise from acts of deception and lying by maintaining a self-perception of undertaking an objective necessity or even an imposed moral duty.

Thus, Shoko Asahara convinced his followers that by killing all humans they will be doing them a favor by bettering the lot of those who need to be killed. In his message to his adherents, Asahara used a perverse version of the concept of *poa*, which in Buddhist thinking means transforming oneself onto a higher plane of being. Asahara perverted the meaning of *poa* to killing people for their own good by providing them with a death that will help them transit onto a more elevated plane of being.[61]

A strikingly similar idea, and closer to the immediate theme of this book, is Khomeini's message to his people a few years after the Iranian revolution:

> If one allows the infidels to continue playing their role of corrupters on Earth, their eventual moral punishment will be all the stronger. Thus, if we kill the infidels in order to put a stop to their [corrupting] activities, we have indeed done them a service. For their eventual punishment will be less. To allow the infidels to stay alive means to let them do more corrupting. [To kill them] is a surgical operation commanded by Allah the Creator. . . . Those who follow the rules of the Qu'ran are aware that we have to apply the laws of *qissas* [retribution] and that we have to kill. . . . War is a blessing for the world and for every nation. It is Allah himself who commands men to wage war and kill.[62]

Khomeini was a venerated leader, not a marginal lunatic or some local agitator. The newspeak here, delivered to the masses, not only inverts evil by renaming it as good, but, in particular, it calls brutalization a caring act designed for the welfare of the receivers of the brutality.

Viewing one's actions as obligatory responses to external imposition creates a perception of oneself as innocent, a victim who deserves justice, or at least a well-intentioned, righteous person. There is a falsely exhibited innocence in it, a disingenuousness that works in subtle, devious ways to deny the other's perception and judgment and to render the victim confused and helpless in the face of the pervert's dissimulative tactics concealing his predatory intentions.[63] In the religious version of perversion, one becomes an actor on God's behalf; one presents oneself—to others and to oneself—as no more than the tool and medium of God's will. This is a central strategy of perversion, whereby the object ("God") of the perverse person is accorded a false entitlement and the perverse person plays at being merely God's instrument and gets his share of enjoyment at these developments.[64]

Thus what is no less (if not more) intriguing than the cruelty and violence, is their not being acknowledged as such. This raises the question of whether, and to what degree, the terrorists believe themselves. Do they believe their own lies, or do they know deep down that these are lies? In a certain sense the question is superfluous, since the answer is self-evident: yes, the terrorists certainly believe in what they are doing, as does everyone with a highly moral mission. The terrorists believe they are ridding the world of evil. And their leaders also believe this, for otherwise they might not be able to infuse their followers with the heat of conviction. But one is still perplexed as to the degree and depth of their belief in regard to what they profess, so that one cannot abstain from the question regarding genuineness in the face of sanctimonious evil. In contrast to my past experience with fundamentalist believers (mainly in Israel and in Iran, as I mention in the Preface), some researchers of religious terrorism express certainty that the leaders cannot be religious in good faith. I think that posing the question in this way simplifies matters; religious leaders are often not cynical Machiavellians, neither are many of them totally wrapped up in belief. One would want to ask whether in these alienated self-states there is not still a small voice in the mind of the evildoer that knows and is aware that the atrocity committed is a great subterfuge, a play-acting, and a self-allowance that is known to be unacceptable. Of course, psychoanalysts (and others) know that the disavowal, the silencing of an undeniable voice, a voice of truth utterly indispensable yet beleaguered, is the essence of perversity, and I am aware that the question may seem naïve, flying in the face of what we human beings living in this world, even analysts, seeing different people at close quarters, know about the extraordinarily versatile capacities of the human mind to deceive itself. And yet I cannot cease asking it.

A further observation concerns the onlooker's occasional perverse need to believe the perverse person. There is a notable similarity in the experience of reading some fundamentalist arguments and listening to the reasoning of a perverse patient. Although one senses that the patient is lying, one is occasionally taken in by her, particularly as one immerses oneself in her being, which a good analyst does. One may feel one still wants to believe her, and the analyst wonders whether the speaker believes herself, that is, whether she might believe that what she says is the truth; eventually, one wonders what she "really" thinks about what she is doing: in other words, at what point, if there is such point, does the perverse person take leave of her senses and totally believe her production. One finds oneself vacillating between believing the patient's words that profess her innocence and knowing that one has been duped for believing her. At the same time, in the process of trying to clarify one's attitude of belief and disbelief regarding such a person, one realizes that one is profoundly manipulated and fooled. It seems that the only thing one can do with such knowledge is to follow one's minute affective responses to it and listen to one's a priori background knowledge and to one's hunches; momentary changes in this state of knowledge can provide useful information about what is going on. Finally, the only bulwark against this subtle deceitfulness and the doubt about whether the patient believes her own deceptiveness, is the analyst's self-awareness of her own seducibility and gullible corruptibility, knowing full well that her seductibility can be made to look and feel pathetic, occasionally even disingenuous, to the other. But it is the only option one has.

At times, the truth behind the deception and passive provocation opens up.[65] I once knew a woman whose husband was a Jewish fundamentalist. What most enraged her were the ways in which he used to deny, rename, and justify his cruelty toward others. One day, when she brought this up, again and again confronting him with his lies, he reluctantly blurted out his secret: "But I'm lying honestly!" he said, and he meant it. After all—and this is a common characteristic of fundamentalist sects—what counts as a lie in ordinary human transactions is for fundamentalist groups a truth in the service of God. Fundamentalist enclaves set apart from other parts of society use two different languages: a genuine, transparent language serving the insiders of the group, and a dissimulative language that functions to communicate with—that is, disinform—the rest of the world.[66] This duplicity is allowed, even recommended, as a means of protecting the believer's thoughts and those of his group.[67]

Sartre's concept of "bad faith," although not identical to these perverse practices, is germane to our concern here. Bad faith pertains to the intricacies that frame the lying to oneself and its difference from lying to others. Whereas lying (to others) implies a cynical knowledge of the truth that is denied to others and replaced by a conscious nontruth, in bad faith lying and truth occupy more ambiguous positions, since the one to whom the lie is told and the one who lies are one and the same person. Hence the religious fanatic is not necessarily a cynical liar—although he may be. One might say that like Sartre's anti-Semite, the person of bad faith is afraid "of his conscience, of his instincts, of his responsibilities, of solitude, of change, of society, of the world,"[68] and like Sartre's anti-Semite who turns the Jew into a thing in order to deny his own faults and failures, the Islamist turns the lesser believer into a thing, an animal, thereby "choos[ing] himself as a person with the permanence and the impenetrability of a rock, the total irresponsibility of the warrior who obeys his leaders [but is] . . . afraid of his own fate."[69] He is certainly a fervent believer in his own preaching (at least most of the time), since he is a product of his culture and religious upbringing, and his religious feelings and acts are in an important sense authentic. After all, he holds *his* values to be true for *all other* humans, or, in Kant's language, he universalizes the particular. On this level, it is a truism that religious acts committed by the believer are ipso facto believed in. But philosophical thinking goes a step further, conceiving of bad faith as the flight from existential responsibility. It asks whether a perverse act, or an act done in bad faith, is not in the nature of lying to oneself and avoiding one's realization, blurring one's knowledge (one's con-science). As Sartre put it, bad faith means denying one's responsibility to choose in one's life, by presenting the other as a thing, and then presenting oneself as a thing as well. When the terrorist ascribes his vengeful destructive lust to God, he denies and disavows his ownership of his desire by positioning the responsibility for these acts on God: being afraid of life, of "his fate," he not only lies to himself, he estranges himself from his reality as a free individual.[70]

Radical Evil, Diabolical Evil

Perversion is the rephrasing of evil, cruelty, and hatred as love and compassion, so that evil and hatred are clad in the garb of rectitude, even concern, for the other. The possibility of the cohabitation of morality and evil has been highlighted in recent discussions of Kantian ethics, the paradigm of Western moral theory. According to Kant, to act morally I must not merely do my duty; I must also do it for duty's sake. An action springing from any other motive than duty may be *lawful*, but for Kant it is, properly speaking, not *moral*, since the motive is ulterior to the duty. Only that action is moral that is motivated by reverence for the moral law itself.[71] To behave ethically, one must behave in a way that is applicable to a universal maxim, the categorical imperative, which says, "Act as if the maxim of thy action were to become by thy will a universal law of nature."[72] Such notions imply that one must be able to identify with the will behind such a maxim. This becomes problematic insofar as the Kantian will can be read in various ways, some of which are liable to make the will a sponsor of evil. Formally following one's will as law can lead to acts that are rule-bound but at the same time abstract, detached, and even hostile, as we saw in the case of Khoumeini and Asahara. Thus, for the al-Qaeda jihadist, the will behind the maxim became, "the will of Allah," and the categorical imperative became, "One must behave in such a way that Allah the all-knowing will approve." The same idea featured in the Nazis' description of their morality, namely, "Act so that if the Führer knew, the Führer would approve." Eichmann's protest in his trial that he had no "pathological" hatred of the Jews, as did many around him, that, further, he had "special reasons" for liking the Jews, is the hallmark of a law-sanctioned Evil that is not done out of hatred or for immediate benefit.

Pure morality can be evil. This is what Kant called "diabolical evil," neatly differentiating it from "radical evil," which seems to be a simpler notion. Radical evil is the refusal, out of self-interest, to do one's duty. It is the will to attain advantages for the self, to acquire money, influence, power, pleasure. Obviously, acting in one's self-interest reflects a deeply rooted and ineradicable human tendency,[73] which when it clashes with others' interests is called radical evil. Radical evil,[74] in the sense of enrooted, ingrained evil, amounts to making a choice against objective morality, a choice that is based on emotional, subjective motives (Kant calls it "pathological," using *pathos* in its etymological Greek sense as affectedness, or suffering). Such motives are fueled by what Kant calls "inclinations," desire for personal benefit. Diabolical evil, by contrast, is the perpetration of evil out of duty, without any self-interested motives, ostensibly without any subjective inclinations. Diabolical evil means obeying some superior, objectified law and by implication, the erasure and annihilation of subjective accountability. Such accountability helps to sharpen the discernment of acts that are evil toward other human beings and would signal the need to abstain from committing them. In obeying superior law, diabolical evil amounts to the surrender of personal judgment, that which Kant called "final judgment." Diabolical evil is the giving up of responsibility for one's own deeds and the embracing of a blind, unqualified adherence to an ideal or ideology. In this situation, one's personal accountability, which presupposes the weighing of the various factors that constitute an ethically demanding situation and the complex solutions it may require, is abdicated and replaced with submission to a vertically positioned Superlaw. Such eradication of "final judgment" is what enabled the Nazis to perpetrate genocide "for the sake of the German *Vaterland*," and what enabled the Taliban to persecute their population in their own country for the glory of Islam.

Abolishing one's "final judgment" requires the unconditional internalization of duty and the silencing, through dissociation or splitting, of the human, multiply-conceivable meanings of one's deeds. It implies the liquidation of considerations and hesitations regarding whether and to what degree one's deeds are moral or immoral, ethical or unethical. Abolishing one's "final judgment" is the ultimate in pseudoneutrality, whereby one voids oneself of overt desire and desires what the Law or God desires, thus remaining ostensibly neutral and "objective" about what is required.[75] The point here is that the diabolic character of calling evil good is all the more trenchant precisely by virtue of its being devoid of any possible pathological interest or justification, and by virtue of its not respecting the privacy and the unique separateness of each individual,[76] thus making everything a matter of equal objectivity.[77]

The traditional Kantian distinction between radical evil and diabolical evil is thus the distinction between interested and disinterested commitment of evil acts. Taking a closer, psychoanalytically informed look, however, reveals the differences between radical evil and diabolical evil as less useful and more limited. It is phenomenologically interesting indeed to distinguish between manifest self-interest and manifest selfless motivations. But beyond a certain point, it becomes evident that so-called diabolical evil is certainly not without self-interest either, only the self-interest is subtler and will be seen as such only from a psychoanalytic perspective. These are forms of self-interest that are not immediately obvious to simplistic ways of seeing. Unacknowledged self-aggrandizement posing as righteousness; the narcissistic seeking of perfection and infallibility; the act of identifying with an omnipotent person or entity in order to become like it; various maneuvers of erasing one's guilt through rationalization and bad faith; subtly pursuing manic, self-righteous entitlement; as well as the sanctimonious spiritualization of violence—all are part of a list of sundry forms of base self-interest that pose as lofty ideals or selfless morality. Here psychoanalysis joins great literature in the realization that the term *diabolical evil* is nothing but a hyperbole and a refusal to look further into human motivation. Diabolical evil is not really diabolical, but very human and suffused with subtle forms of self-interest.[78] There are so many ways in which self-interest can pose as self-denying, narcissistically-inflected asceticism, whose self-seeking character poses as the Nietzschean moralizing and ascetic ideal[79]—in short, the self-interest that lies in ideological adherence.[80]

Diabolical Evil and the Death Drive

Looking for concepts to express the immorality that lies in certain moralities, we find a correspondence between the concept of diabolical evil and Kant's categorical imperative: both denote, or are easily made to denote, righteousness and morality that is corrupted or easily corruptible into evil. More specifically, Kant's moral philosophy has been criticized for its separation of the moral law, that universal human compass of morality, from any particular, contingent contents or situational factors. The classical example of whether stealing drugs for one's moribund mother is a greater evil than letting her die; or whether helping another human out of compassion, breaking some minor rules in the process, is more evil than not helping, are examples for the possible rigidity of the Kantian imperative under a literal reading. The separation of the most general, universal moral precept from the particular and immediate human context, and its absolute universalization, claim Kant's critics, eventually makes the moral law, in its demand for ostensibly selfless moral obedience, indistinguishable from diabolical evil with its manifest impersonal character. Ultimately, both the moral law and diabolical evil appear inhumane and impersonal in their call for obedient self-erasure.[81] Freud attempts to explain why this is so in a work in which he addresses the complex relations between self-aggression and morality in masochism. In this work, he presents Kant's categorical imperative as the best philosophical expression of the concept of the cruelty of the superego:

> This super-ego is in fact just as much a representative of the id as of the outer world. It originates through the introjection into the ego of the first objects

of the libidinal impulses in the id, namely, the two parents. . . . Now the super-ego has retained essential features of the introjected persons, namely their power, their severity, their tendency to watch over and to punish . . . the conscience at work in it, can then become harsh, cruel, and inexorable against the ego which is in its charge. The categorical imperative of Kant is thus a direct inheritance of the Oedipus-complex.[82]

Freud draws a direct line from the ruthless id to the cruel superego, a transition made via the introjected parent representations that have become impersonal. One could say that Kant and Freud elucidate the insidious workings of a force of "impersonalization," or "universalization" in terms of social theory, or "depersonalization" in terms of psychoanalytic theory. Common to both terms is the desire for a final solution which will achieve permanent exemption from moment to moment worries, decisions, complexities, the other's fluctuating subjectivity, life events. Freud's complex notions of the death drive conceive it as the striving for perfect rest and immutability that can be expressed in the desire for universalization and impersonalization. These two related forms of deanimation cancel the individual's momentary concerns, her local ambivalences, inner debates, temptations, delinquencies, and strange pursuits of happiness—in short, varieties of thinking and feeling. Kant's diabolical evil and Freud's death drive both point toward a striving for deindividuation and for the certainty that comes from the cessation of the need to decide and be responsible for oneself. Freud talks about a death drive that strives toward an inanimate state,[83] and Kant analyzes diabolical evil that impersonalizes the moral law and liquidates the need for exercising personal judgment, which is replaced here by a literal version of the moral law as the ultimate imperative. Not surprisingly, both concepts, Kant's diabolical evil and Freud's death drive, are controversial; each has attracted considerable criticism. Both concepts deal with limit states that challenge simplistic notions of human motives, and both have been criticized on account of their inherent pessimism and their subversion of habitual motivational explanations in terms of utilitarian or hedonistic, and hence rationally comprehensible, human motives. They both indicate a turning away from the "simple" vices and pleasures of straightforward self-interest and toward seemingly self-abnegating, self-destructive, and other-destructive lethal acts or motives. The affinity between the two concepts and a certain overlapping of their fields of meaning makes them illuminative of one another.

The idea behind diabolical evil becomes clearer when viewed through a psychoanalytic lens that moves "beyond the pleasure principle" into human destructiveness and the lure of the death drive.[84] Aspiring toward the gratifying grandiosity and total control afforded by superhuman systems with their attendant ideologies can be immeasurably more alluring and exciting to some people than the messy, unpredictable small life with its mundane satisfactions, prosaic compromises and ever reappearing frustrations. When one adds to this the excitement and arousal that killing can bring, the way is open for tremendous yields of pleasure. This is the other side of the equation between ideology, or Superlaw, and obstacle-abolishing destructiveness: destructive temptations are sponsored and nourished by a corresponding "law." Explaining human motivation in terms of simple gratifications and profits misses the point of the awesome complexity and self-opposition of the human mind. It ignores the layeredness of the psyche, which can create cultures and extremist versions of religions and traditions to lend strong expression to fears and suspicions.[85] The human psyche hopes and longs for immortality and transcendence of "regular" existence and craves to deny the body's frailty and death.[86] The manic triumph of overcoming the limits and barriers that stand in the way of total fulfillment of all wishes holds the fantasized promise of utter solace and total bliss. We often get our thrills in life from loftier and darker motives, for those loftier and darker motives allow us to "go all the way."

The phrase *going all the way* helps us understand further what is meant by triadic evil. We said that collective evil has a triangular form, encompassing a cultural or religious group, its ideal, and the others outside of the group. When the outsiders are perceived as standing in the way of attaining the group's ideal, or rather, as barring the merger of the group with the ideal or challenging the identity of the group, the group is liable to turn to perpetrating evil deeds against the outsiders. Evil deeds are committed by ideological groups to remove outsiders from barring the way to merger with the coveted ideal aspect of itself. The triangle then becomes that of perpetrator, fusional ideal, and victim, and evil consists in the attempt of the perpetrator to erase anything between himself and his ideal, including the distance to the ideal. This eradication is made possible through an ideology that requires of its subjects to "go to the end," with no regard for the human consequences of their acts. Ideology, such as the ideology of instituting Allah's reign on earth and uniting the world under divine law, functions here to enable the perverse renaming of destructiveness as exalted goodness, and further, to proclaim this goodness as universal and applicable to all.

Going All the Way

In the preface to this book I mentioned the epiphanic moment that brought me a sudden visceral grasp of the triumph and exhilarating power the planners of the 9/11 events felt or may have felt on visualizing the straight way to heaven that opened up when the Twin Towers and their human inhabitants went up in flames and smoke.[87] At that paradigmatic moment—mythical or metaphorical as it may have been—it was as if all barriers between the believer and God had been removed, all boundaries had been overcome, a realm of pure triumph had been entered. It was an archetypal image of "going all the way," condemned by Kantian ethics as leading to diabolical evil. Slavoj Žižek writes that Kant reasserts the ethics of proper distance, of consideration and self-limitation, of avoiding the temptation to "go right to the end." When he goes "right to the end," writes Žižek, "the subject is swallowed up by the abyss of total self-disintegration, he accomplishes the . . . step into diabolical evil, morality breaks down, reality itself dissolves into the Monstrous."[88] Philosopher Iavor Rangelov writes that the possibility for diabolical evil is given the very moment ideology requires from the subject to "go right to the end," completely and irreversibly "disregarding the human dimension of his deeds."[89] Neutralizing one's "final judgment," that is, relinquishing one's personal deliberation on the ethical meaning of an act to be committed, releases the destructive and omnipotent self to overcome and extinguish all personal reflectiveness regarding one's acts. Abdication of *personal* responsibility and letting oneself "go all the way" blinds one to the (Sartrean) recognition that every decision is an individual, particular choice that can have a questionable character and that one is liable to bear its consequences and pay its price all by oneself.

Diabolical evil, the apparent "lack of self-interest," universalizes an individual moral vision and recasts it as absolute and universally valid by means of ideology, which regularly functions to universalize the particular by rephrasing it as absolute truth. Ideology falsely seizes the status of a universally binding truth for a particular, local, contingent interest, but also works in the opposite direction. Ideology can devalue universal ethical rules as invalid when a Superlaw or "supermorality" is called for. Part of diabolical evil is the claim that universal moral laws of human commonality (with all the problematics such a term involves) are contingent, even hypocritical, and need to be superseded in an extreme situation, a situation of "exception," in Agamben's phrase, or a situation of ultimate truth, as totalitarians claim. In the face of the Superlaw, human laws become secondary, even invalidated, and are violently overridden by divine truth, itself invoked as a utopian ideology, a superiority doctrine, an eschatological or millenarian ideal state, or another highly abstract metaphysical category. The list is endless: God, *Raison d'Etat*, National Security, Freedom, *Volk und Heimat*, *Blut und Boden*, Peace, Progress, Empire, Historical Imperative, Sacred Order, Natural Necessity, and so on. Ideological militants such as coercive fundamentalists claim, following Sayyid Qutb's formulations, that laws outside their own faith are mendacious and false since they are legislated by men, and men are fallible and unreliable, compared with Allah's infallibility and endless justice. Only the divine Truth will never need any modification and will stand forever. Diabolical evil means absolute self-valorization and devaluation of everything else. Going beyond one's contingent and specific belief by declaring it universal constitutes omnipotence, with the self-idealization and self-absolutization that come with it. Both the universalization of oneself and the particularization and invalidation of the other are used to abolish in fantasy the painful gap between a wished-for ideal and what actually exists. Psychoanalyst Joseph Sandler explains the experiential quality of psychic pain as the awareness, in varying degrees of consciousness, of the distance between one's "actual" self from one's ideal self.[90] It is this gap between the actual and the ideal self-state that can under certain circumstances be extremely painful and feel like a narcissistic insult. Overcoming these feelings is the work of mourning, considered by many psychoanalysts, and I among them, as a most basic psychic activity. It is the emotional work of coming to terms with loss, guilt, and limitation, and it sometimes makes for a great part of work in analysis. Mourning, or coming to terms with pain, involves a back-and-forth movement between realization of the thing that causes pain and the protective dissociation from awareness of it, acknowledgement of it and renewed obliviousness to it, in a way that keeps the gap from becoming an abyss. Omnipotence is the denial and annulment of this realization; evil is the use of omnipotence to erase the necessary recognition of this gap.[91]

Abdication of final judgment signals the loss of the barrier, of the protective device against self-loss and mind-loss, against "going all the way." The subject becomes separated from his moral self, detaches from his human discernment, even as he tragically and ironically merges with "God." In this way, the enemy, the depository of the unconsciously rejected parts in oneself, becomes a negative binding link between the believer and his god. The shared fantasy of merger and symbiosis with the omnipotent idealized-persecutory object creates a myth,[92] an ideology that implements this fantasy. Abdicating one's own "final judgment" parallels the sidestepping of the necessary internal process of developing one's own autonomous voice and individualized ethics, one's exit from mindless obedience to authority,[93] and the sidestepping of the necessary internal process of "killing the father"; it is a giving up of the revolt against a controlling, mass-tailored Superlaw; it is, as we saw in the preceding chapter, a "regression to the father."

The demarginalization of evil and the foregrounding of evil's positivity was a long historical process. Modern thought since Kant sees this evil as the product of the will: if we have acted badly, it is because we have chosen to do so; therefore we are fully responsible for our actions. Evil is not the Devil, and it is not beyond discourse. Evil is perpetrated by humans for human reasons. Kant went even further and talked about a profound malignity in the human being that causes him to be bad even when he is good: there is always self-interest at play, there is always a radical and ineradicable evil. As Kant writes, there is "a secret falsity in even the closest friendships . . . a propensity to hate him to whom one is indebted . . . a hearty well-wishing which allows the remark that 'in the misfortunes of our best friends, there is something which is not altogether displeasing to us.'"[94]

Detheologizing and humanizing evil also meant—and Kant understood this—the subverting of the longstanding religious and metaphysical view of evil as negative, as nothing more than the lack or deficit of the good.[95] It is not only our weak nature that cannot resist temptations ("inclinations") that prevents us from doing good; more deliberate mental action is involved.[96] In Kant's *Religion Within the Limits of Reason Alone*, evil no longer has a shadowy, insubstantial existence compared to the reality of the good it had in religious (particularly Augustinian) writings before him. Evil became for Kant and for most of us today a positive fact, firmly rooted in reality.[97] Evil is no longer seen, Socratically, as the result of human limitations of understanding, or of the weakness of the resistance to temptation, but as tightly linked to human freedom, that is, to the freedom that is existentially given, or rather, imposed on us, to choose and simultaneously be aware of the "unfreedom," the false freedom, enfolded in our aspirations for immortality, the same aspirations that threaten us with an illusionary liberation from human bonds, from time, and from death. Evil is a matter of choice, and as Kant taught us, should be regarded as evil if it is governed by the free adoption of a bad maxim.[98]

Radical Islam and the Question of Judgment

I have made an effort to show how Islamist terrorism is determined to commit actions we have always understood and interpreted as evil.[99] A central, vexing question that poses itself when judging a system of values such as Islamic totalitarianism concerns the legitimacy of deeming another cultural system, or rather, the radical wing of a religious system, evil. The quandary of delineating and attributing evil becomes compounded in our minds by the awareness of the atrocities committed on the Western, or American, or non-Muslim side. There is no doubt that evil deeds were and are committed by the West, by America, by Israel, by Europe. The ancient Israelites as recounted in the Old Testament, fought and exterminated the peoples of Canaan, and, after centuries of being harshly victimized, are now causing suffering, some of it preventable, to the Palestinians. The history of Christianity is bloodied by its inquisitional and colonial persecutions of outsiders, and twentieth-century Europe with its hypernationalistic, pseudo-religious totalitarian systems exterminated many millions of people. Radical Islam is certainly not the only violent movement in history. We should not forget all the other atrocities that were and are still committed in the world.

The question of judgment becomes particularly poignant in our postmetaphysical era, suffused as it is with our awareness that there might be no external, objective system for adjudication regarding cultures. There is a wide array of different vocabularies, conversational communities, language games, and conceptual schemes with their differing value systems, all sustained by different conceptions of good and evil. Every culture has its own particular and venerated conception of the good, that is, its own ethics. Even Nazi culture had its own ethics. Can we judge a culture that is different from ours as evil? Would difficulty in judging be resolved if we used more general, neutralizing terms, such as *socially structured order*, as does Adi Ophir when analyzing evil, or the *nation-state*, as do Badiou and others? It might sound less culturally judgmental, less "us-versus-them," to use such terms in criticizing evils and terrors. But even given such modulations, some of us are still reluctant to see the jihadist culture for what it is, as some contemporary scholars and those who have left the system have articulated it.[100] It seems to me that the objection concerning the right to criticize another culture is more problematic in relation to cultures and religious systems that differ from one's own. Coercive fundamentalism, and in particular jihadism, is such an instance of another culture with its specific ethics.[101] Alessandro Ferrara attempts to answer the question of perceiving evil in other cultures (and hence the issue of cultural relativism) by setting as a generally valid criterion the lack of "some reflection, however minimal or implicit, of an understanding of good as being that which is good for humanity as a whole."[102] Every culture holds relative ideals and values that are specific to it alone, but no culture can see itself as exempt from some modicum of accountability for *the human collective as a whole*. The determining and binding power of judgment should be ethics that apply to all of humanity, ethics that are based on the assumption of a basic human solidarity. Such solidarity-based ethics (even if the all-human concern comprises a small part of that culture's ethics) should constitute the binding power and the measuring rod for judging the culture's merits and faults, however complicated such judging of another culture may be. Extreme Islamism displays a belief system so narrow and exclusivist that any deviation from it results in lethal punishment, since difference or even doubt threatens its existence. The totalitarian cast of this movement, its acknowledged call to dominate the world by the sword and to annihilate those who do not believe in its tenets, the cruel practices with which women, moderate Muslims, and nonbelievers are treated, all point to the willful suspension of the central significance of a humanitarian ethics. The West has been slow to realize that Islamic terrorism has all the features of the totalitarian mindset, diabolical—that is, self-abnegating, "superhuman"—evil posing as righteousness (or even *being* a certain form of righteousness). This evil seeks to transcend the human order. The absolutist cast of the religious mode is its natural language, which Islamist jihadism liberally uses. Nonrecognition of this phenomenon and the attempt to understand jihadism in terms of Western modernism without paying more serious attention to its language, its professed intentions, and its historical background, results in considerable misunderstanding, confusion, and guilt.

An example of such confusion and guilt, leading to a moral crisis generated by the impact of 9/11, is found in Christopher Bollas's *Dark at the End of the Tunnel*. Bollas traces the changes that the world has undergone since, as he sees it, good and evil were reversed. The main character, called the psychoanalyst, of the particular episode in a book bringing together reflections on life, death, and 9/11, called the catastrophe, launches into a conversation with Westin Moorgate, an intelligent though ironically portrayed journalist. Their dialogue at lunchtime over a salad (consumed by the thoughtful analyst) and pizza (gulped down by the journalist) reveals the psychoanalyst's painful struggle with the idea, following the catastrophe, that "having thought we were the good, we are now the evil."[103] The "world's character is destroyed," he says, "the form of our character was gone . . . we have ceased to exist. We are meaningless. We don't mean anything anymore."[104] This mayhem, he feels, is due to the fact that the categories of Western culture, established over two thousand years ago— our way of being—have been devastated in the current reversal that has taken place between good and bad people. The antagonists before and after 9/11 increasingly resemble one another, since in fighting terrorism we Westerners emulate the terrorists' behavior, and we have become terrorists ourselves. We are becoming involved, he argues, voluntarily or not, in escalating and self-perpetuating cycles of violence and brutalization, emulating our antagonists until we become indistinguishable from them. The psychoanalyst does not go into details of how we have become like our antagonists; he portrays the world becoming unhinged, out of character, morally disordered, following the catastrophe. Actually, the reversal goes much further, says the psychoanalyst, in a manner revealing his having contemplated the situation for a long time. For him, the 9/11 tragedy is a total moral inversion, a chiasmic reversal of good and evil. Even more than our becoming evil, he tells Westin Moorgate, who is now joined by another acquaintance, the lovely art therapist Valerie Stone, we become aware that our adversaries have become good because they have suffered more than we have, and suffering establishes its own order of vindication.

Bollas presents us with an affecting scenario, yet his views exemplify the nefarious work of guilt and angst that destroys the awareness that such simple reversal is just a flight from a dialectical view of things that is needed to overcome a simplified "us and them" thinking. To say that good and evil are defined by suffering and sacrifice, as the psychoanalyst's speech makes clear, is to weaken any moral traction regarding the significance of the terrorist act itself. Chosen suffering, or even inflicted suffering, does not make one good. The fact that the suicide bombers are ready to die does not make their killing any less horrible (even if they tell themselves—or us—otherwise, taking a readiness to die as a proof of truth). Values should not be allowed to be so relative, and reversals should not be so direct and swift. The greatest evil is less in the nature of retaliation, even if we grant that America's "war on terror" is often wrongly conceived and causes much suffering. Rather, such evil may lie in the mentality that attempts to kill what stands in its way to self-enthronement, an enthronement it aims to achieve via an abject abdication of the mundane and individual self to a cruel Big Other. It is a mood, a state of mind, generalized into a truth about the state of the West, which I challenge here, in the context of our caution not to be judgmental about other cultures and consequently indicting ourselves instead to an extreme degree and blaming ourselves as evil and deserving of the "catastrophe." The key to the difference between good and evil (rather than between "us" and "them") lies rather in what I am calling the triadic structure of collective evil, a structure that encompasses a superhuman ideal and a will to supremacy over the human lot, that seeks to overcome the human. It is there, rather than in the dyadic chain reaction where suffering grants the right to kill, and even makes one good, as the psychoanalyst believes. The abject and slyly self-deceptive reliance on a divine alibi and scapegoat, a compelling ideal furnishing unbounded justification for attacking the different other, is one side of the coin of moral irresponsibility. The other side of it is the failure to deal with the situation, and giving in to a despairing contrition, blaming ourselves to the effect that we have deserved this calamity because of the other's pain. "We" are not evil because we have been attacked; neither would "they" be evil had they not been inculcated with a religious culture pitched to extremes, whereby its ideal, "God," blocks the recognition that collectively or religiously based killing resembles the individual kind in its cycle of revenge, whereby the victim of today can become the perpetrator of tomorrow. The idea of a certain "God" puts a stop to reflection by legitimizing the self-serving narcissism of a collective, blinding it to the common humanity of all peoples.

Reference Matter

Appendix A

Mohammed Atta's Letter

00:33 29Sep2001 RTRS-Text of suspected hijacker document

WASHINGTON, Sept 28 (Reuters)—Here is the complete text of the four-page document found in the luggage of Mohammed Atta, the 33-year-old Egyptian who helped hijack one of the two planes that hit the World Trade Center in New York on Sept. 11. This is a Reuters translation from handwritten Arabic. Portions in square brackets are explanatory additions. Other bracketed portions are bracketed in the original.

The Last Night:

1. Making an oath to die and renew your intentions.
   - Shave excess hair from the body and wear cologne.
   - Shower
2. Make sure you know all aspects of the plan well, and expect the response, or a reaction, from the enemy.
3. Read Al-Tawba and Anfal [traditional war chapters from the Holy Koran] and reflect on their meanings and remember all of the things that God has promised for the martyrs.
4. Remind your soul to listen and obey [all divine orders] and remember that you will face decisive situations that might prevent you from 100 percent obedience, so tame your soul, purify it, convince it, make it understand, and incite it. God said: "Obey

God and His Messenger, and do not fight amongst yourselves or else you will fail. And be patient, for God is with the patient."

5. Pray during the night and be persistent in asking God to give you victory, control and conquest, and that He may make your task easier and protect us.

6. Remember God frequently, and the best way to do it is to read the Holy Koran, according to all scholars, as far as I know. It is enough for us that it [the Koran] is the words of the Creator of the Earth and Heavens, the One that you will meet [on the Day of Judgment].

7. Purify your soul from all blemishes. Completely forget something called "this world" [or "this life"]. The time for play is over and the serious time is upon us. How much time have we wasted in our lives? Shouldn't we take advantage of these last hours to offer sacrifices and obedience?

8. You should feel complete tranquility, because the time between you and your marriage [in heaven] is very short. Afterward begins the happy life, where God is satisfied with you, and eternal bliss "in the company of the prophets, the companions, the martyrs and the good people, who are the best company." Ask God for his mercy and be optimistic, because [the Prophet], peace be upon him, used to prefer optimism in all his affairs.

9. Keep in mind that, if you fall into hardship, how will you act and how will you remain steadfast and remember that you will return to God and remember that anything that happens to you could never be avoided, and what did not happen to you could never have happened to you. This test from Almighty God is to raise your station and atone for your sins. And be sure that it is a matter of moments, which will then pass, God willing, so blessed are those who win the great reward of God. Almighty God said: "Did you think you could go to heaven before God knows whom amongst you have fought for Him and are patient?"

10. Remember the words of Almighty God: "You were looking to the battle before you engaged in it, and now you see it with your own two eyes." Remember: "How many small groups beat big groups by the will of God." And His words: "If God gives you victory, no

one can beat you. And if He betrays you, who can give you victory without Him? So the faithful put their trust in God."

11. Remind yourself of the supplications and of your brethren and ponder their meanings. (The morning and evening supplications, and the supplications of [entering] a town, and the [unclear] supplications, and the supplications said before meeting the enemy.

12. Bless your body with some verses of the Koran [done by reading verses into one's hands and then rubbing the hands over things over whatever is to be blessed], the luggage, clothes, the knife, your personal effects, your ID, your passport, and all of your papers.

13. Check your weapon before you leave and long before you leave. (One of you must sharpen his blade and you must not discomfort your animal during the slaughter).

14. Tighten your clothes well [a reference to one making sure his clothes will cover his private parts at all times], since this is the way of the pious generations after the Prophet. They would tighten their clothes before battle. Tighten your shoes well, wear socks so that your feet will be solidly in your shoes and do not stick out. All of these are worldly things [that humans can do to control their fate, although God decrees what will work and what will won't] and the rest is left to God, the best One to depend on.

15. Pray the morning prayer in a group and ponder the great rewards of that prayer. Make supplications afterward, and do not leave your apartment unless you have performed ablution before leaving, because (The angels will ask for your forgiveness as long as you are in a state of ablution, and will pray for you). This saying of the Prophet was mentioned by An-Nawawi in his book, The Best of Supplications. Read the words of God: "Did you think that We created you for no reason" from the Al-Mu'minun Chapter.

The Second Step:

When the taxi takes you to (M) [this initial could stand for *matar*, "airport" in Arabic] remember God constantly while in the car. (Remember the supplication for entering a car, for entering a town, the supplication of place and other supplications).

When you have reached (M) and have left the taxi, say a supplication of place ["Oh Lord, I ask you for the best of this place, and ask you to protect me from its evils"], and everywhere you go say that prayer and smile and be calm, for God is with the believers. And the angels protect you without you feeling anything. Say this supplication: "God is more dear than all of His creation." And say: "Oh Lord, protect me from them as You wish." And say: "Oh Lord, take your anger out on them [the enemy] and we ask You to protect us from their evils." And say: "Oh Lord, block their vision from in front of them, so that they may not see." And say: "God is all we need, He is the best to rely upon." Remember God's words: "Those to whom the people said, 'The people have gathered to get you, so fear them,' but that only increased their faith and they said, God is all we need, He is the best to rely upon." After you say that, you will find [unclear] as God promised this to his servants who say this supplication:

1. They will come back [from battle] with God's blessings.

2. They were not harmed.

3. And God was satisfied with them.

God says: "They came back with God's blessings, they were not harmed, and God was satisfied with them, and God is ever-blessing."

All of their equipment and gates and technology will not prevent, nor harm, except by God's will. The believers do not fear such things. The only ones that fear it are the allies of Satan, who are the brothers of the devil. They have become their allies, God save us, for fear is a great form of worship, and the only one worthy of it is God. He is the only one who deserves it. He said in the verses: "This is only the Devil scaring his allies" who are fascinated with Western civilization, and have drunk the love [of the West] like they drink water [unclear] and have become afraid of their weak equipment "so fear them not, and fear Me, if you are believers."

Fear is a great worship. The allies of God do not offer such worship except for the one God, who controls everything. [unclear] with total certainty that God will weaken the schemes of the non-believers. God said: "God will weaken the schemes of the non-believers."

You must remember your brothers with all respect [?]. No one should notice that you are making the supplication, "There is no God but God," because if you say it 1,000 times no one will be able to tell whether you are quiet or remember God. And among its miracles is what the Prophet, peace be upon him, said: ("Whoever says, 'There is no God but God,' with all his heart, goes to heaven." The Prophet, peace be upon him, said: ("If you put all the worlds and universes on one side of the balance, and 'No God but God' on the other, 'No God but God' will weigh more heavily." You can repeat these words confidently, and this is just one of the strengths of these words. Whoever thinks deeply about these words will find that they have no dots [in the Arabic letter] and this is just one of its greatnesses, for words that have dots in them carry less weight than those that do not. And it is enough that these are the words of monotheism, which will make you steadfast in battle [unclear] as the prophet, peace be upon him, and his companions, and those who came after them, God willing, until the Day of Judgment.

Also, do not seem confused or show signs of nervous tension. Be happy, optimistic calm because you are heading for a deed that God loves and will accept [as a good deed]. It will be the day, God willing, you spend with the women of paradise.

Smile in the face of hardship, young man/For you are heading toward eternal paradise.

You must remember to make supplications wherever you go, and any-time you do anything, and God is with his faithful servants, He will protect them and make their tasks easier, and give them success and control, and victory, and everything.

Appendix B

From Dr. Ali Shariati's *After Shahadat*

The following text is from a speech of Dr. Ali Shariati (1933–77), an Iranian sociologist and Islamologist, a charismatic speaker and prolific writer. Shariati refers to both Islamic and Western sources in inciting Iranians to a simultaneous religious revolution and social reform. His mix of Third Worldism and Shiite Islam was a potent impetus for the spectacularly popular Iranian revolution of 1979. Note the idealistic, ideological, and self-sacrificial tone of this appeal, the frequent rhetoric of blood in his inflaming message for his Shiite countrymen who revere Hussein as their saint-martyr. The text is revolutionary and martyrological at the same time. It calls for its audience to assume the global responsibility of a community which can be a model for humanity as a whole by serving as witnesses to Hussein's martyrdom (at the hands of Yazid, the treacherous caliph). The speech is a passionate call to continue where Hussein, and his family and supporters left. Shariati's rhetoric makes it sound as if the Shuhada, the martyrs, just left the stage a few minutes ago, and the listeners should turn now to pursuing the heroic deeds of Hussein and his entourage as "we have remained in eternal mourning." Timelessness, or rather, ever-presence is of the essence here. Ever-presence seems to signify the overcoming of the humiliation of defeat and the finality of death. Accordingly, there is no end to mourning, and the spilt blood of the martyrs becomes a life-dispensing liquid for humanity. The frequent mention of children evokes powerful images of victimhood, innocence, sacrifice and offerings. Like Atta's letter, this is not a letter of hate, but one of love and hope and the active, willing embracing of martyrdom. The Shiite branch of Islam is the minority compared to the Sunnis who generated the 9/11 terrorists, yet this is just a more blatant example of the valorization of blood and death as life-giving. Shariati's speeches had a spellbinding power over his hearers, yet they did not contain incitement to hate. This is a reason of appending a great part of it,[1] like Atta's letter, to the text of this book.

Sisters and brothers! The *shuhada* ["witnesses" to Allah's grandeur, essentially the martyrs whose place in paradise is guaranteed by waging war for Islam] are now dead, and we the dead are alive. The shuhada have conveyed their message and we the deaf are their audience. Those who were bold enough to choose death, when they could no longer live, have left, we the shameless have remained. We have remained for hundreds of years. It is quite appropriate for the whole world to laugh at us because we, the symbols of abjection and humility, are weeping for Hussein and Zaynab, the manifestations of life and honor.[2] This is another injustice of history: that we the despicable should be the mourners of these mighty ones. Today the shuhada delivered their message with their blood and sat opposite us in order to invite the seated ones of history to rise.

In our culture, religion, and history in Shiis [the Shi'is] the most valuable jewels [jewelry] that mankind has created, and the most life-giving substances that bestow vitality, pulsation, and movement upon history and teach mankind the most divine lessons, elevating him as high as God, are concealed. The heritage of all these valuable divine treasures has fallen into our hands. We, the abject and humble, we are the heirs of the most beloved trusts, prepared by jihad, *shahadat* [the statement of faith that all Muslims affirm, namely, "There is no God but God and Muhammad is His Prophet"] and great human values in the history of Islam. We are the heirs of all this. We have a responsibility to make ourselves a community which can be a model for humanity.

"Thus we have made you a mediating community, that you may be shuhada over the nations, and the Apostle may be a shahid [witness, model] over you" (2:143).

[This *ayah*] is addressed to us.[3] We have a responsibility to make from the mighty and beloved heritage of our shuhada, warriors, imams, leaders, faith, and Book—a model community, in order that we might be shahid (martyrs) and shahid (witnesses) for the people of the world, as the Apostle should be the model and shahid for us.

Such a heavy responsibility, that of bestowing vitality and movement to humanity, rests upon our shoulders, yet we are unable to carry out our routine daily life.

God! What wisdom is there in this?

And we drowned in the filthy swamp of our animalistic lives must be the mourners of such men, women, and children, who in Karbala proved forever their shahadat and presence in history before God and in the presence of freedom.

God! What oppression is this which is again committed against the family of Hussein?

Now the shuhada have completed their task. We declare its end by mourning tonight. Behold that we under the cloak of weeping for and loving Hussein are allied with Yazid, who wished this story to end.

Now the shuhada have completed their task and have left in silence. All of them, one by one, have played their role well: the teacher, the caller, the old, the young, men and women, master and slave, and even a baby. Each of them, as representative, lesson, and model to mankind, old and infant, man and woman . . . chose such a beautiful and live-giving death.

They carried out two tasks: from Hussein's baby to his brother, from his slave to himself, from the reciter of the Koran to the teacher of the children of Kufah, from the one who called out at the time of prayer to others, both stranger and kin, from the one who was noble and respectable to the one deprived of social honors all stood as brothers, face to face with shahadat men and women, the children, the old and young of history in order to teach mankind how they should live if they are able and how they should die if they are not.

This is the first task.

These shuhada carried out another task as well. With their blood, not with words, in the court of the history of mankind, each as a representative of his social group, they witnessed that all human groups and human values are condemned in the one system ruling over the history of mankind, a system which employs politics economy, religion, art, philosophy, thought, feeling, ethics, and one word, humanity, as tools for sacrificing men to their own interests, which makes everything support the rule of oppression, aggression, and crime. There is one ruler over all history, or oppressor who rules history, and one executioner who martyr. Throughout history, many children have been victims of the executioner. Many women have been silenced under the whips of the executioner who rules history. At the price of much blood, endless appetites have been appeased. Many cases of starvation, slavery, and massacres in history have been suffered by women and children, by men, heroes, slaves, and teachers, in all times and in all generations.

And now Hussein has come with all his existence to the court of history, so that he may witness on the banks of the Euphrates. He has come to witness for all the oppressed people of history, for all those condemned by the executioner ruling history, to witness how this merciless executioner, Dahhak, continues to eat the brains of the youth throughout history. He has come to witness with his Ali Akbar. He has come to witness how the heroes have died in the criminal regimes.[4]

He has come to witness with himself. He has come to witness with his sister Zaynab that in the regimes ruling history, women must either choose slavery and thus remain in the harems or choose freedom and thus become shuhada, thereby leading to the caravan of the captives and being heirs to the shuhada.

He has come to bear witness with his nursing child, Ali Asghar, that in the regime of oppression, aggression, and crime, the executioner does not show mercy, not even to a nursing baby.

And Hussein, with all his existence, has come to bear witness in the criminal court of history for the benefit of those for whom there has never been a witness and thus have died defenselessly in silence.

Now the court has ended, and the witnessing of Hussein, all his dear ones, and all his existence, the best that anyone other than God is capable of, have completed their great divine mission.

Friends! In Shiism—which has presently taken this form—we see such that anyone who wishes to speak of genuine, dynamic, and awakening Shi'ism is victimized by his friends before the enemy has access to him—great lessons and messages, abandoned treasures, divine values, mighty capitals, and life-giving souls for the revival of society, nation, and history are hidden.

One of the best life-giving sources in the history of Shiism is shahadat.

As Jalal has said, "Since the time that we have forgotten the tradition of shahadat and have become the guardians of the cemeteries of the shuhada, we have submitted to the black death." Since the time that we, instead of being Shiites of Ali, Shi'ites of Hussein, and Shiites of Zaynab, that is to say, being followers of the shuhada our men and women have become mere mourners for the shuhada, we have remained in eternal mourning. How intelligently the message of Hussein and his great, dear, and immortal friends has been metamorphosized—a message addressed to all mankind.

After he sees all his dear ones fallen on the battlefield, and when he has no audience except the vengeful and plundering enemy, Hussein cries, "Is there anyone to stand at my side?" Does he not know that there is no one to stand by his side? This is the question posed to future generations, to each one of us. This question revealed Hussein's expectations of those who love him. It is an invitation addressed to all those who respect and revere the shuhada.

We belittled this invitation, this expectation, and this message by misreading its content. Instead of, "Hussein demands followers in every age and generation," we read, "Hussein demands only tears and weeping. He has no other message. He is dead and demands mourners. He is not a living shahid in every time and place in search of followers." Thus we have been told.

For every revolution, there are two visages, the first is "blood" and the second is "message."

Shahid means "present." The ones who personally choose the red death as a symbol of their love for a dying truth—as the only weapon of jihad for the sake of the great values which are being altered—are referred to as shahid. They are alive, present, witnesses, and observers. They are not only so in the sight of God, but also in the sight of the masses in every age and every land.

Those who submit to any humiliation in order to remain alive are the silent, dirty, dead of history. Which ones are alive? Those who choose their own death and with selflessness have come with Hussein to be slaughtered, while hundreds of religious excuses permit them to remain alive, but who do not seek excuses and thus die; or those who left Hussein and thus submitted to abjection and obedience to Yazid—which ones are still alive?

Anyone who considers life as more than just an animate corpse sees and feels with his whole existence the life and presence of Hussein and the death of those who submitted to humiliation in order to remain alive.

In confronting oppression and aggression, the shahid shows, teaches, and argues against those who think, "Inability means exemption from jihad," and those who say, "Triumph means victory over the enemy." The shahid is the one who, in the age of inability to conquer, triumphs over the enemy by his own death, disgracing him if not defeating him.

A shahid is the heart of history. The heart gives blood and life to the otherwise dead blood-vessels of the body. Like the heart, a shahid sends his own blood into the half-dead body of the dying society. whose children have lost faith in themselves, which is slowly approaching death, which has accepted submission, which has forgotten its responsibility, which is alienated from humanity, and in which there is no life, movement, and creativity. The greatest miracle of shahadat is giving to a generation a renewed faith in itself.

A shahid is ever-present and ever-lasting.

Who is absent?

Hussein has taught us another lesson more important than his shahadat. Leaving *hajj* [the pilgrimage to Mecca, a spiritual journey which is the duty of every Muslim to do, at least once in his or her life] unfinished and proceeding to shahadat. He leaves half-finished the revival of the pilgrimage for which all his ancestors, his grand-father and father, struggled. From the half-finished hajj, he proceeds to shahadat in order to teach all pilgrims in history, all worshippers in history, and all the believers in the tradition of Abraham that if there is no imamate and leadership, if there is no goal, if there is no Hussein, and if instead there is Yazid, circumambulating the house of God is the same as circumambulating the idol houses. The ones who continue their circum-ambulation in the absence of Hussein are equal to those who moved around the Green Palace of Muahwiyah [a palace built by Muahwiyah, the ruler of Damascus, which was built by enslaving the population and which wallowed in earthly riches]. A shahid, who is present in all the battlefields of truth and falsehood, reveals to all humanity: "If you are not in the battlefield of truth and falsehood, it makes no difference where you are. When you are not a witness in the battlefield of truth and falsehood of your time, be anywhere else you wish. Stand for prayer or sit down for wine. Both are the same."

Shahadat means presence in the battlefield of truth and falsehood of the eternity of history . . .

Where Hussein is present, and he is present in every century and every age, anyone who does not stand beside him, be they believers or non-believers, criminal or virtuous, are all equal. This is the meaning of the Shiite principle that the nature of each act depends upon imamate, leadership, and *wilayat* [*wila* means power, and *vilayat* is the authority invested in the Prophet]. Without it everything is meaningless and we see that it is meaningless. And now Hussein has declared his presence in all ages and for all generations, in all wars, struggles, and battlefields of any time and land. He has died in Karbala, so that he may be resurrected in all generations and ages.

You and I must weep over our own misery that we are not present.

Yes, for every revolution, there are two visages: blood and the message. Hussein and his companions undertook the first mission, that of blood. The second mission is to bear the message to the whole world, to be the eloquent tongue of this flowing blood and these resting bodies among the walking dead. The mission of conveying the message begins today. Its responsibility rests on the fine shoulders of Zaynab, a woman from whom mankind is to learn virtue. The mission of Zaynab is more difficult and heavier than that of her brother. Those who have the courage to choose their own death have simply made a great choice. But the responsibility of those who survive is heavy and difficult. Zaynab has survived. The caravan of the captives follows behind her. The ranks of the enemy, as far as the eye can see, are in front of her. The responsibility of conveying her brother's message rests solely upon her shoulders. Leaving behind a red garden of shahadat and the perfume of roses, spreading from her skirts, she enters the city of crime, the capital of power, the center of oppression and execution.

With peace and pride, she victoriously announces to the power and cru-elty of the slave-agents and executioners, to the remnants of colonialism and dictatorship: "Thank God for all the generosity and glory which He has be-stowed upon our family. The honor of prophethood and the honor of sha-hadat." Zaynab bears the responsibility of announcing the message of the alive but silent shuhada. She has survived the shuhada and it is she who must be the tongue for those whose tongue has been cut off by the sword of the executioner.

If blood does not have a message, it remains mute in history . . .

The eyes of the shuhada are upon us. They are conscious, alive, and present. They are the paradigms, the witnesses of truth and falsehood, and the witnesses of the destiny of mankind.

And shahid has all these meanings.

For every revolution, there are two visages: blood and message.

Anyone who has accepted the responsibility of accepting the truth, and anyone who knows the meaning of the responsibility of being Shiite, of being a freedom-lover, knows he has to choose in the eternal battle of history, everywhere and in every land. All battlefields are Karbala, all months are Muharram [the first month in the Islamic calendar, a sacred month associated with many auspicious events in Islamic history], all days are Ashura [Muharram is the month when the Shia imam Hussein ibn-Ali, the grandson of Muhammad, was killed. Ashura, the tenth day of Muharram, is the day when Hussein was treacherously killed by the Ummayad caliph Yazid]? One has to choose either the blood or the message, to be either Hussein or Zaynab, either to die like him or survive like her, if he does not choose to be absent from the battlefield.

I apologize to you. It is too late, and there is no further opportunity. There is much to be said, but how can one sufficiently explain the miracle that Hussein has performed and Zaynab has completed. What I want to say is a long story, but I can summarize it as the mission of Zaynab after the shahadat: those who died committed a Hussein-like act. Those who survive must perform a Zaynab-like act. Otherwise, they are the followers of Yazid.

Notes

Preface

1. Hours later we saw its verbally outspoken expressions on Al-Jazeera.

2. I was told that on this day all foreigners should stay inside and not show their faces for fear of being attacked.

3. *Kharijieh*, the word for foreigner in Farsi, is allied etymologically to "standing out" (*kharig* in Hebrew).

4. Islamic scholar Johannes Jansen (2001), however, suggests that "the Muslim world, for very sad reasons, is much more violent than Christian or Israeli societies. If you are a fundamentalist in an Arabic country, force seems to be the only logical choice, as there are so very few means to spread your views peacefully. You cannot be elected and you have no right to elect. If these two rights are denied and you have fundamentalist leanings, the possibility of a violent reaction is much more to be expected than in an American, European, or Israeli context. To a large extent, the present leaders in the Muslim world, the present political elite of the Middle East, are responsible for the violent character of Muslim fundamentalism. Fundamentalists almost mirror the violent character of their own societies."

Introduction

1. The letter is reproduced as Appendix A to this volume.

2. Heinrich Racker (1968) suggests that "the intention to understand creates a certain predisposition . . . to identify oneself with the analysand, which is the basis for comprehension. . . . The analyst may achieve this by . . . identifying each part of his personality with the corresponding psychological part in the patient" (p. 134). But the analyst not only identifies with the analysand, experiencing

these identifications consciously. The analyst also identifies with the patient's "internal objects," that is, with the representations of relations with people the analysand has internalized in his psyche which are often partially or wholly unconscious. The process of understanding the patient's "transference" depends on such identifications as well as on accepting the analyst's own "countertransference," that is, identifying with the analyst's own, repressible, but unavoidable emotions and impulses. Heinz Kohut (1971) views empathy as vicarious introspection, a mode of cognition which is specifically attuned to the perception of complex psychological configurations in the other. He distinguishes between the use of empathic observation when it is necessary to gather "psychological data," and the use of "nonempathic modes of perception when the data [gathered] . . . do not concern the area of the inner life of man" (p. 300). Thomas Ogden (1994), suggests that with Melanie Klein's introduction of the concept of "projective identification" (later developed by Wilfred R. Bion to encompass a deeply communicative function), "the idea of the interdependence of subject and object became fundamental to the analytic understanding of the creation and development of subjectivity" (p. 8). Projective identification is understood as "a psychological-interpersonal process in which there is a partial collapse of the dialectic of subjectivity and intersubjectivity" (p. 9).

3. Peter Fonagy and Mary Target (1998, 2007) link emotions to the capacity to think about the other person. They posit that grasping that the other person possesses an interiority and has intentions is a cognitive capacity that is acquired thanks to the child's caretaker's ability to "play" with the child with both reality and imagination, that is, take both into account when playing and responding to the child verbally, as well as with self and other. The responses of a good mother are unconsciously geared to enable the infant to grasp that its feelings *can be understood* from the inside of another human being, at the same time as they are *not equivalent* to the other's feelings. Simultaneously, the child also learns that its own feelings are, so to speak, a version of reality but not reality itself. This capacity to grasp that one's fantasy is a *representation* of reality rather than reality itself, as well as the ability to distinguish one's own affects from those of others, are fragile and profoundly dependent on a certain capacity for attachment. Also see: Joseph E. LeDoux (1998), Colwyn Trevarthen (2006), and Edward Tronick et al. (1999).

4. Guillaume Bigot (2002) makes a case that Islamic fundamentalist terrorists know us much better than we know them.

5. In Hebrew, the root *e'l'm'* (*aleph, lamed, mem*) means both violence and muteness, suggesting that violence renders the victim with no voice or speech, that is with no sovereign mind.

6. In Islamic theology, all countries that are not under Islamic law (*shar'ia*) are called "house(s) of war" or "house(s) of chaos" (*dar al-harb*), the assumption being

that countries that do not accept Allah's law are necessarily filled with strife, or, alternatively, that they deserve the sword to bring them under Muslim dominance.

7. Raymond Ibrahim (2007), p. 175.

8. Ibid., p. 13.

9. *Jizya* is the per capita tax paid by *dhimmis*, non-Muslims subjects, to the Islamic state.

10. This is part of bin Laden's request of the Saudis "to clarify this matter to the West," although in his letter to the Americans, bin Laden relies on "humanitarian, political, and even emotional arguments," such as "self-defense, biased U.S. support for of Israel, U.S. support for oppressive, dictatorial regimes, unjust war in Iraq, etc., as to why al-Qaeda has declared war on the United States. . . . However, at no time does al-Qaeda's letter to the Americans clarify that the terrorist organization's aggression is ultimately rooted in what they understand to be principles intrinsic to Islam" (ibid., pp. 19–20).

11. Giacomo Rizzolatti, Leonardo Fogassi, and Vittorio Gallese (2001, 2006); Vittorio Gallese, Christian Keysers, and Giacomo Rizzolatti (2004).

12. Teresa de Lauretis (2004), p. 366.

13. Ibid.

14. Roxanne L. Euben (1999).

15. Alain Badiou's (1982, 2001) writings seem to exemplify this trend, among others; see Calvin O. Schrag (1992); also, Foucault's endorsement of Khoumeini as a freedom fighter is well known.

16. I agree with Euben though, as well as with Mary Habeck (2006), regarding the need to discard a self-centered, functionalist prism that neglects to recognize the fundamentalist self-understanding *in its own terms,* and that erroneously sees the religious aspect of fundamentalism as an epiphenomenon.

17. Franz Fanon (1961).   18. Alain Badiou (2001).

19. Giorgio Agamben (1995).   20. Michel Foucault (1961).

21. Schrag's (2002) phrase "God as otherwise than being," Jacques Derrida's (1995) "gift of death" or "religion without religion," Jean-Luc Marion's (1991) "God without Being": all are attempts to work beyond the fact that classical theism leads to atheism in philosophy and that it is therefore necessary to replace theological approaches that rely on metaphysics and/or epistemology with posttheistic and post-atheistic, postmodern ways of speaking about God without ascribing to him being in the ordinary sense of the word.

22. Slavoj Žižek's (e.g., 2001, 2003) post-Marxist, pro-Catholic perspective is an exception in that he talks about religion differently than most contemporaries, but he does not deal extensively with Islamic religiosity, so that he ultimately assimilates the terrorist mentality into a political-economic viewpoint.

23. Žižek (2003) talks about a new spirituality that is "in" in our "postsecular" age, such as the Lévinasian ethico-religious turn, which recognizes the demise of

traditional onto-theology (where God is asserted as a supreme being), but which assumes that a radical human Otherness confronts us with an absolute ethical responsibility. This is not religious faith in (religious) Žižek's view, but a kind of "disavowed spirituality."

24. Terry Eagleton (2005), p. vi.

25. According to Islamic law, a country that was once under Muslim dominance has to be reconquered and become Islamicized again. This applies thus not only to Palestine, but to parts of Europe, Africa, and East Asia.

26. Max Weber (1919) contrasts value rationality to instrumental rationality, the latter being the pragmatic, self-interested, means-ends considerations that, I suggest, are insufficient to account for fundamentalist movements. See also Hans H. Gerth and C. Wright Mills (1946).

27. This is the conclusion drawn on the basis of interviews with religious terrorists, as in Scott Atran (2003, 2007); Farhad Khosrokhavar (2005), p. 166. See also Jessica Stern (2003).

28. See Robert Jay Lifton (1999), Charles B. Strozier (1994), Oliver Roy (2004), Paul Berman (2003), Farhad Khosrokhavar (2005).

29. See Sayyid Qutb (1964). Although moderate (and apologist) Islamic philosophers like Seyyed Hossein Nasr say that "human laws not derived from Divine Law can become integrated into the Islamic legal system as long as they do not oppose the edicts of the *Shari'ah*. This occurred often throughout Islamic history" (Seyyed Hossein Nasr, *The Heart of Islam* [2002], p. 121), their opinion is that of a minority of thinkers in Islamic thinking.

30. Emmanuel Sivan (1985). See also Roger Scruton's (2003) analysis of the state, the city, and the elements of citizenship in Islam and in the West.

31. Raymond Ibrahim (2007) who translated and compiled the key texts of the al-Qaeda organization, notes that "perhaps the most disturbing aspect of these works [the key texts of the al-Qaeda movement] is how grounded they are in the traditional sources of Islamic theology" (text on back of book).

32. Mark Juergensmeyer (2003a), too, remarks on the fuzziness of religious groups regarding their political aims. He concludes that "although some movements for religious nationalism are indeed serious alternatives to secular rule, proponents of religious terrorism often have a less tangible goal. These acts are often devices for symbolic empowerment in wars that cannot be won and for goals that cannot be achieved" (p. 218).

33. Lee Harris (2004, 2007) and Anthony Pagden (2008) document the historical continuity of war between Western civilization and "its enemies," and warn that we may be making a mistake by regarding our present civilization and cultural achievements as more robust and invulnerable than they really are.

34. Hannah Arendt (1958).

35. Michael Ignatieff (2004).

36. Avishai Margalit (2005), p. 209.

37. Ian Buruma and Avishai Margalit (2004).

38. Buruma and Margalit draw striking parallels among diverse anti-Western ideologies that began in Europe and spread to prewar Japan and Nazi Germany, and recent Islamist movements. They call the latter *occidentalism*; it denotes a totalizing, homogenizing prejudice against the liberal, secular, materialistic West. Occidentalism is the counterpoint to Edward Said's famous concept of orientalism. Said (1979) had claimed that the "Orient" has been prejudicially viewed by the West as homogeneous, crude, backward, and dangerous. Buruma and Margalit describe occidentalism as the way Islamist extremists reduce the West into a caricature of greedy materialism, animalism, and soulless mechanicality.

39. Paul Berman (2003).

40. Berman (2003), Buruma and Margalit (2004), Bartov (2000), Küntzel (2005), and others. Supporting this view of extremist Islam as not much different from other totalitarian movements of the last century, see the work of Matthias Küntzel (2005, 2007); Omer Bartov (2000), or Paul Berman (2003). Other authors, such as Farhad Khosrokhavar (2005), however, compare this movement to groups such as the European (mostly French) *Gauchistes* (Lefties of different stripes) or the Latin American revolutionaries of the 1970s, a comparison I find too minimalist and normalizing in view of the ideology of radical Islam.

41. Juergensmeyer (2003a) quotes Mahmud Abouhalima, one of the men convicted of the 1993 bombing of the World Trade Center, whom he interviewed in his detention in 1997. Asked to clarify what he meant when he said that something was missing in America, and that we did not understand, Abouhalima said: "The soul . . . the soul of religion. . . . Without it . . . Western prosecutors, journalists and scholars like [you] will never understand who I am." Juergensmeyer tells us that Abouhalima "compared a life without religion to a pen without ink. An ink pen," he said, "a pen worth two thousand dollars . . . it's useless if there's no ink in it. That's the thing that gives life . . . the life in this pen . . . the soul . . . . the soul, the religion, you know, that's the thing that's revived the whole life. Secularism . . . has none, they have none, you have none . . . [secular people] they're just moving like dead bodies" (p. 70).

42. Some authors have argued that occupying foreign lands is the primary reason for terrorism, but as Olivier Roy argues, terrorist activity in America or Europe is unconnected to the conflict in the Middle East, to Iraq or to Afghanistan, or, for that matter, to the presence of "infidel" troops In Islam's holy lands. See also Jerry Piven (2005).

43. Walter Laqueur (2005) notes the persistence against all evidence of the general belief that there is a fatal link between poverty and violence. He is one of an increasing number of researchers who have found no such correlation. He also notes that in the world's fifty poorest countries there is little or no terrorism.

In the Arab countries, the terrorists originated not from the poorest and most neglected districts but from places with concentration of radical preachers, but from educated strata. Al-Qaeda was founded and 9/11 occurred not because of territorial dispute or the feeling of national oppression, but because of a religious commandment.

44. Mary M. Habeck (2006); see also Bernard Lewis (2002).

45. The concept of the contemporary "hyphenated identity" of Islamic terrorists began to be elaborated by Paul Berman (2003), Gilles Kepel (2005), and others.

46. Farhad Khosrokhavar (2001) describes how contemporary Islamic writings use a modern and personal style to interpellate young Muslims. This is a style that is more pertinent and attractive to young adherents than the impersonal, formal, stilted classical Islamic texts of the past.

47. *The Economist* (2008) had an article on cyberwar between Russia and Estonia that discussed the possibilities of such wars being waged in various terrorist settings.

48. Notably Mary M. Habeck (2006), Raymond Ibrahim (2007), Gil Kepel and Jean-Pierre Mileli (2008).

49. To some observers (e.g., David Rapoport [1990], Johannes Jansen [1997]), myself included, the speech directed toward the inside likewise rationalizes and normalizes deep impulses, but it rationalizes to itself, that is, unwittingly and unconsciously.

50. Hans Kippenberg (2008), p. 180.

51. See Emanuel Sivan's (1983, 1985, 1991, 1995) research on the double (and duplicitous) language of fundamentalist groups.

52. But not only Islamic fundamentalists: Jewish fundamentalists too.

53. Paul Berman (2003) attributes the glaring inability of America to detect the imminent 9/11 attack that was in preparation for years to the belief held here that "around the world people behave rationally." It was this belief, he maintains, rather than bureaucratic "glitches," that was responsible for the blindness. Likewise, it was the refusal to believe in the possibility of such hostility materializing that overrode the visible signs of this unpleasant truth. Differently put, it was the (understandable) narcissistic need to feel that one is sufficiently loveable and powerful to have created a safe place for one's omnipotent sense of self-value that produced the inertia and the subsequent disbelief.

54. Hans Kippenberg and Tilman Seidenstricker (2004), p. 48. All translations are mine unless otherwise stated.

55. Lee Quinby (forthcoming).

56. Ernest Becker (1973). See Tom Pyszczynski, Jeff Greenberg, and Sheldon Solomon (1997, 2003) for examples of findings and thinking in terror management theory.

57. Although perhaps it is within culture that values are made more visible and explicit and endow the members of the specific culture with a sense of coherence.

58. Walter Davis (2001) is one of the most important writers on the tragic in contemporary culture. He views it as an ineluctable dimension of human existence that is powerfully resisted.

59. Jessica Benjamin (1988).

60. Peter Sloterdijk (2007) brilliantly analyzes the struggle for hegemony and domination that is endemic to the three monotheisms by virtue of their genealogy and their structure.

61. Usama bin Muhammad bin Ladin (2001). Mary Habeck (2006) who quotes this declaration, notes that it went unnoticed by the West because it relied on language largely incomprehensible to non-Muslims (p. 70).

62. Shaykh al-Islam Ibn Taymiyya (1263–1328) taught that jihad is the "best of all voluntary (good actions) which men perform," and in another place he equated jihad with the love of God: "Jihad involves absolute love for that which Allah has commanded and absolute hate for that which He has forbidden, and so whom He loves and who love Him is . . . fighting in the Way of Allah and never afraid of the reproaches of such as find fault" (Habeck [2006], p. 21).

63. See Mark Juergensmeyer (2003a) and also Lee Harris (2004), who interpret this observation in similar ways. Hans G. Kippenberg (2008) shows how the 9/11 hijackers were instructed to reproduce a holy war as specified in the Quran, including the act of taking spoils, which they were instructed to actualize by getting a glass of water in the plane before the action (p. 182).

64. Michael Ignatieff (2004).

65. The description of Christians, Jews, or liberals as corrupt, treacherous, and forgers of the truth makes any dialogue with them unthinkable. Thus Abu Hamza says, "Only the most ignorant and animal-minded individuals would insist that prophet killers (Jews) and Jesus worshippers (Christians) deserve the same rights as us." But the complete rejection "is more than a simple refusal to accept these belief systems as valid or to acknowledge them at least as equals, but is rather a declaration that they must be destroyed" (quoted in Habeck [2006], p. 80).

Chapter 1: Evil as Love and as Liberation

1. It seems that the letter was intended for inner circulation among the hijackers of the planes, although we cannot rule out the less likely possibility that it was deliberately left there to be found after the attack or that it was "forgotten" there as a Freudian symbolic action for us to read. It has been translated and published in the American press through Reuters.

2. Hans G. Kippenberg and Tilman Seidenstricker (2004), p. 36.

3. Psalm 3:1–3; my translation from the Hebrew.

4. In his interviews with suicide bombers in Gaza, Nasra Hassan (2001) confirms this impression when he quotes interviewees who assured him that the bliss is not sensual" (p. 39).

5. Jessica Benjamin (1988), p. 124.

6. Rajneesh was an Indian guru who preached sexual liberation in the early 1980s (quoted in Robert J. Lifton [2000], p. 113).

7. William James (1901), p. 32.

8. Charles Lindholm, quoted in Lifton (2000), p. 113.

9. Daniel Boyarin (1999).

10. Robert Jay Lifton (1979), p. 97.

11. Christopher Bollas (1995).

12. Nasra Hassan (2001; italics added).

13. Neil Macfarquhar (2001).

14. Terry McDermott (2005), pp. 20–26.

15. PsyBC discussion (October 2001). Psy Broadcasting Corporation, www .psybc.com, Continuing Professional Development for Mental Health Clinicians, owned by Dan Hill, Ph.D.

16. Mark Juergensmeyer (2000) points out the social marginality of the young men who become religious terrorists. Coming from traditional societies that are built around family units, these men are insecure about their careers, social location, and sexual relationships. Experiencing humiliation and helplessness, they become vulnerable to powerful leaders who explain their misery and give them hope by promising a glorious victory in an imminent cosmic holy war. "Terrorist movements provide a community that supplies a family and an ideology that explains the source of their problems and gives them hope" (p. 191).

17. Luce Irigaray (2002) poetically describes how Western subjectivity is normatively masculine, and suggests that the "male cultural object of religion and philosophy," as she calls him, builds himself on the absence of the mother. Irigaray contends that "theology and metaphysics join together in their attempt to hide that which founds the "monocratic, patriarchal truth . . . its order, its word, its logic," to wit, the concealment and sacrifice of the mother's body (p. 27).

18. Emmanuel Ghent (1990).

19. Some are reminiscent of the laws mentioned in the Old Testament that apply to going to war, such as keeping one's clothes tight and being modest in bodily hygiene (Keter Yerushalaim, Deut. 23:13).

20. If "intention" here is similar to what is called intention in Jewish theology, then it has the significance of close adherence to and concentration on whatever religious act (including prayer) one is performing (occasionally, as in Kabbalah, "intention" means religious meditation). The idea is mystical and

valorizes intention as elevating the significance of any act into a ritual intended to put the divine into earthly actions.

21. In the text of the letter, written as a manual for performing a holy war ritual, the addressees become increasingly identified and merged with the early Islamic holy warriors, while the enemy gradually becomes the early heretics and enemies.

22. Cf. "The time has come; the kingdom of God is upon you; repent" (Mark 1:15; International Standard Version); "Repent, for the Kingdom of Heaven is at hand" (Matt. 3:2).

23. "I asked," Hassan writes, "about the problem of fear." The boy has left that stage far behind", [his interlocutor] said. "The fear is not for his own safety or for his impending death. . . . It is awe, produced by the situation. He has never done this before and, *inshallah*, will never do it again! It comes from his fervent desire for success, which will propel him into the presence of Allah. It is anxiety over the possibility of something going wrong and denying him his heart's wish" (Hassan [2001], p. 40).

24. In a similar vein, Quaker Robert Griswold (2003) preaches that "fear makes us act in ways that increase the force of whatever we fear." He points out that "in fear, we magnify what we fear and attribute to it great importance."

25. Fear easily melds into awe in the German *Ehrfurcht*, which, more visibly than its English homologue, *reverence*, concretely combines respect and fear by signifying a fear that honors of the object of fear.

26. Sigmund Freud (1921) writes about the abolition of the distance between ego and ego-ideal (the ego-ideal functions here mainly as the superego). In this state, "the person, in a mood of triumph and self-satisfaction, disturbed by no criticism, can enjoy the abolition of his inhibitions, his feelings of considerations for others, and his self-reproaches" (p. 132). He also notes that the individual in the group, "in obedience to the new authority [of the group] . . . may put his former 'conscience' out of action, and so surrender to the attraction of the increased pleasure that is certainly obtained from the removal of inhibitions" (p. 85; see also p. 113).

27. Melanie Klein (1958) regards the superego as produced by the splitting of the ego struggling with the perennial conflict between love and hate, or the life instincts and the death instincts. The superego can be protective but it can also be savage and terrifying. Klein also affords insights into the difference between protective, even if disciplinarian, internal object representations that, because of their affinity with the ego, win over the ego to identify with them, and internal figures that are too cruel and terrifying for the ego to identify with and are therefore experienced as alien and persecutory (pp. 240–41).

28. Robert Jay Lifton (1979), p. 35.

29. Jacques Lacan (1953–54), p. 259. The reduction of the symbolic father to the imaginary father is conceived in Lacanian theory (e.g., Jacques Lacan

[1956–57], pp. 275–76), as being involved, in different ways, in psychosis and in perversion.

30. Georges Bataille (1957); Robert Jay Lifton (2000); William Sargent (1957).

31. Heinz Kohut (1971), p. 9.

32. Robert Jay Lifton (1979), p. 206 (italics in the original).

33. Karl Abraham (1924).

34. Islamic as well as Jewish law commands merciful animal slaughter (the mercifulness of which, however, has come into question recently). To the question of how he gets along with people at his work, all nonreligious, a (Jewish) fundamentalist smilingly replied, "They are not people. They only look like people, but in truth they are monkeys." He was saying in effect that the difference between himself and them (his being different and not quite integrated and belonging) did not bother him at all, since they were not really his human equals.

35. Paul Oppenheimer (1996), p. 95.

36. Roy Baumeister (1996).

37. To say that these acts are authentically religious is to put forward a strong claim, but even so-called authentic religious fakes, that is, phenomena that seem to be religious but typically are not considered religious, "still do authentic religious work," as David Chidester shows (2005, p. vii).

38. While I am editing this manuscript, the terrorist atrocities in Mumbai are weeks behind us.

39. See for example, Klein (1940); See also Stein (1991).

40. The Holy Inquisition tortured its victims in order to save their souls; Aum Shinrikyo killed people in order to transform their lives and redeem them, through *poa*, Buddhist improvement of reincarnation, from their bad karma (Lifton [2000], pp. 66–67).

41. Christopher Bollas (1995), p. 189.   42. Ibid.

43. Sue Grand (2002a), p. x.   44. Ibid, p. 5.

45. Ibid, p. 6.   46. Ibid.

47. Donald Moss (2003a), p. 325.

48. Paul Oppenheimer (1996) believes that terms such as *criminal* and *sociopathic* fail adequately to describe the monstrous acts they address. Evil, according to Oppenheimer, is not a primitive notion that has lost its usefulness as an explanation, and the reality of evil cannot be made to disappear.

49. Robert Jay Lifton (2000).

50. The profile of moderately successful low- or average-level academics applies also to Mohammed Atta, for instance, who did not fully succeed in his career as an architect and could not obtain a higher degree as he had wanted.

51. William G. Joffe and Joseph Sandler (1965).

52. Sigmund Freud (1921), p. 127.

53. Jessica Benjamin (1988).

54. I suggest that this slavish, self-immolating love could be added to Freud's (1911, his Schreber essay) transformations from homosexuality to paranoia. In addition to Freud's "I love him" turning into "He loves me—he persecutes me," or "I don't love him—I love her," and so on, we could say: "I love him—I love him more, and more, and I'll enslave, even annihilate myself, and everything I have (my life) and everything I am (my identity), to eventually gain his love."

55. Among the numerous examples are Hieronymus Bosch, Michelangelo Buonarotti, Paul Rubens, and a memorable fourteenth-century print from the British Library, depicting the „mouth of hell swallowing the damned, who are tormented by demons as Christ locks them in."

56. Remarkably, the letter repeatedly tells the addressees to smile.

57. Ana-Maria Rizzuto (personal communication, 2003) objects to my hypothesis, and thinks that behind the father hides the primal mother, who is more terrifying and therefore has to be disguised behind the appearance of the father. Her view represents the reluctance of many psychoanalysts to accord the "pre-Oedipal" father the same archaic, and therefore potentially terrifying, status as that of the "pre-Oedipal," "oral," or "phallic" mother. In Chapter 4, I deal with this error of conflating the pre-Oedipal with the maternal by developing the concept of a "pre-Oedipal" "phallic" father.

58. Jean Laplanche and Jean-Bertrand Pontalis (1967), p. 386.

59. Freud (1900) mentions Chronos, who devoured his children, as an example of the murderous father (p. 256). Another instance of the depiction of God as an evil cannibal, is «the Creator» in Lautréamont's *Les chants de Maldoror*. The image of the cannibalistic God eating the human beings he had created, who swim in a pond of boiling blood, is horrifying. "Sometimes, he would shout: "I created you, so I have the right to do whatever I like to you. You have done nothing to me, I do not deny it, I am making you suffer for my own pleasure" (Comte de Lautréamont [1965], p. 77).

60. Sigmund Freud (1913b).

61. Janine Chasseguet-Smirgel (1986) suggests that the "Jewish" Freud put the barrier of reason in the face of chthonian maternal forces in psychoanalysis. At the same time, however, as she emphasizes the father's role of separator of the child from the mother and from symbiotic relations(or God's separateness from human beings), she also writes that "in the Jewish religion this percept [to separate, divide, and isolate] also concerns the separation between God and man" (p. 137). This separation between the divine Father and his sons, both in Judaism and Islam, may be the problem, not its solution.

62. "[A] filial piety: love as a modulation of fear, gratitude flowing from an abrupt sense of relief" (David Lee Miller [2003], p. 20).

63. Paul Oppenheimer (1996) writes: "Evil frequently masquerades as love, that must indeed be acknowledged as one of the most profound, if horrific,

forms of love . . . evil may fascinate, mesmerize . . . it may enchant with ecstasy and . . . offer a release from the mundane. At its most vivid, evil . . . opens doors on frightful possibilities, those that reach behind the sickening final insults of death and oblivion, into suggestions that a good deal of life, even as it is lived by those with the best of intentions, may contain in its opaqueness something ugly, chaotic, foul, which has, perhaps only for a brief while, achieved a beautiful appearance" (pp. 2–3).

64. Mark Juergensmeyer (2000) has attempted to explain this phenomenon from a sociological rather than an intrapsychic angle. Writing about young men disempowered in both their original and their secondary societies, he suggests that violent "acts are often devices for symbolic empowerment in wars that cannot be won and goals that cannot be achieved. . . . For some activist groups the awareness of their potency is all that they desire. . . . What they have in common, these movements of cowboy monks, is that they consist of anti-institutional, religio-nationalist, racist, sexist, male-bonding, bomb-throwing young guys. Their marginality in the modern world is experienced as a kind of sexual despair that leads to violent acts of symbolic empowerment" (pp. 204–5).

65. Sigmund Freud (1913b), p. 141.   66. Mikkel Borch-Jacobsen, (1991).

67. Sigmund Freud (1913b), p. 156.   68. Lee Harris (2007), p. 133.

69. Ibid, p. 114. Harris, who makes the case for blatant social Darwinism, succinctly contrasts cultures that obey ethical, rational laws with cultures that obey "cosmic law," and reveals the inherent weakness of liberal individualism in the face of the allegedly superior survival value of fanaticism.

70. René Girard (1972), p. 31.

71. See Georges Bataille (1954, 1970); Emile Durkheim (1912), Henri Hubert and Marcel Mauss (1899).

72. Sigmund Freud (1913b).

73. Sigmund Freud (1920).

Chapter 2: Fundamentalism as Vertical Mystical Homoeros

1. Ernest Becker's (1973, 1975) theory of denial of death, Robert Jay Lifton's (1979, 1999) thinking on the "death taint" and the "broken connection," Robert Langs's (1997) writings on death anxiety and extremes of violence, and Jerry Piven's (2000) work on delusion and death are some among numerous articulations regarding this type of human predicament.

2. Hegel's master-slave dialectics (1806), Jean-Paul Sartre's theory (1945) about becoming alienated and feeling shame through the other's look, and Melanie Klein's notion (1940, 1957) of dependency and envy that cause pain and that crystallize defenses are relevant here. On the group level, there is the fear of whatever serves to relativize the group's world, whatever is different and suggests

the possibility of other ways, which may be both threatening and alluring, and thereby threatens the identity of the closed society.

3. Peter Berger (1999), p. 2.

4. Gabriel A. Almond, R. Scott Appelby, and Emmanuel Sivan (2003).

5. Ibid., p. 7.

6. Karen Armstrong (2000); Mark Juergensmeyer (2000, 2003a).

7. Jürgen Habermas, in Giovanna Borradori (2004), p. 69.

8. For additional arguments against the globalist and counterglobalist characteristics of fundamentalism, particularly Islamic fundamentalism, see Juergensmeyer (2000, 2003a, 2003b).

9. Adorno 1992, quoted by Pecora 2006, p. 19.

10. There are nonmonotheistic religions or movements that are violent. Examples are: the Buddhist- and Shinto-inspired Aum Shinrikyo cult in Japan, or the Hindu and Sikh altercations. These religious groups are not monotheistic but they operate under powerful patriarchal leaders.

11. Still, the interesting point has been made by Max Horkheimer and Theodor W. Adorno (1944), and amplified by recent thinkers (cf. Gilbert Germain [1993]), that our technological environment has paradoxically acquired magical qualities, becoming incomprehensible and mysterious due to its sheer complexity, which is the reason for our ignorance of the sophisticated technological tools we use (in contrast to simple tools that were completely mastered by earlier humans). Furthermore, as they note, contemporary art's preoccupation with form seeks to strip away all sentimentality and becomes ipso facto sacred in its focused starkness.

12. Christopher Rhoades Dÿkema (2001). See also Egyptologist Jan Assman's "Mosaic turn," which, he suggests, necessitated a sharp distinction between true and false and the harshly intolerant, exclusionary attitudes that came in its wake (2003).

13. Although Nazism is not usually regarded as a religion, and certainly not as patriarchal monotheism, Nazism was a father-leader cult, and Hitler talked about Germany as the *Vaterland*, saying: "We do not want to have any other God, only Germany" (Richard Koenigsberg [2009], p. 5).

14. Hans Horkheimer and Theodor W. Adorno (1944).

15. Freud spoke in *Moses and Monotheism* (1939) of the "advance in intellectuality" achieved via abstinence and renunciation of instinct.

16. See Ansor Rabinbach (2000).

17. Fatema Mernissi (1992), p. 98.

18. Ibid., p. 97.

19. Although I make no essential distinctions between Muslim, Jewish, and Christian fundamentalism, I focus mostly on radical Islam, since, aided by existing political circumstances (including negative American politics and corrupt Arab regimes) it has become at present a brutally violent politico-religious form.

Tawhid, the Islamic doctrine of God's Oneness, Unity, and Indivisibility, of there being no other God's than Allah, is central to Islamic belief. This credo is pronounced as *La Ilahha Ilallah*. It designates a single, absolute Truth that transcends the world.

20. In contrast to Anglo-American psychoanalytic terminology, which makes little use of the concept of desire, I find it useful to follow continental, mostly Hegelian-inspired, French, particularly Lacanian psychoanalysis, that uses *desire*, taking it for granted that desire subtends even the most abstract cognitive and cultural ostensibly rational endeavors.

21. Homa Hoofdar (2002).

22. Ibn Warraq (2003). Despite the gaudy title of his book (at the same time as it is modeled on Bertrand Russell's "Why I Am Not a Christian"), *Why I Am Not a Muslim* is a well-researched, scholarly compilation of sources and references of Islamic writings, regarding Islam and women. See chap. 14, pp. 290–327.

23. Ruth Stein (1998b). 24. Daniel Boyarin (1997), p. 11.

25. Stein (1998b). 26. Heinz Kohut (1971).

27. Sigmund Freud (1921), p. 113. 28. Ibid., p. 116.

29. Theodor W. Adorno (1950); Donald Moss (2003a, 2003b).

30. See Hannah Arendt's (1951) description of the structure of totalitarianism as "the iron band of terror, which destroys the plurality of men and makes out of many the One who unfailingly will act as though he himself were part of the course of history or nature" (p. 466).

31. See Madeleine Sorkin's (2004) Girardian analysis of al-Qaeda's and bin Laden's mimetic desire for America's world power. On this view, the jihadists envy what America has, namely world dominion. This is the cause for scapegoating America and the violent desire to destroy it.

32. Johannes J. G. Jansen (1997), pp. 5–6. Jansen notes that the Muslim fundamentalist movement has all the characteristics of a religious movement at the same time as it also has all the characteristics of a modern political movement. Fundamentalists aspire to come to power. However, "power in [their] . . . perception is not something that can be divided or shared with other groups" (p. 2).

33. Shaykh Abdalqadir as-Sufi (1978).

34. As-Sufi probably means here religious awareness, specifically, Allahic awareness. Farhad Khosrokhavar (2005) notes that as-Sufi was the founder of the Murabitun movement, the members of which believe that the West with its democratic systems is dying; they have therefore "attempted to establish a gold-based Islamic monetary system to challenge the dollar-based system, in order to reestablish Islamic networks of caravans to challenge the West's monopoly on distribution and to re-establish a so-called Islamic economy" (p. 170).

35. Abdalhaqq Bewley (1999) is the husband of Aisha Abdurrahman Bewley, a British academic woman who converted to Islam and hosts as-Sufi's doctrines

on her Web site. There are innumerable sources describing how Islamists see history, namely in terms of a continuous war between Christians (and Jews) and Muslims. A continuous, unceasing war of religions is by far the most compelling narrative line of a great part of the Islamic world.

36. Regarding Shariati, see Appendix B.

37. This view is strikingly symmetrical to the view the West has of itself as democratic and ethically more evolved than the "rest" (as conservative philosopher Roger Scruton [2003] calls it), which is regarded as undemocratic, indifferent to human rights, and sunk in a state of a long decline.

38. Karen Armstrong (2000).

39. See Gabriel A. Almond, R. Scott Appelby, and Emmanuel Sivan (2003); Robert Jay Lifton (2000); Ahmad S. Moussali (1992).

40. There are numerous moderate Muslim voices that reject and condemn these fanatical ideas and actions. There is in fact an enmity between radical Islamists who consider moderate Muslims as apostates, with all the practical implications of how therefore to handle them, and the moderate Muslims themselves.

41. Erik H. Erikson (1959) talks about identity diffusion as the sense of weakness, alienation, and confusion that comes about when no "identity crisis" occurs in the arduous struggle to forge an identity for oneself through trial and experimentation. Identity diffusion is a state of deep anxiety about choices and life commitments and hence it is tantamount to paralyzed development (p. 134).

42. Cf. Mircea Eliade (1968); Rudolph Otto (1958).

43. This is why a simple thesis like Armstrong's, where fundamentalism would be a normal response to a world shorn of transcendence and spirituality, is unsatisfactory.

44. Fatema Mernissi (1992), p. 128.

45. Ibid.

46. Robert B. Altmeyer and Bruce Hunsberger (1992), p. 114.

47. Allah is all-merciful, all-compassionate, all-knowing and eternal. Ascribing total perfection to a monotheistic deity is typical; however, in Islam, the attributes of perfection are repeated on a daily basis, in fact, five times a day.

48. Fundamentalism could be metaphorized as aiming at imitating God's creation of a new world (or New World) by partitioning an earth and heaven out of chaos, at the same time as locating Earth down and low and Heaven up and high, by separating them in an absolute manner.

49. Freud's theoretical notions of castration are propounded in several of his writings. See also Jürgen Reeder's (1995) work.

50. Lee Harris (2004) adduces Hegel and Marx to make the case that "when people are force to create their own material world through their own labor . . . whether they will or not, they are also, at every step of the way, acquiring a keener grasp of the objective nature of the world" (p. 26). He claims that most

Arab countries did not create their wealth by engaging in the struggle that is needed to measure one's aspirations and one's work against harsh reality and learn therefrom, since "wealth has come to them by magic," by virtue of their oil, which "allows them to live in a feudal fantasyland" (p. 27). In this way they did not build a more sustained work ethic and did not develop their countries long after the European colonizing forces left the area.

51. Eric Hoffer (1951), p. 59.

52. Sigmund Freud (1921). See also Hans Nunberg (1932).

53. Walter A. Davis (2006), p. 110.

54. Michael Eigen (2001a), p. 138.

55. Ibid.

56. Notably, this core often constitutes the axis or denouement in dramas and tragedies, when the main character reveals it, as in Hamlet's portraying himself as "a dull and muddy-mettled rascal . . . unpregnant of my cause . . . I am pigeon-liver'd and lack gall to make oppression bitter" (*Hamlet*, 2.2.561–66); in Richard the Third's self-description as "rudely stamp'd," "curtail'd of this fair proportion" and "so lamely and unfashionable/that dogs bark at me as I halt by them" (*Richard the Third*, 1.1.22–23). This self-loathing is narrated in Gregor Samsa in *Metamorphosis* (Kafka); or with the son in *Letter to His Father* (Kafka). The letter, addressed to the father, is full of seething fear, hatred, contrition, and masochistic love for Franz's powerful, disdainful, bullying father. It is permeated with fear and hatred, combined with self-loathing and a deep wish to comply with the father's destructive motives toward his son. "My writing was all about you; all I did there, after all, was to bemoan what I could not bemoan upon your breast. It was an intentionally long-drawn-out leave-taking from you," writes Nicholas Murray, Kafka's biographer, and states: "The alternative to slaying the father is self-destruction" (2004, p. 125).

57. See Marion Milner (1969); Hannah Green (1989).

Chapter 3: Purification as Violence

1. Islam distinguishes between *jism*, the body, *nafs*, the personality or character, and *rooh*, spirit. *Nafs*, here translated as soul, is impressionable and relatively static, even base, compared with *rooh*, which is capable of transcendence and transformation; it is called the "inner prophet."

2. Annemarie Schimmel (1994), p. 95.

3. Many of the characteristics of purification rituals fit the pattern of anorectics, the "terrorized and terrorizing little girls and young women," as Ellen Pearlman wrote in a response to a PsyBC discussion (April 2005). She goes further to write that the "cause" these girls and women "are willing to risk themselves for is recognition of self by some higher power, parents or culture. The purity they

aim for is an absence of need, an absence of 'shameful' frustrated desire, and the absence of feminine characteristics."

4. René Girard (1972); Terry Eagleton (2005).

5. Ernst Cassirer (1962).

6. Ibid., p. 104.

7. Quoted in Eli Edward Burris (1931), p. 12. In his study of purificatory rites in ancient Roman religion, Burris reminds us that "magic acts which are intended to avert evils resulting from contact with a tabooed object . . . involved the use of purifying instruments . . . such as water, fire, wool, the skin of sacrificial animals, laurel . . . salt, sulphur, and any object used to cleanse their bodies. . . . Evils may be washed or burned away by the use of these objects" (p. 146).

8. Quran, 74:4. See Schimmel (1994), p. 95.

9. Mary Douglas (1966).

10. Ibid., p. 3.

11. Ibid., p. 50.

12. See the first four chapters of the Book of Numbers.

13. Ruth Stein (1998a).

14. This struggle roughly corresponds to Melanie Klein's conceptualization of the paranoid-schizoid and depressive positions, to wit, the struggle between idealization cum devaluation as they are affected by psychic splitting (the paranoid-schizoid position), and the recognition of loss, harm done, and "contagion" of love with hate, "purity" with "impurity" (the depressive position).

15. For sources of peaceful jihad, see the Quran, 2:214, 4:76–79, 8:39–42, 9:5, 6, 29. See also Thomas P. Hughes (1994), pp. 243–45.

16. Ibid. See also Amir Taheri (1987), pp. 241–43, 251.

17. The distinction, to my mind, is largely quantitative; it is a question of the degree of fear and alarm that necessitates ever stronger means of appeasement and protection. It would be fascinating to inquire about the contingent and circumstantial conditions that trigger movement into the second stage, but such inquiry would be at a level that cannot be gone into here.

18. See, for example, Almond, Appelby, and Sivan (2003); Juergensmeyer (2000, 2003b).

19. The lines between orthodox, particularly ultraorthodox, and fundamentalist groups are not always clear-cut. Thus the term *fundamentalists* seems to apply more to the Mormons than to the Amish, whereas there are some fine distinctions in Jewish religious groups between the orthodox and the fundamentalist, and the same must apply to Muslim religious groups. The Haredim are Jewish ultraorthodox fundamentalists who do not recognize the State of Israel and its administrative, judiciary, and legislative authority (which is mostly secular and does not follow Halakhic law). The Haredim have established their own judiciary and executive systems and keep an isolationist lifestyle in Israel, in the

United States, and to a lesser degree in some western-European countries. Most Haredim refrain from "preempting the Redemption" that is expected when the Messiah Ben-David will be sent by God on earth and will turn Israel into the theocracy they wish it to be.

20. A group of Jewish fundamentalists planning to build the Third Temple on Temple Mount in Jerusalem have found the red heifer mentioned in the Old Testament whose ashes will purify the attendants of the Temple when they renew the sacrificial rites the Temple will be built for. Since these preparations precede the purging of the holy site of the impure Al-Aqsa Mosque, this constitutes a minor purification that will precede the major purging to come (see Con Coughlin [2007]).

21. Although he meant it in a somewhat different sense, we can still borrow Derrida's concept of "autoimmunitary suicide." See Giovanna Borradori (2003).

22. Robert Jay Lifton (1979), p. 97.

23. See René Girard (1972); Gil Baillie (1995, 2005); Mark Juergensmeyer (2000).

24. René Girard (1972), p. 23.

25. The great Greek tragedies enact evolving Greek thought about seemingly unavoidable spiraling violence and the place of the law in this conundrum.

Chapter 4: Regression to the Father

1. Ernst L. Abelin (1971, 1975); Dorothy Burlingham (1973); Peter Blos (1985); James Herzog (2001); Kyle D. Pruett (1983, 1992).

2. Ernst L. Abelin (1975); Peter Blos (1985); James Herzog (2001); Hans W. Loewald (1951); Margaret S. Mahler (1966); John Munder Ross (1979).

3. Sigmund Freud (1927, 1940); Robert Bak (1968); Janine Chasseguet-Smirgel (1964); Lawrence S. Kubie (1974); Nancy Kulish (1986).

4. Peter Blos (1989), p. 10.

5. Sigmund Freud (1913, 1933); Jacques Lacan (1956–57); Janine Chasseguet-Smirgel (1973).

6. Jessica Benjamin (1988); David Braunschweig and Michel Fain (1971).

7. Sigmund Freud (1911, 1921); Jacques Lacan (1971, 1977); Heinz Kohut (1971, 1978); Jessica Benjamin (1988).

8. Sigmund Freud (1923).

9. Nine years earlier, in 1914, Freud had realized how desperately the ego needed to take itself as a love object. This idea is then repeated in 1923 (p. 30). No wonder that the paper Freud wrote just a year later, in 1924(a), deals with the problem of masochism.

10. See, for instance, Psalms 42, 54, 55, 57, and so on.

11. The biological father in many contemporary Moslem cultures is, by contrast, a disappointing figure, who offers no strong support for his son(s). See, for example, Stefania Pandolfo's (2007) interviews with Moroccan youth who attempted dangerous illegal emigrations to Europe.

12. Jacques Lacan (1953–54), p. 156; (1959–60), p. 308.

13. Sigmund Freud (1923); Theodor W. Adorno (1951).

14. See Jacques Lacan's (1959–60) seminar 7.

15. This horrifying "father" would sometimes shout, "I created you, so I have the right to do whatever I like to you. You have done nothing to me, I do not deny it, I am making you suffer for my own pleasure" (Comte de Lautréamont [1869], p. 85).

16. Jürgen Reeder (1995), p. 142.

17. Sigmund Freud (1913b) (I remind the reader that the same story is repeated in *Moses and Monotheism* [1939]).

18. Sigmund Freud (1913b).

19. Sigmund Freud (1939), p. 101.

20. The picture they present may superficially resemble that of a negative Oedipus complex, where the boy loves his father, and even competes with mother for his father's heart. But these men were neither submissive to their fathers, nor were they inhibited in their narcissistic ambitions, their "masculine" pursuits.

21. See Melanie Klein (1928), who writes about the "combined parental couple," who, though fantastically violent in the child's unconscious phantasies, has a strong cohesive relationship. A milder version of the idea of parents bonding among themselves, rather than gender-wise, is David Braunschweig and Michel Fain's (1971) notion of the "mother of the day and the mother of the night," whereby the mother at daytime is devoted to her child, at night she is with another, the father. We could speculate that where a father-son emotional dyad has developed, the mother would have to function as an emotional third, holding a relation that gives added depth and perspective that enables the son to acquire a more lucid viewpoint than the one he could get in the distance-less collapsed space created by the imaginary symbiotic tie between father and son. This seems not to have happened with these patients.

22. Sigmund Freud (1922), p. 82.

23. Johann Wolfgang von Goethe (1808); Roman Polanski (1968).

24. Heinz Kohut (1971), pp. 61–62.

25. Harry Stack Sullivan (1953), p. 216. Such patients were often children who came to experience their needs as bad and repulsive. They often tax the analyst's endurance by their rejecting attitudes, or alternatively, they are compliant and do not dare "put their weight" and be themselves with the analyst, for fear of overburdening her.

26. Or his "soul", to use an apt Rankian term. See Sándor Ferenczi (1932).

27. Jessica Benjamin (1988).

28. Ruth Stein (2002, 2003, 2006a). See Chapter 2.

29. Stanley H. Cath (1982), p. 624.

30. When the parent survives the child's destruction (Winnicott, 1969), the child learns about the other human as separate and acquires skills and "know how" to relate to others. James Herzog (2001).

31. Hans W. Loewald (1979), p. 390.

32. Charles Shepherdson (2000), p. 75.

33. Sigmund Freud (1913b). Later still, Freud wrote about the harsh Semitic God (*Yahweh*), who took the place of the enlightened Egyptian God in *Moses and Monotheism* (1939).

34. On this subject, the central thesis of *Totem and Taboo* is that the actual bearer of prohibition, who prevents our access to the incestuous object, is not the living father (like in the Oedipus complex), but the father who, after his death, becomes the embodiment of the symbolic law or prohibition. In Lacan's words, the dead father returns as his Name (this is the source of Lacan's "name of the father, which in his early work served as a term for paternal prohibition and the laying down of the incest taboo, but later in his writings became hyphenated and capitalized (as the Name-of-the-Father) and became the fundamental signifier which permits signification to proceed normally" (Dylan Evans [1996], p. 119), and which represents the whole symbolic order).

35. Dr. Daniel Gottlieb Moritz Schreber, the popular German educator and father of Daniel Schreber, whose psychotic ideation Freud interpreted in his theory of paranoia, recommended that a blackboard be hung in the children's room on which should be recorded each child's act of disobedience, forgetfulness, or impulsivity, throughout the month. Erez had a list of sins for which he had to atone, one by one. The parallel between Schreber and Erez was sometimes uncanny. Both persons expressed a deep wish to become women and submit, sexually and/or otherwise, to God's might. Both feared mechanization and yet wanted it too, both expressed covert sarcastic rebelliousness but both were tempted to give up their masculinity for love of the father.

36. Never before (or later) in my professional life did I serve as God Himself in a patient's transference. Nowhere in the literature did I find a template for such a phenomenon. But this configuration proved highly instructive for my thinking on these themes.

37. A relationship which I am leaving out in the present account of the case (see Ruth Stein [1995]).

38. Sigmund Freud (1913b) writes that in primitive fantasy, a person dies because he has been killed.

39. Sigmund Freud (1911).

40. Wilhelm G. Niederland (1951; 1959; 1960).

41. Wilhelm G. Niederland (1951), p. 583. In a way, Schreber could not sustain the self-protective "malevolent transformation" mentioned above, and became psychotically ill when he realized how great and extreme his need was for tenderness, to the point of wanting to become a woman to get his father's love.

42. Daniel Gustav, Daniel Paul Schreber's brother, committed suicide in his early thirties.

43. Erez apparently referred to me when he said, " . . . everything you say is not words of love . . . ," but at those moments, I was his father (and/or his mother) in the transference.

44. See Jacques Lacan (1956–57); Charles Shepherdson (2000).

45. This savage father, according to Gilles Deleuze (1997), can be seen as a counterpart of the oral mother, a mother who is the ideal of desire and death and is located between the womb mother and the Oedipal mother (who always already includes the father within her).

46. Marvin P. Osman (2004), p. 976.

47. Ibid., p. 979.

48. The Aztec culture is notorious for the numerous human beings it sacrificed to the sun god, who demanded more and more human hearts and blood in order to keep the world in motion. According to Marvin P. Osman (2004) and Nigel Davies (1987, quoted by Osman), the Aztecs believed that world events occurred in cycles, and that the sun's rays expired periodically. According to them, all life on earth would have perished had the sun god not been continuously regenerated with a steady flow of blood and human hearts. First, it was the gods' deaths that gave the sun life and made possible the birth of living beings. Later it was "the precious blood of human beings that was needed to sustain and make restitution to the sun god to ensure that his countenance would continue to shine down upon them" (p. 992). "It was thus that the actual living fiber and substance of the victim was directly transferred to the vulnerable and thirsty gods of the Aztecs" (p. 994).

49. As Stefania Pandolfo (2007) describes it, *al-qanat*, despair, "is a sense of withdrawal of life, of life shrinking. It is as if by the aftershock of an impact, human beings have been ejected from the space of life—the blood drawn out of their bodies, thrown into an Elsewhere which is also a different time, a temporality which is not of this world, and which, at the same time, is the bodily record of a zone of exclusion" (p. 348). This despair, which religion warns against as dangerous to sanity and faith, carries images of "imprisonment, lack of space, extreme boredom, and a cause of madness or suicide" (p. 348). The despairing heroic figures in the Old and New Testaments, such as David, who is besieged by his enemies, Job who is stuck down with the worst of calamities, Jesus on

the Cross crying out to God why He had forsaken him, are all implicated in a struggle between faith and a despair that threatens to lead to the denial of Divine Providence and God's reliability and goodness.

50. Ruth Stein (2005b).

51. Erikson (1950); Kernberg (1984).

52. Note that the 9/11 hijackers more often became fanatical Muslims in Europe (Germany) than in their mother countries.

53. In *Moses and Monotheism* (1939), Freud discusses Islam and compares it disadvantageously, and perhaps disparagingly, with Judaism as Father-religion and Christianity as Son-religion. Islam, in his view, recuperated Judaism, "but the internal development of the new religion soon came to a stop, perhaps because it lacked the depth which had been caused in the Jewish case by the murder of the founder of their religion." (pp. 92–93).

54. These transformations, I believe, form the core of mind control (or "brainwashing"; cf. Ruth Stein [2007]), whereby hate and fear, whether artificially induced or accumulating over one's life, are transformed into perverted, enthralled "love."

55. Usama bin Muhammad bin Laden (2002). "A Nation Challenged: Al Qaeda; Verses from bin Laden's War: Wielding the Pen as a Sword of the Jihad." *New York Times*, April 7, 2002, section 1, p. 20.

56. David Lee Miller (2003).

57. "The firstborn of your sons you shall give to me" (Ex. 22:29).

58. The Jewish Easter is called Pesach, which carries the etymological root meaning of "to skip over" (*psch*'), signifying God's skipping over the houses of the Israelite families with firstborns. The families were instructed to smear blood from sacrificial animals on their thresholds and door jambs as a sign for God not to strike the firstborns of His people on the night He struck down the firstborns of Egypt.

59. Richard Koenigsberg (2009).

60. John Hackett, in Gwynne Dyer (2004), p. 129.

61. Cited in Koenigsberg (2009), p. 21.

62. In the preface to the second edition of his *The Interpretation of Dreams* (1900), which Freud began writing a year after his father's death, he says: "[This book] was, I found, a portion of my own self-analysis, my reaction to my father's death—that is to say, to the most important event, the most poignant loss, of a man's life" (p. xxvi). Freud's words carry an intensity that seems to come from recesses of personal knowledge. Even if few analysts would totally accept such a sweeping, exclusivist statement, and most analysts unhesitatingly would give primary importance to the mother, we should take Freud very seriously here, particularly as he dwells on the absence, elusiveness, death of the father in a person's life, on the rich presence of varieties of absence.

Chapter 5: The Triadic Structure of Evil

1. Mahdi, the child Imam who disappeared in a well in 879, will come only if the non-Muslim world is destroyed first, and/or most of the world plunges into chaos, great misery, and suffering before his messianic reappearance. The word *ma'ad* means "return" (to God), and refers to Islamic ideas of eschatology—whence this name.

2. Svetozar D. Stojanovi (2005).

3. Some authors, such as Robert Jay Lifton (2000), Charles B. Strozier (1994), James W. Jones (2008), call it apocalyptic, with all the differences and similarities that obtain between utopia and apocalypse. These categories are often confounded in religious eschatological thinking, which sees the end of time simultaneously as the destruction of the world and the consummation of God's perfection.

4. Serbian philosopher Svetozar Stojanović (2005) calls auto-apocalypse "the possibility and probability of the self-destruction of a good part of humanity, if not of the [*sic*] entire humanity." Such an apocalyptic scenario would involve a struggle for survival that would supplant the more ordinary struggles for recognition between master and servant. Stojanović believes that our morals and moral philosophies have failed in this respect, since they have all evolved "in communities incapable of putting in jeopardy the survival of the human species." In such a situation, writes Stojanović, "a part of humanity would have to be sacrificed in order for humanity to survive." "Principle-ist" ethics will be supplanted by "consequentialist" ethics, with negative, rather than positive terms: rather than producing the greatest good for the greatest number of people, its criterion will be to prevent absolute evil, that is, the destruction of the entire humanity (p. 149).

5. The subject of mind control (what used to be called "brainwashing") is outside the scope of this book, but there is ample evidence regarding the systematic indoctrination and religious training that radical Islamists receive in madrassas, training camps, and mosques, as well as on the Internet. Fascinating research findings show the effectiveness of the induction of trance states that change brainwave patterns and shape altered states of experience, both sensitizing and blunting sensory and cognitive functions. When these mechanical methods (which include sensory deprivation and intense repetitive behaviors) are used in a group setting, with a charismatic leader or guide, and accompanied by the skillful manipulation of certain emotions, the effects are powerful (Ruth Stein [2007]). In a way, mind control strategies not only create altered states of consciousness; they also help transpose the person's personal balance of impulse and conscience, into a thing of the group.

6. Israeli philosopher Adi Ophir (2005) talks about the socially structured order of "superfluous evils," preventable suffering that is perpetrated on others.

7. Leonard Shengold (1989); Christopher Bollas (1995).

8. W. Ronald D. Fairbairn (1952); Melanie Klein (1946); Franco Fornari (1966); Peter Fonagy (2008); Peter Fonagy and Mary Target (1998, 2007).

9. See Betty Joseph (1982); Donald Meltzer (1975); Herbert Rosenfeld (1971); John Steiner (1993).

10. See Ruth Stein (1990). The subjective bent of Kleinian theory produces the following conclusions: a good person, let us say, a good mother, is perceived as bad because she is more frustrating, absent, or withholding than her child can tolerate. At the same time, a mother who is not kind or loving, but cruel, narcissistic and seductive, or indifferent, can nonetheless be felt to be an ideal, loving figure by a child who needs to idealize her, or who needs to protect her against his own aggression and sadism.

11. Melanie Klein (1957); Wilfred R. Bion (1967).

12. Vamik Volkan (2004), p. 132.

13. Theologian Karl Niebuhr (1932) argues for a basic difference between the morality of the individual, who is capable of care and goodness, and collectives which are "inherently selfish and uncaring." Niebuhr believes that there is a baseness in human nature that is more obvious and massive in the life of the group, which responds only to power. Since the evil of the collective is more intractable than the evil of the individual, coercion is needed to maintain society, and violence is merely the ultimate form of coercion. His view seems to me to be too categorical, after all, groups also bring out good things in individuals, yet there is definitely a different balance of restraint and license in individual and in group situations.

14. One of the most notorious and painful to me as I am editing this chapter is the Israeli-Palestinian conflict.

15. See Claudia Card's (2002) analysis of what she calls the "atrocity paradigm."

16. Gil Baillie (2005), p. 21.

17. Sigmund Freud (1921) regards the group leader as instantiating the (ego-) ideal that has come to replace the superego and conscience of the individual.

18. Michael Sebek's (1996) concept of "totalitarian objects," coercive internalized objects that force the individual into submission and obedience, blocking individual development at the same time as they provide a sense of safety and importance, are quite relevant here.

19. Sigmund Freud (1915), p. 280, sees "evil" as the expression of primal, "egoistical" instincts, ruthlessly bent on satisfaction. These instincts can be controlled from the outside by upbringing, and from the inside by eroticism, that is, "by the human need for love, taken in its widest sense," which acts on selfish instincts and turns them into social ones. "We learn to value being loved as an

advantage for which we are willing to sacrifice other advantages," he writes (p. 282). Here we have a Freudian ethics of love, the care a human infant is born into and gets in most human families. Holding on to the value of being loved and not giving up on this impulse, protects against the nihilism and jouissance of violence.

20. Ninian Smart (2003b), pp. 122–23.

21. Scott Atran (2003, 2007).

22. Martin Kramer (2008).

23. Zygmunt Bauman (1992), p. 66

24. For examples, Hassan Hanafi in Egypt, Rashid Ghanouchi in Tunisia, Mohammed Arkoun in Algeria. Regarding Christianity, Matthias Beier (2004) publicized the stance of spiritual leader Eugen Drewermann.

25. Gil Baillie (2005), p. 20.

26. Osama bin Laden and his cohorts did not expect the Twin Towers to collapse, contends Joseph Heath from the University of Toronto. The fact that they did was for them an indication that God willed it, and a proof of His grandeur and Truth.

27. The editor of Rasoulallah.net (whose identity I have not been able to obtain), a Muslim Web site with apologeticist aims, claims that Islam "broke away from the longstanding [sacrificial] tradition of appeasing an 'angry God' and instead demanded personal sacrifice and submission as the only way to die before death and reach '*fana*'' or 'extinction in Allah'" (Rasoulallah.net [2008]). He makes the point that the notion of "vicarious atonement of sin" (absolving one's sins through the blood of another) is nowhere to be found in the Quran. Neither is the idea of gaining favor by offering the life of another to Allah; rather, what Islam demands as a sacrifice is one's personal willingness to submit one's ego and individual will to Allah. Girard (2003) concurs with this view regarding the non-sacrificiality of Islam, based on the fact that human sacrifice is not part of the Muslim tradition, and is not justified by any Quranic phrases. But he allows for the exception represented by fundamentalist terrorism, which is, as I claim in this book, obviously sacrificial. Fundamentalist terrorism, according to Girard, is "a contradiction that plays upon the ambiguity … between religion and the sacred." What he seems to mean, if I read him correctly, is that while religion, following Christ's ultimate sacrifice for humanity, does not need sacrifices anymore, Islamic fundamentalism functions on the need for the sacred through human sacrifice, which means "making sacred" by ritual killing.

28. The vexing question as to why, while both biblical Judaism and Islam decry (animal) blood sacrifice, Anspach's notion applies less to Judaism than to Islam cannot be fully addressed here. One hypothesis (Küntzl, 2004) is that Judaism has more contentious aspects than Islam and would therefore tend to absorb violence intramurally, maintaining an elevated self-vision at the same

time. Linguistically, the difference between the two Abrahamic religions (each in its own language) is telling. While "Israel" is etymologically derived from "contending with" (Jacob received the name Israel following his nightlong struggle with an angel, Genesis, 32:29), Islam, on the other hand, means, etymologically, submission and making peace with that to which one submits. This explanation by a German Islamic scholar is highly metaphorical and literary and leaves much by way of speculation. I think that other aspects in Jewish history, including loss of political sovereignty (with its attendant adaptation to being a cosmopolitan minority), were among the many factors that contributed to the decrease of violence in this religion.

29. Mark Anspach (1991), p. 25.

30. Roger Scruton (2003) talks about the "stark, unmediated confrontation between the individual and his God" (pp. 92–93).

31. It is harder to find such messages in the Quran, but see Wendell Berry and Reza Shah-Kazemi (2007).

32. Noah Feldman (2006) describes the growing permissiveness of Islamic legal authorities toward Muslims striking at noncombatant populations in pursuing divine justice.

33. Heinz Kohut (1971), p. 8. Kohut also offers an interesting explanation for psychic degradation (a decompensation that, on an individual level, causes psychopathology). When cohesive structures are destroyed, their disconnected fragments can become secondarily organized, rearranged into delusions, and then rationalized through the efforts of remaining integrative functions of the psyche—or ideology.

34. Regarding mind control, see note 54 in Chapter 4, as well as note 5 in the current chapter.

35. Judaism and Islam, but see also some of the Gospels and, particularly, the Book of Revelation.

36. The Freudian concept of disavowal, or denial, a major constitutive mechanism in perversion, offers useful insight into the originating contexts and defense mechanisms of this psychodynamic. The understanding is useful even if one does not apply it to individual psychopathology (Sigmund Freud [1924], pp. 184–85; [1940], p. 203).

37. I have in mind the way nothingness and nonbeing in the context of God is treated by Kierkegaard (1849). See also Sartre's (1945) analysis of being and nothingness, and the belief in God as a form of bad faith.

38. As is clear in this study, I assume that God is a creation of man, an externalization and expression (a projection) of parts of the human psyche, a constant and perpetual grand projection, ubiquitous in the arts and in relation to others. The fact that we create myth and art and culture in our template does not invalidate their quality, their value, and their novelty and impact on us, even their

sacredness. After all, we cannot relate to anything that is too alien to us, that is, to anything that we have not created in some sense.

39. Obviously, God has been depicted as loving or vengeful, good or evil. If we assume that the construct of God encompasses both, then focusing on one aspect to the exclusion of the other means that the other aspect is dissociated or split off.

40. Rudolph Otto (1923), p. 24.

41. Wendy Doniger-O'Flaherty (1976).

42. I assume the liberty here to talk about polytheistic Hinduism and its deities as "God," following Doniger-O'Flaherty's generic use of the term.

43. Ibid., 141 ff.

44. It would be most intriguing to study the alterations in consciousness and the variations in what is deemed acceptable for a believer to be able to worship a god of this stripe.

45. In addition, the Hindu belief, according to Doniger-O'Flaherty, has historically undergone a progressive shift regarding the notion of sacrifice: from feeding the gods to give them the strength for maintaining cosmic order; to offering sacrifices designed to expiate sins; to the current situation, in which the gods appear as subordinate to the sacrificer. Perhaps after all the pragmatic realism that I find so praiseworthy in this system is too transparent to sustain the mystification needed to sustain a Godhead.

46. The investigation of such geo-historical facts is outside the scope of this work, although it does seem that there is a fair amount of violence in Hindu cultures as well, as the recent violent Hindu attacks against Christians in India makes clear.

47. Hinduism is a henoistic religion (it recognizes a single deity, and views other gods and goddesses as manifestations or aspects of that supreme God). Henotheistic and polytheistic religions have traditionally been among the world's most religiously tolerant faiths. The recent attacks of Hindu believers on Christians in India, however, seem to belie this image. Some blame it on the Hindu nationalistic political party that controlled the government of India until recently. The linkage of religion, the national government, and nationalism led to a degeneration of the separation of church and state in India. This, in turn, has decreased the level of religious tolerance in that country. The escalation of anti-Christian violence was one manifestation of this linkage. With the recent change in government, the level of violence will diminish, says the Ontario Council for Religious Tolerance, an independent research body (see their Web site). Obviously this is just a hypothesis and much more study is needed in this domain.

48. This is basically a leitmotif in how psychoanalysis regards people's struggles and dealings with their lives, and a substantial portion of clinical writings are basically devoted to portrayals of varieties of this tension.

49. Robert Stoller (1986); Ruth Stein (2001, 2005b).

50. In individual perversion, the object of desire is at the same time the persecutory object (that needs to be "persecuted," that is, seduced, exploited for one's psychic needs, following which it is most often discarded). The details of psychoanalytic thinking on individual perversion are outside the scope of this book (see Ruth Stein [1995, 2001, 2005b]).

51. Ideology can have a brief and inchoate form, or can take the shape of a formally argued procedure. A deliberate structure of ideology was described by Jean-Pierre Mignard (2005). The Wansee Conference resolution of the Final Solution for the Jews and kindred decisions were represented in documents that were all underwritten and consented to by lawyers and historians who had been *supporters and creators of notions of the liberal state and regulatory legislation*. Ideology, it is clear, can function to transform a regressive desire into a progressive force.

52. Louis Althusser (2001).

53. Peter L. Bergen (2006); Christiane Amanpour (2007).

54. Giorgio Agamben (1995).

55. Omer Bartov (2000), p. 153, distinguishes between the "higher" morality of genocidal regimes that aspire toward utopia (Robert Jay Lifton calls it apocalyptic) and ordinary morality. From the utopians' perspective, ordinary morality must be destroyed along with those undesirable elements so that the "higher" morality of utopia can be achieved.

56. Theodor W. Adorno (1950).

57. In existential thinking (Ernest Becker [1973, 1975]; Giorgio Agamben [1995]; Carolyn Marvin and D. W. Ingle [1999]), power is the power to deal with life and death issues through administering death. Ernest Becker calls "social evil" the successive and increasing usurpation of people by rulers and priests who appropriated more and more power for themselves until the advent of the megamachines of power such as the state and the military, which express their sovereignty through holding and exercising the power to kill.

58. James Bernauer (1989).

59. Alessandro Ferrara (2001), p. 175.

60. Cf. Ruth Stein (1999).

61. Robert Jay Lifton (1999), pp. 8, 312.

62. In Peter L. Berger et al. (1999).

63. Christopher Bollas (1992) uses the concept of "violent innocence" to describe patients who provoke and taunt the analyst but act in bewildered surprise when the analyst draws their attention to anything they might have said or done (p. 191). Thomas Ogden (1997) and Ruth Stein (1995, 2001, 2005b) have traced patterns of this ostensibly irreproachable, sterling self-presentation of certain patients who specialize in effectively rendering the analyst confused, embarrassed, and

deeply frustrated with a facade of innocence, muffled initiative, and concealed intention. Very often, the perverse person wants to bring the other to his side of seeing things; he wants to strike a "perverse pact" with the other person, in which both will share a warped worldview that becomes validated through their partnership.

64. I have written about the sense of self-entitlement some perverse people are adept at giving to the objects of their seduction, subversion, or collusion (Stein [2001]).

I developed this specific idea regarding perversion in my clinical work, but later found it in the writings of Slavoj Žižek (2003b), who likewise believes that the characteristic perverse enjoyment comes from adopting the position of the pure instrument of the big Other's will: "It's not my responsibility, it's not me who's effectively doing it, I am merely an instrument of the higher Historical Necessity" (pp. 4–5). Žižek tells us about his shock at reading some speeches by Commandant Marcos of the Zapatistas: "'Behind a mask, Marcos says, 'I am nobody. Through me, you have this poetic explosion. Through me, dispossessed peasants in Brazil, poor drug addicts and homeless people in New York, sweatshop workers in Indonesia, all of them speak, but I am nobody'" (p. 5). Marcos's position appears modest, but the manifest self-erasure conceals an extreme arrogance. As do other leaders like him, Marcos speaks like one who annihilates himself for his people, when in fact it is they who are annihilated through him. Perversion is the willingness of a leader and a group, a seducer and seduced, to undergo this process. When such a "self-negating" leader begins to demand his followers' selves, even lives, the perversion is gradually or abruptly revealed as the disavowed and mutated hatred it is, and the followers find themselves—whether they are aware of it or not, or only partially so—subjugated and exploited. Sooner or later, it becomes a question of killing in the service of the leader, rephrased as fulfilling a righteous cause, of preserving Truth and Divine Will.

65. In my clinical work over the years, I have had several experiences with difficult patients who operated on perverse levels, who, at a late stage in their analysis, confessed to me about how they had repeatedly provoked me into the behavior they wanted me to enact, and what tactics they had used to deceive me and hide from me. Perhaps such a crack may also open up regarding the perverse duplicity of the fundamentalist mind.

66. The term *taqiyya*, "to fear," writes Raymond Ibrahim (2007), is based primarily on Quran 3:28 and 16:106. It denotes an Islamic doctrine allowing Muslims to dissemble their true beliefs when fearing persecution. Based on certain hadiths, some *ulema* (legal scholars) expand the meaning of *taqiyya* to permit general lying in order to "advance any cause beneficial to Islam" (pp. xxi, 72–73).

67. Emmanuel Sivan (1983) talks about the two languages (or the double language) of fundamentalist groups a long time ago.

68. Robert C. Solomon (1987), p. 287.

69. Ibid., p. 292.

70. *Disavowal* is a psychoanalytic term denoting a typical mechanism of perversion.

71. Emil I. Fackenheim (2005), p. 61.

72. Immanuel Kant (1793), p. 72.

73. Sigmund Freud (1915) explicitly rejects the idea that we can eradicate evil human tendencies and replace them by good ones under the influence of education and a civilized environment (pp. 280–81).

74. For Kant, a key voice of the Enlightenment, there is no diabolical evil, since there is no explicit, direct denial of the authority of the law. Man is born free and his freedom is deeply embedded in his being a rational agent; according to Kant, this implies knowledge of the moral law. Acting against the moral law, according to Kant, would imply a devilish entity rather than a human being.

75. The Jewish fundamentalist husband of the above-mentioned woman presented himself to her, during their courtship, as "first and foremostly God's slave." "You should know," he told her, "that I'm doing anything God asks me to do, even walking in the streets with a yellow tail if needed."

76. Masud R. Khan (1979) quotes Muhammad, with no further references, as saying: "Whoever invades people's privacy corrupts them" (p. 197).

77. "Law," says Slavoj Žižek (1997), "is the name for the limitation the subject imposes on himself—say, with regard to another human being, the name for the 'respect' which enjoins me to maintain a distance toward him or her, to abstain from trying to penetrate all of his/her secrets" (p. 238).

78. One could say that radical evil comes from the id, whereas diabolical evil resides in the superego. In the following pages I shall develop this idea.

79. Nietzsche (1887) talks about the ascetic ideal as pertaining to the will to absolute, unquestioned truth. Absolute truth is taken as explaining suffering as a result of sins, which, man hopes, can be expiated through rigorous self-discipline and self-denial. "The ascetic treats life as a wrong road" (1887, p. 83). The ascetic priest achieves this valuation of life by juxtaposing against it an otherworldly „life" that is deemed to be the only *true* form of life. In this way, the resentment of the weak against the strong is changed by giving the feeling a religious rationalization as sin and guilt. In this way, "the ascetic priest [is] the predestined savior, shepherd, and advocate of the sick herd. . . . *Dominion over ones who suffer is his realm*" (ibid., p. 90).

80. There is an interesting affinity between this understanding of self-interest and Heinz Kohut's demonstrations of how the picture of narcissistic patients that was prevalent before his contributions—that they are inaccessible to analytic treatment for their lack of transferential engagement with the analyst—is simply false. There are powerful transferential and object-relational motivations in even the most self-centered, self-sufficient narcissistic disturbances. Narcis-

sistically disordered people can develop intense transferences to the analyst, but their nature is that of gaining narcissistic regulation from her as self-object; in other words, the attachment, more than in individuals with less-accented narcissism, revolves around self-interest.

81. Max Horkheimer and Theodor W. Adorno (1944) contend that Kantian reason leads ineluctably to the calculating rationality of a totalitarian order, and that it finds a counterpart in the systematic mechanization of pleasures in Sade's perverse utopias (see also Jacques Lacan's [1966], "Kant avec Sade").

82. Freud (1924a), p. 167.

83. Freud (1920). Other versions of the death drive, developed after Freud, see it as a static repetition (Lacan), envy and the hatred of life (Melanie Klein), and the lure of destructiveness and self-destructiveness—all signifiers of an attraction to the death of the human.

84. The lure of the death drive exists whether we think of it as a desire for quietude and the abolition of any tension or as idealized destructiveness and self-destructiveness.

85. I believe, together with Norman O. Brown (1959), Kirby Farrell (1998), and others that one very useful way to view culture is to see it as an externalization of privately formed psychic events and strivings into publicly acceptable ways, and that this externalization can come in very different forms across time and space. Jihadism is one of them.

86. Ernest Becker (1973); Jerry Piven (2004).

87. A critique of this kind of transcendence is found in Luce Irigaray (2002), where she criticizes Plato's allegory of the cave, deemed as representing the classical account of transcendence. She regards the cave as the womb from which male philosophers have been trying to escape, so that transcendence for them expresses a disdain for being born of flesh. "No soaring airless freedom of the soul from the body for this Irigarayan transcendence" (2002, p. 14).

88. Slavoj Žižek (1997), p. 238.

89. Iavor Rangelov (2003).

90. William G. Joffe and Joseph Sandler (1965).

91. Jessica Benjamin (1995) discusses omnipotence from an intersubjective perspective as the loss or obliteration of the outside other . . . [an] intersubjective correlative of what Freud calls the death instinct (p. 191). She notes that mental omnipotence is the fantasy counterpart to death. Omnipotence for her means the complete assimilation of the other into the self.

92. Roland Barthes believes that myth "does not deny things, on the contrary, its function is to talk about them; simply, it purifies them, makes them innocent, gives them a natural and eternal justification and a clarity which is not that of explanation but that of a statement of fact" (Andrew Robinson [2005], quoting Barthes, p. 35).

93. The allusion to Kant's "What Is Enlightenment?" and to Foucault's discussion of Kant's article will not be lost on some readers. According to Kant, Enlightenment is the exit from self-imposed tutelage and the assumption of the courage to use one's own reason without excessive privileging of authority figures. The inability to do so does not come from lack of understanding but from lack of courage and resolve. Foucault basically adds to Kant's criticism of reason the criticism of our own experience of difference as subjects, that is, the criticism of the singular and the contingent.

94. Quoted in Joan Copjec (1996), p. vii.

95. See my essay on *Schadenfreude*; Ruth Stein (1992).

96. This traditional theological negative view of evil considered disease, natural catastrophe, social injustice, and other kinds of suffering as illusions created by the limitations of our human understanding, or as realities generated by weak human resistance to earthly temptations.

97. Adi Ophir (2005) sets out to reverse the marginalization of evil in recent philosophical work by strongly positing evil's positive existence. Ophir also reminds us that attempts to clarify the nature of the good have failed. "We know nothing about the good . . . other than some clear knowledge of those specific elements . . . which make life more tolerable" (p. 11). The good is always missing, always in a state of not-yet or no-longer, and every discussion of the good is founded on allegories. It is more significant, he suggests, to focus on the concept of evil.

98. In his studies of nonmilitant Christian fundamentalists, Charles B. Strozier (2009) notes that they can be "good people with bad theory." Augustine and other medieval thinkers talk about freedom of choice to do evil, where evil is defined as turning away from God—a definition of free choice and evil very different from Kant's formulations. See below.

99. Michael Scheuer, who once headed the CIA's bin Laden unit, tells CNN international correspondent Christiane Amanpour (2007) that bin Laden and al-Qaeda have been authorized by the Saudi Sheikh Nasir bin Hamadal-Fahd to "use nuclear weapons against the United States . . . capping the casualties at 10 million." Amanpour tells us of her response to this news: "'He's had an approval, a religious approval for 10 million deaths?' I asked him. 'Yes,' Scheuer responded" (Amanpour [2007]).

100. See the courageous account by Ibn Warraq (2003), who left Islamic orthodoxy and who has to write under a pseudonym to protect his physical safety.

101. Mary M. Habeck (2006) articulates this useful distinction between the Islamic religion and its dangerously violent manifestations.

102. This quote is from Ferrara (2001), who contends that one cannot condemn a culture as perpetrating evil when it acts according to its own "comprehensive conception of good," such as the Nazi culture did (pp. 180–81).

103. Christopher Bollas (2004), p. 106.
104. Ibid., p. 108.

Appendix A: Mohammed Atta's Letter

The text of this appendix is taken from "A nation challenged: Notes found after the hijackings." A version of this text appeared in print on Saturday, September 29, 2001, on section B, page 3, of the New York edition of the *New York Times*, and is now available at www.nytimes.com/2001/09/29/us/a-nation-challenged-notes-found-after-the-hijackings.html?scp=7&sq=september%2029%20200 (accessed June 25, 2009).

Appendix B: From Dr. Ali Shariati's After Shahadat

The text of this appendix was originally delivered as a speech the day after Shahadat, in the Grand Mosque of Narmak in Tehran, the night after Ashura, 1970. It was published in *Jihad and Shahadat: Struggle and Martyrdom in Islam*, edited by Mehdi Abedi and Gary Legenhausen (Houston: The Institute for Research and Islamic Studies, 1986), pp. 244-52. Reprinted with permission.

1. I have left out some redundant passages.
2. Zaynab was the granddaughter of Muhammad, the daughter of Muhammad's daughter Fatimah, and the sister of Hussein. Hussein was a prophet and the Shiite's second Imam, martyred in the Battle of Karbala by his enemy, the heretic Yazid. Zaynab is known for her support of Hussein and his family, and by her speech to the people of Kufa, who were ruled by Yazid.
3. *Ayah* (plural *ayat*) is a sign or miracle (it is cognate with the Hebrew *ot*). Each of the Quran's 6,236 verses is called *ayah*, and is considered a sign from Allah.
4. "Dahhak is a mythical Arab king who conquered Iran. In Firdowsi's epic *Shahnamah*, he is said to have had two snakes which came out of his shoulders which had an insatiable appetite for the brains of young boys. Kavah, a blacksmith with seven sons, refused to give up the last of his sons, after having lost the other six to Dahhak. He mounted a rebellion against Dahhak and won popular support. The staff and apron of Kavah became symbols of Iranian nationalism. . . .
"In the Shi'ite literature, Ali Akbar refers to the second son of Husayn, who was martyred on Ashura (there are also some reports to the effect that Ali ibn al-Husayn al-Akbar was the only son of Husayn . . . [and] was the only son of Husayn to survive Karbala. He became the fourth Imam)" (*Jihad and Shahadat*, p. 252).

References

Abelin, Ernst L. (1971). The role of the father in the separation-individuation process. In John B. McDevitt and Calvin F. Settlage, eds., *Separation-Individuation*, pp. 229–52. New York: International Universities Press.

———.. (1975). Some further observations and comments on the earliest role of the father. *International Journal of Psychoanalysis* 56: 293–302.

Abraham, Karl (1924). A short study of the development of the libido, viewed in the light of mental disorders. In *Selected Papers on Psychoanalysis*, trans. Douglas Bryan and Alix Stratchey, pp. 418–503. London: Hogarth Press, 1927.

Adorno, Theodor W. (1950). Prejudice in the Interview material. In *The Authoritarian Personality*, ed. Theodor W. Adorno, Else Frenkel-Brunswick, and Daniel J. Levinson, pp. 605–53. New York: W. W. Norton, 1969.

———. (1951). *Minima Moralia: Reflections from Damaged Life*. Trans. Edmund F. N. Jephcott. London: Verso, 2000.

———. (1992). *Notes to Literature*. Vol. 2. Ed. Rolf Tiedemann. Trans. Shierry Weber Nicholsen. New York: Columbia University Press.

Agamben, Giorgio (1995). *Homo Sacer: Sovereign Power and Bare Life*. Trans. Daniel Heller-Roazen. Stanford, CA: Stanford University Press, 1998.

Alford, C. Fred (1997). *What Evil Means to Us*. Ithaca, NY: Cornell University Press.

———. (2006). *Psychology and the Natural Law of Reparation*. Cambridge: Cambridge University Press.

Allison, Henry E. (2001). Reflections on the banality of (radical) evil: A Kantian analysis. In *Rethinking Evil: Contemporary Perspectives*, ed. Maria Pia Lara, pp. 86–100. Berkeley: University of California Press.

Almond, Gabriel A., R. Scott Appelby, and Emmanuel Sivan (2003). *Strong Religion: The Rise of Fundamentalism around the World*. Chicago: University of Chicago Press.

Althusser, Louis (2001). Ideology and ideological state apparatus. In *Lenin and Philosophy and Other Essays*, pp. 85–126. New York: Monthly Review Press.

Altmeyer, Robert B., and Bruce Hunsberger (1992). Authoritarianism, religious fundamentalism, quest, and prejudice. *International Journal of Psychology and Religion* 2: 113–33.

Amanpour, Christiane (2007). *God's Warriors*. CNN, August 27.

Anspach, Mark (1991). Violence against violence: Islam in comparative context. *Terrorism and Political Violence* 3: 9–29.

Appleby, R. Scott, Gabriel A. Almond, and Emanuel Sivan (2003). *Strong Religion*. Chicago: University of Chicago Press.

Arendt, Hannah (1951). *The Origins of Totalitarianism*. New York: Harcourt Brace Jovanovich.

———. (1958). *The Human Condition*. Chicago: University of Chicago Press.

———. (1964). *Eichmann in Jerusalem: A Report on the Banality of Evil*. New York: Viking Press.

———. (1970). *On Violence*. Orlando, FL: Harvest Books.

Armstrong, Karen (2000). *The Battle for God*. New York: Ballantine Books.

as-Sufi, Shaykh Abdalqadir (1978). *Islam and the Death of Democracy*. Tucsan Discourses. http://ourworld.compuserve.com/homepages/abewley/tucson .html. Aisha Bewley's Islamic Home Page (accessed April 28, 2009).

Assman, Jan (2003). *Die Mosaische Unterscheidung order der Preis des Monotheismus*. Munich: Carl Hanser Verlag.

Atran, Scott (2003). Genesis of suicide terrorism. *Science* 299: 1534–39.

———. (2007). Sacred barriers to conflict resolution. *Science* 317: 1039–40.

Augustine, Saint. *On Free Choice of the Will*. Trans. Thomas Williams. Indianapolis: Hackett Publishing, 1993.

Badiou, Alain (1982). *Théorie du suject: L'ordre philosophique*. Paris: Seuil.

———. (2001). *Ethics: An Essay on the Understanding of Evil*. Trans. Peter Hallward. London: Verso.

Baillie, Gil (1995). *Violence Unveiled: Humanity at the Crossroads*. New York: Crossroad Publishing.

———. (2005). Two thousand years and no new God. In *Destined for Evil? The Twentieth-Century Response*, ed. Predrag Ciovacki, pp. 19–43. Rochester, NY: University of Rochester Press.

Bak, Robert (1968). The phallic woman: The ubiquitous fantasy in perversions. *Psychoanalytic Study of the Child* 23: 15–36.

Bartov, Omer (2000). *Mirrors of Destruction: War, Genocide, and Modern Identity*. Oxford: Oxford University Press.

Bataille, Georges (1954). *Inner Experience*. Trans. Leslie A. Boldt. Albany: State University of New York Press, 1988.

————. (1957). *Eroticism: Death and Sensuality.* Trans. Mary Dalwood. San Francisco: City Lights Books, 1986.

————. (1970). *Visions of Excess: Selected Writings, 1927–1939.* Minneapolis: University of Minnesota Press, 1985.

Baudrillard, Jean (1983). *Fatal Strategies: Crystal Revenge.* New York: Pluto Press.

Bauman, Zygmunt (1992). *Modernity and the Holocaust.* Ithaca, NY: Cornell University Press.

Baumeister, Roy F. (1996). *Evil: Inside Human Violence and Cruelty.* New York: W. H. Freeman.

Becker, Ernest (1962). *The Birth and Death of Meaning: An Interdisciplinary Perspective on the Problem of Man.* New York: Penguin Books.

————. (1973). *The Denial of Death.* New York: Free Press, 1997.

————. (1975). *Escape from Evil.* New York: Free Press, 1985.

Beier, Matthias (2004). *A Violent God-Image: An Introduction to the Work of Eugen Drewermann.* New York: Continuum.

Benjamin, Daniel, and Steven Simon (2002). *The Age of Sacred Terror.* New York: Random House.

Benjamin, Jessica (1988). *The Bonds of Love: Psychoanalysis, Feminism, and the Problem of Domination.* New York: Pantheon Books.

————. (1995). *Like Subjects, Love Objects: Essays on Recognition and Sexual Difference.* New Haven, CT: Yale University Press.

Bergen, Peter L. (2006). *The Osama Bin Laden I Know: An Oral History of Al Qaeda.* New York: Free Press.

Berger, Peter L., et al. (1999). *The Desecularization of the World: Resurgent Religion and World Politics.* Grand Rapids, MI: Ethics and Public Policy Center and Eederman Publications.

Berman, Paul (2003). *Terror and Liberalism.* New York: W. W. Norton.

Bernauer, James (1989). *Nazi-Ethik: Uber Heinrich Himmler und die Karriere der Neuen Moral. Babylon* 6: 46–62.

Berry, Wendell, and Reza Shah-Kazemi (2007). *My Mercy Encompasses All: The Qu'ran's Teachings of Compassion, Peace, and Love.* Berkeley, CA: Counterpoint Books.

Bewley, Abdalhaqq (1999). *The West Wakes Up to Islam.* http://ourworld.compuserve.com/homepages/abewley/tucson.html, Aisha Bewley's Islamic Home Page (accessed April 28, 2009).

Bigot, Guillaume (2002). *Le zombie et le fanatique.* Paris: Flammarion.

bin Ladin, Usama bin Muhammad (2001). Declaration of war against the Americans occupying the land of the two holy places (expel the infidels from the Arab Peninsula). *The Idler,* September 13. In *Knowing the Enemy: Jihadist Ideology and the War on Terror,* ed. Mary M. Habeck, pp. 70, 161–77. New Haven, CT: Yale University Press, 2006.

————. (2002).On exile and betrayal. *New York Times*, April 7.

Bion, Wilfred R. (1967). *Second Thoughts*. London: Heinemann.

Bloom, Mia (1987). Freud and the father complex. *Psychoanalytic Study of the Child* 42: 425–41.

————. (2007). *Dying to Kill: The Allure of Suicide Terror*. New York: Columbia University Press.

Blos, Peter (1985). *Son and Father: Before and Beyond the Oedipus Complex*. New York: Free Press.

————. (1989). The place of the adolescent process in the analysis of the adult. *Psychoanalytic Study of the Child* 44: 3–18.

Bollas, Christopher (1992). *Being a Character: Psychoanalysis and Self-Experience*. New York: Hill and Wang.

————. (1995). *Cracking-up: The Work of Unconscious Experience*. New York: Routledge.

————. (2004). *Dark at the End of the Tunnel*. London: Free Association Books.

Borch-Jacobsen, Mikkel (1991). *The Emotional Tie: Psychoanalysis, Mimesis, and Affect*. Trans. Douglas Brick and others. Stanford, CA: Stanford University Press, 1993.

Borradori, Giovanna (2004). *Philosophy in a Time of Terror: Dialogues with Jürgen Habermas and Jacques Derrida*. Chicago: Chicago University Press.

Boyarin, Daniel (1997). *Unheroic Conduct: The Rise of Homosexuality and the Invention of the Jewish Man*. Berkeley, CA: University of California Press.

————. (1999). *Dying for God: Martyrdom and the Making of Christianity and Judaism*. Stanford, CA: Stanford University Press.

Braunschweig, David, and Michel Fain (1971). *Eros et Anteros*. Paris: Petit Bibliothèque Payot.

Breen, Margaret S., ed. (2003). *Understanding Evil: An Interdisciplinary Approach*. Amsterdam: Rodopi.

Brown, Norman O. (1959). *Life Against Death: The Psychoanalytic Meaning of History*. Middletown, CT: Wesleyan University Press.

Burkert, Walter (1983). *Homo Necans: The Anthropology of Ancient Greek Sacrificial Ritual and Myth*. Berkeley: University of California Press.

Burlingham, Dorothy (1973). The preoedipal infant-father relationship. *Psychoanalytic Study of the Child* 28: 23–48.

Burris, Eli Edward (1931). *Taboo, Magic, Spirits: A Study of Primitive Elements in Roman Religion*. New York: Kessinger Publishing, 2003.

Buruma, Ian, and Avishai Margalit (2004). *Occidentalism: The West in the Eyes of Its Enemies*. New York: Penguin Books.

Butler, Judith (2004). *Precarious Life: The Power of Mourning and Violence*. London: Verso.

Caputo, John D., ed. (2002). *The Religious*. Malden, MA: Blackwell Publishers.

Card, Claudia (2002). *The Atrocity Paradigm: A Theory of Evil.* New York: Oxford University Press.

Cassirer, Ernst (1962). *An Essay on Man: Introduction to the Philosophy of Human Culture.* New Haven, CT: Yale University Press.

Cath, Stanley H. (1982). Adolescence and addiction to alternative belief systems: Psychoanalytic and psychophysiological considerations. *Psychoanalytic Inquiry* 2: 619–75.

Chasseguet-Smirgel, Janine, ed. (1964). *Female Sexuality.* London: Virago, 1981.

———. (1973). *The Ego-Ideal: The Malady of the Ideal.* Trans. Paul Barrows. London: Free Association Books, 1985.

———. (1986) *Sexuality and Mind: The Role of the Father and the Mother in the Psyche.* New York: New York University Press.

Chidester, David (2005). *Authentic Fakes: Religion and American Popular culture.* Berkeley: University of California Press.

Cicovacki, Predrag, ed. (2005). *Destined for Evil? The Twentieth-Century Response.* Rochester, NY: University of Rochester Press.

Conway, Flo, and Jim Siegelman (1978). *Snapping: America's Epidemic of Sudden Personality Change.* New York: Stillpoint, 1995.

Cooke, Maeve (2001). An evil heart: Moral evil and moral identity. In *Rethinking Evil: Contemporary Perspectives*, ed. Maria Pia Lara, pp. 113–30. Berkeley: University of California Press.

Copjec, Joan (1996). Evil in the time of the finite world. Introduction to *Radical Evil*, ed. Joan Copjec, pp. vii–xxviii. London: Verso.

Coughlin, Con (2007). Jews hail birth of red cow as sign to start Third Temple. *Electronic Telegraph*, March 16.

Davies, Nigel (1987). *The Aztec Empire: The Toltec Resurgency.* Norman: University of Oklahoma Press.

Davis, Walter A. (2001). *Deracination: Historicity, Hiroshima, and the Tragic Imperative.* Albany: State University of New York Press.

———. (2006). *Death Dream Kingdom: The American Psyche Since 9/11.* Ann Arbor: University of Michigan Press.

de Lauretis, Teresa (1994). *The Practice of Love: Lesbian Sexuality and Perverse Desire.* Bloomington: Indiana University Press.

———. (2004). Statement due. *Critical Inquiry* 30: 365–68.

Deleuze, Gilles (1997). Nietzsche and Saint Paul, Lawrence and John of Patmos. In *Essays Critical and Clinical*, trans. Daniel Smith and Michael Greco, pp. 36–52. Minneapolis: University of Minnesota Press.

Derrida, Jacques (1995). *The Gift of Death.* Trans. David Wills. Chicago: University of Chicago Press.

Doniger-O'Flaherty, Wendy (1976). *The Origins of Evil in Hindu Mythology.* Berkeley: University of California Press.

———. (2006). Many gods, many paths: Hinduism and religious diversity. Paper presented at the Martin Marty Center, Institute for Advanced Study of Religion, University of Chicago, February.

Douglas, Mary (1966). *Purity and Danger: An Analysis of the Concepts of Pollution and Taboo.* New York: Routledge, 2006.

Durkheim, Emile (1912). *Selected Writings.* Ed. Anthony Giddens. New York: Cambridge University Press, 1972.

Dyer, Gwynne (2004). *War: The Lethal Custom.* New York: Random House.

Dÿkema, Christopher Rhoades. (2001). Comment on evil as love and liberation. In *Psyche Matters,* http://psychematter.com (December 29, 2001). Web page (no longer active, as of May 2009) owned by Cheryl Martin.

Eagleton, Terry (2005). *Holy Terror.* Oxford: Oxford University Press.

Ehrenreich, Barbara (1997). *Blood Rites: The Origins of the Passions of War.* New York: Henry Holt.

Eigen, Michael (2001a). *Damaged Bonds.* London: Karnac Books.

———. (2001b). *Ecstasy.* Middletown, CT: Wesleyan University Press.

Eliade, Mircea (1968). *The Sacred and the Profane: The Nature of Religion.* New York: Harvest Books.

Erikson, Erik H. (1959). *Identity and the Life Cycle.* New York: W. W. Norton, 1994.

Euben, Roxanne L. (1999). *Enemy in the Mirror: Islamic Fundamentalism and the Limits of Modern Rationalism; A Work of Comparative Political Theory.* Princeton, NJ: Princeton University Press.

Evans, Dylan (1996). *An Introductory Dictionary of Lacanian Psychoanalysis.* London: Routledge.

Fackenheim, Emil I. (2005). Kant and radical evil. In *Destined for Evil? The Twentieth-Century Response,* ed. Predrag Cicovacki, pp. 59–73. Rochester, NY: University of Rochester Press.

Fairbairn, William Ronald D. (1952). *Psychoanalytic Studies of the Personality.* London: Tavistock Publications.

Fanon, Franz (1961). *The Wretched of the Earth.* New York: Grove Press, 1963.

Farley, Edward (2005). Fundamentalism: A theory. *Cross-Currents* 55(3): n.p.

Farrell, Kirby (1998). *Post-Traumatic Culture: Injury and Interpretation in the Nineties.* Baltimore: Johns Hopkins University Press.

Feldman, Noah (2006). Islam, terror, and the second nuclear age. *New York Times Magazine,* pp. 50–57, 72–79.

Ferenczi, Sándor (1932). Confusion of tongues between adults and the child. In *Final Contributions to the Problems and Methods of Psychoanalysis,* pp. 156–67. London: Hogarth Press, 1955.

Ferrara, Alessandro (2001). The evil that men do: A meditation on radical evil from a post-metaphysical point of view. In *Rethinking Evil: Contemporary Perspectives,* ed. Maria Pia Lara, pp. 173–97. Berkeley: University of California Press.

Fisher, Robert N. (2003). The catheter of bilious hatred. In *Understanding Evil: An Interdisciplinary Approach*, ed. Margaret S. Breen, pp. 33–42. Amsterdam: Rodopi.

Fonagy, Peter (2008). A developmental theory of sexual enjoyment. *Journal of the American Psychoanalytic Association* 56: 11–36.

Fonagy, Peter, and Mary Target (1998). Mentalization and the changing aims of child psychoanalysis. *Psychoanalytic Dialogues* 8(1): 87–114.

———. (2007). Playing with reality. Part 4, A theory of external reality rooted in intersubjectivity. *International Journal of Psychoanalysis* 88: 917–37.

Fornari, Franco (1966). *The Psychoanalysis of War*. Trans. Alenka Pfeifer. Bloomington: Indiana University Press, 1974.

Foucault, Michel (1961). *Madness and Civilization: A History of Insanity in the Age of Reason*. Trans. Richard Howard. New York: Routledge, 1988.

———. (1984). What is Enlightenment? In *The Foucault Reader*, ed. Paul Rabinow, pp. 32–50. New York: Pantheon Books.

Freud, Sigmund (1900). *The Interpretation of Dreams*. In *The Standard Edition of The Complete Psychological Works of Sigmund Freud*, ed. James Strachey, vols. 4–5. London: Hogarth Press, 1981. All citations from the *Standard Edition of The Complete Psychological Works of Sigmund Freud* are from this 1981 edition.

———. (1909). Notes upon a case of obsessional neurosis. *Standard Edition*, 10: 151–318.

———. (1911). Psycho-Analytic notes on an autobiographical account of a case of paranoia (*dementia paranoides*). *Standard Edition*, 12: 9–82.

———. (1913a). The theme of the three caskets. *Standard Edition*, 12: 289–301.

———. (1913b). *Totem and Taboo. Standard Edition*, 13: 1–162.

———. (1914). The *Moses* of Michelangelo. *Standard Edition*, 14: 209–36.

———. (1915). Thoughts on the times of war and death. *Standard Edition*, 14: 274–300.

———. (1920). Beyond the pleasure principle. *Standard Edition*, 18: 1–63.

———. (1921). Group psychology and the analysis of the ego. *Standard Edition*, 18: 65–143.

———. (1922). A seventeenth-century demonological neurosis. *Standard Edition*, 19: 67–105.

———. (1923). The ego and the id. *Standard Edition*, 19: 1–65.

———. (1924a). The economic problem of masochism. *Standard Edition*, 19: 155–70.

———. (1924b). The loss of reality in neurosis and psychosis. *Standard Edition*, 19: 184–85.

———. (1927). The future of an illusion. *Standard Edition*, 21: 1–56.

———. (1933). *New Introductory Lectures on Psychoanalysis. Standard Edition*, 22: 1–249.

————. (1939). *Moses and Monotheism. Standard Edition*, 23: 3–137.

————. (1940 [1938]). An outline of psycho-analysis. *Standard Edition*, 23: 139–207.

Gallese, Vittorio, Christian Keysers, and Giacomo Rizzolatti (2004). A unifying view of the basis of social cognition. *Trends in Cognitive Science* 8: 396–403.

Gambetta, Diego, ed. (2005). *Making Sense of Suicide Missions*. New York: Oxford University Press.

Germain, Gilbert G. (1993). *A Discourse on Disenchantment: Reflections on Politics and Technology*. Albany: State University of New York Press.

Gerth, Hans H., and C. Wright Mills (1946). *Essays in Sociology*. Oxford: Oxford University Press.

Ghent, Emmanuel (1990). Masochism, submission, surrender: Masochism as a perversion of surrender. *Psychoanalytic Dialogues* 26: 108–36.

Girard, René (1972). *Violence and the Sacred*. Trans. Patrick Gregory. Baltimore: Johns Hopkins University Press, 1979.

————. (1978). *Things Hidden Since the Foundation of the World*. Trans. Stephen Bann and Michael Metter. Stanford, CA: Stanford University Press, 1987.

————. (2003). God of the Apocalypse. Interview with René Girard, by Attilio Scarpellini. *L'Espresso*, June.

————. (2005). *The Girard Reader*. Ed. James G. Williams. New York: Crossroad Publishing.

Goethe, Johann Wolfgang von (1808). *Faust: The Tragedy, Part One*. Trans. Walter W. Arndt. New York: W. W. Norton, 2000.

Grand, Sue (2002a). *The Reproduction of Evil: A Clinical and Cultural Perspective*. Hillsdale, NJ: Analytic Press.

————. (2002b). Discussion of Ruth Stein's Evil as love and as liberation. Colloquium, New York University Postdoctroral Program for Psychotherapy and Psychoanalysis, April.

Green, Hannah (1989). *I Never Promised You a Rose Garden*. London: Pan Macmillan.

Griswold, Robert (2003). Quaker peace testimony in times of terrorism. *The Henry J. Cadbury Library of Philadelphia Yearly Meeting of the Religious Society of Friends*, www.pym.org/peace-and-concerns/comments.php?id=25880_0 _152_0_C_23k, Philadelphia Yearly Meeting Peace Testimony, 2000 to 2006; or: Torrance, CA: Friends Bulletin, 2003.341/15.Gri, under the care of the Web Working Group (accessed May 18, 2009).

Grossman, Dave (1995). *On Killing: The Psychological Cost of Learning to Kill in War and Society*. Boston: Little, Brown.

Habeck, Mary M., ed. (2006). *Knowing the Enemy: Jihadist Ideology and the War on Terror*. New Haven, CT: Yale University Press.

Halbertal, Moshe, and Avishai Margalit (1998). *Idolatry.* Trans. Noemi Gold-blum. Cambridge, MA: Harvard University Press.

Harris, Lee (2004). *Civilization and Its Enemies: The Next Stage of History.* New York: Free Press.

———. (2007). *The Suicide of Reason: Radical Islam's Threat to the West.* New York: Basic Books.

Hassan, Nasra (2001). An arsenal of believers: Talking to the "human bombs." *New Yorker*, November.

Heath, Joseph (2008). The fear factor could be vastly overrated. Canwest News Service, www2.canada.com/reginaleaderpsot/news/story.html?id=058baf1a-e8ee-4a27-a985-408846da4cbb (accessed May 7, 2009).

Hegel, Georg Wilhelm Friedrich (1806). *Phenomenology of Spirit.* Trans. A. V. Miller, New York: Oxford University Press, 1977.

Herzog, James (2001). *Father Hunger.* Hillsdale, NJ: Analytic Press.

Hoffer, Eric (1951). *The True Believer: Thoughts on the Nature of Mass Movements.* New York: Harper and Row, 1989.

Hoffman, Bruce (1998). *Inside Terrorism.* New York: Columbia University Press.

Hoofdar, Homa (2002). Bargaining with fundamentalism: Women and the politics of population control in Iran. Formerly available at www.hsph.harvard.edu/rt21/globalism/hoofdar.html. Also printed in *Reproductive Health Matters* (1996): 30–40.

Horkheimer, Max, and Theodor W. Adorno (1944). *Dialectic of Enlightenment.* New York: Herder and Herder, 1974.

Hubert, Henri, and Marcel Mauss (1899). *Sacrifice: Its Nature and Functions.* Trans. W. D. Halls. Chicago: University of Chicago Press, 1981.

Hughs, Thomas P. (1994). S.v. *jihad. Dictionary of Islam.* Chicago: Kazi Publications.

Ibn Taymiyyah, Shaykh al-Islam (2006). Al-Ubudiyyah: Being a true slave of Allah. In *Knowing the Enemy: Jihadist Ideology and the War on Terror*, ed. Mary M. Habeck, pp. 21, 181. New Haven, CT: Yale University Press.

Ibn Warraq (2003). *Why I Am Not a Muslim.* Amherst, NY: Prometheus Books.

Ibrahim, Raymond, ed. and trans. (2007). *The Al-Qaeda Reader.* New York: Random House.

Ignatieff, Michael (2004). *The Lesser Evil: Political Ethics in an Age of Terror.* Princeton, NJ: Princeton University Press.

International Standard Version of the New Testament (2008). Santa Anna, CA: ISV Foundation.

Irigaray, Luce (2002). Belief itself. Paper presented at Cerisy-la-Salle in honor of Jacques Derrida. In *The Religious*, ed. John D. Caputo, pp. 107–27. Malden, MA: Blackwell Publishers.

James, William (1898). *The Will to Believe and Other Essays in Popular Philosophy.* New York: Longmans, Green. Reprint, Elibron Classics Series, 2005.

———. (1901). *Varieties of Religious Experience: A Study in Human Nature.* New York: Collier Publishers, 1961.

Jansen, Johannes J. G. (1997). *The Dual Nature of Islamic Fundamentalism.* Ithaca, NY: Cornell University Press.

———. (2001). Faraj and the neglected duty. Interview with Jean-François Mayer. Amsterdam, December 8. Transcribed by Nancy Grivel-Burke. *Religioscope,* www.religion.info (accessed May 19, 2009).

Jihad and Shahadat: Struggle and Martyrdom in Islam (1986). Ed. and trans. Mehdi Abedi and Gary Legenhausen. Foreword by Mahmud Ayoub. North Haledon, NJ: Islamic Publications International.

Joffe, William G., and Joseph Sandler (1965). Notes on pain, depression, and individuation. *Psychoanalytic Study of the Child* 20: 394–424.

Jones, James W. (2008). *Blood That Cries Out from the Earth: The Psychology of Religious Terrorism.* Oxford: Oxford University Press.

Joseph, Betty (1982). Addiction to near-death. *International Journal of Psychoanalysis* 63: 449–56.

Juergensmeyer, Mark (2000). *Terror in the Mind of God: The Global Rise of Religious Violence.* Berkeley: University of California Press.

———. (2003a). *Terror in the Mind of God: The Global Rise of Religious Violence.* Berkeley: University of California Press.

———, ed. (2003b). *Global Religions: An Introduction.* Oxford University Press.

Kafka, Franz (1976). *Brief an den Vater.* Frankfurt am Main: Fischer Verlag.

Kant, Immanuel (1793). *Religion Within the Boundaries of Mere Reason.* Cambridge: Cambridge University Press, 1999.

———. (1970). An answer to the question "What is Enlightenment?" In *Kant: Political Writings,* ed. H. S. Reiss, pp. 54–60. Cambridge: Cambridge University Press, 2003.

Katz, Fred (1993). *Ordinary People and Extraordinary Evil: A Report on the Beginnings of Evil.* Albany: State University of New York Press.

Kaufman, Gershen (1980). *Shame: The Power of Caring.* Rochester, VT: Schenkman.

Kekes, John (2005). *The Roots of Evil.* Ithaca, NY: Cornell University Press.

Kepel, Gilles (2005). *The Roots of Radical Islam.* London: Saqi Books.

Kepel, Gilles, and Jean-Pierre Mileli (2008). *Al-Qaeda in Its Own Words.* Cambridge, MA: Belknap Press of Harvard University Press.

Kernberg, Otto (1984). *Severe Personality Disorders.* New Haven, CT: Yale University Press.

Khan, Masud R. (1979). *Alienation in Perversions.* New York: International Universities Press.

Khosrokhavar, Farhad (2005). *Suicide Bombers: Allah's New Martyrs*. Trans. David Macey. London: Pluto Press.

Kierkegaard, Søren (1849). *Provocations: Spiritual Writings of Kierkegaard*. Ed. Charles E. Moore. Rifton, NY: Orbis Books, 1999.

Kippenberg, Hans G. (2008). *Gewalt als Gottesdienst: Religionskriege im Zeitalter der Globalisierung*. Munich: Verlag C. H. Beck.

Kippenberg, Hans G., and Tilman Seidenstricker (2004). *Terror im Dienste Gottes*. Frankfurt: Campus Verlag.

Klein, Melanie (1928). Early stages of the Oedipus-Complex. In *Love, Guilt, and Reparation, and Other Works, 1921–1945, The Writings of Melanie Klein*, 1: 186–98. London: Hogarth Press, 1984.

———. (1940). Mourning and its relation to manic-depressive states. In *Love, Guilt, and Reparation, and Other Works, 1921–1945, The Writings of Melanie Klein*, 1: 344–69. London: Hogarth Press, 1984.

———. (1946). Notes on some schizoid mechanisms. In *Envy and Gratitude and Other Works, 1946–1963, The Writings of Melanie Klein*, 3: 1–24. London: Hogarth Press, 1984.

———. (1957). *Envy and Gratitude and Other Works, 1946–1963*. In *The Writings of Melanie Klein*, 3: 176–235. London: Hogarth Press, 1984.

———. (1958). The development of mental functioning. In *Envy and Gratitude and Other Works, 1946–1963, The Writings of Melanie Klein*, 3: 236–46. London: Hogarth Press, 1984.

Koenigsberg, Richard A.(2009). *Nations Have the Right to Kill: Hitler, the Holocaust, and War*. New York: Library of Social Science.

Kohut, Heinz (1971). *The Analysis of the Self*. New York: International Universities Press.

———. (1978). *The Restoration of the Self*. New York: International Universities Press.

Kolakowski, Leszek (1997). *Modernity Under Endless Trial*. Trans. Stefan Czerniawski et al. Chicago: University of Chicago Press.

The Koran Interpreted (1955). Trans. A. J. Arberry. New York: Simon and Schuster, 1996.

Kramer, Martin (2001). Hijacking Islam: A religion in danger of deteriorating into a manifesto of terror. *National Review*, September 19.

———. (2008). *Arab Awakening and Islamic Revival: The Politics of Ideas in the Middle East*. Edison, NJ: Transaction Publishers.

Kulish, Nancy (1986). Gender and Transference: The screen of the phallic mother. *International Review of Psychoanalysis* 13: 393–404.

Küntzel, Matthias (2005). Suicide bombing "for a higher ideal?" Germany's central office for political education on "paradise now." *Transatlantic Intelligencer*, October 10.

————. (2007). *Jihad and Jew-Hatred: Islamism, Nazism, and the Roots of 9/11.* New York: Telos Press.

Kubie, Lawrence S. (1974). The drive to become both sexes. *Psychoanalytic Quarterly* 43: 349–426.

Lacan, Jacques (1953–54). *Freud's Papers on Technique: The Seminar of Jacques Lacan; Book I.* Trans. John Forrester. New York: W. W. Norton.

————. (1956–57). *The Psychoses: The Seminar of Jacques Lacan; Book III.* Trans. Russell Grigg. New York: Routledge, 1993.

————. (1959–60). *The Ethics of Psychoanalysis: The Seminar of Jacques Lacan; Book VII.* Trans. Dennis Porter. London: Routledge, 1992.

————. (1966). *Ecrits.* Paris: Seuil.

Langs, Robert (1997). *Death Anxiety and Clinical Practice.* London: Karnac.

Laplanche, Jean, and Jean-Bertrand Pontalis (1967). *The Language of Psychoanalysis.* Trans. Donald Nicholson-Smith. New York: W. W. Norton, 1973.

Laqueur, Walter (2005). *Voices of Terror.* Naperville, IL: Sourcebooks.

Lara, Maria Pia, ed. (2001). *Rethinking Evil: Contemporary Perspectives.* Berkeley: University of California Press.

Lautréamont, Comte de (1869). *Les chants de Maldoror.* Trans. Guy Wernham. New York: New Directions, 1965.

Layton, Deborah (1998) *Seductive Poison: A Jonestown Survivor's Story of Life and Death in the People's Temple.* New York: Anchor Books.

Lazar, Rina (2003). Knowing hatred. *International Journal of Psychoanalysis* 84: 405–25.

LeDoux, Joseph E. (1998). *The Emotional Brain: The Mysterious Underpinnings of Emotional Life.* New York: Simon and Schuster.

Lefort, Claude (1986). *The Political Forms of Modern Society.* Ed. John B. Thompson. Cambridge, MA: MIT Press.

————. (1989). *Democracy and Political Theory.* Trans. David Macey. Minneapolis: University of Minnesota Press.

Lewis, Bernard (2002). *What Went Wrong? Western Impact and Middle Eastern Response.* New York: Oxford University Press.

Lifton, Robert Jay (1979). *The Broken Connection: On Death and the Continuity of Life.* New York: Simon and Schuster.

————. (2000). *Destroying the World to Save It: Aum Shinrikyo, Apocalyptic Violence, and the New Global Terrorism.* New York: Henry Holt.

Loewald, Hans W. (1951). Ego and reality. *International Journal of Psychoanalysis* 32: 10–18.

————. (1979). The waning of the Oedipus complex. In *Papers on Psychoanalysis*, pp. 384–404. New Haven, CT: Yale University Press.

Lukes, Steve (2002). Interview with Ruth Stein, December.

MacCannell, Juliet F. (1996). Fascism and the voice of conscience. In *Radical Evil*, ed. Joan Copjec, pp. 46–73. London: Verso.

Macfarquhar, Neil (2001). A nation challenged: Disavowal; Father denies "gentle son" could hijack any liner. *New York Times*, September 19.

Mahler, Margaret S. (1966). Discussion of Phyllis Greenacre's "Problems of over-idealization of the analyst and of analysis." Abstract in *Psychoanalytic Quarterly* 36: 637.

Margalit, Avishai (2005). *I. Indecent Compromise. II. Decent Peace.* Tanner Lectures on Human Values, Stanford University, May 4–5. Tanner Humanities Center, www.tannerlectures.utah.edu (accessed May 19, 2009).

———. (2007). A moral witness to the "Intricate Machine." *New York Review of Books*, December 6, pp. 34–37.

Marion, Jean-Luc (1991). *God Without Being: Hors-texte.* Trans. Thomas A. Carlson. Chicago: University of Chicago Press.

Marty, Martin E., and R. Scott Appleby, eds. (2004). *Fundamentalism Comprehended.* Chicago: University of Chicago Press.

Marvin, Carolyn, and D. W. Ingle (1999). *Blood Sacrifice and the Nation: Totem Rituals and the American Flag.* New York: Columbia University Press.

McDermott, Terry (2005). *Perfect Soldiers: The Hijackers; Who They Were, Why They Did It.* New York: HarperCollins.

Meltzer, Donald (1975). The role of narcissistic organization in the communicative difficulties of the schizophrenic. In *Sincerity and Other Works*, ed. Donald Meltzer and Alberto Hahn, pp. 363–73. London: Karnac, 1994.

Mernissi, Fatema (1992). *Islam and Democracy: Fear of the Modern World.* Trans. Mary Joe Lakeland. Cambridge, MA: Perseus Press.

Mignard, Jean-Pierre (2005). Bibliothèque Médicis. TV5 (French international television), February 12.

Miller, David Lee (2003). *Dreams of the Burning Child: Sacrificial Sons and the Father's Witness.* Ithaca, NY: Cornell University Press.

Milner, Marion (1969). *The Hands of the Living God.* New York: International Universities Press.

Moss, Donald (2003a). Does it matter what the terrorists meant? In *Hating in the First Person Plural: Psychoanalytic Essays on Racism, Homophobia, Misogyny, and Terror*, ed. Donald Moss, pp. 323–36. New York: Other Press.

———, ed. (2003b). *Hating in the First Person Plural: Psychoanalytic Essays on Racism, Homophobia, Misogyny, and Terror.* New York: Other Press.

Moussali, Ahmad S. (1992). *Radical Islamic Fundamentalism: The Ideological and Political Discourse of Sayyid Qutb.* Beirut: American University of Beirut Press.

Murray, Nicholas (2004). *Kafka: A Biography.* New Haven, CT: Yale University Press.

Nasr, Seyyed Hossein (2002). *The Heart of Islam*. New York: HarperCollins.

Niebuhr, Karl (1932). *Moral Man and Immoral Society: A Study in Ethics and Politics*. New York: Scribner and Sons.

Niederland, William G. (1951). Three notes on the Schreber case. *Psychoanalytic Quarterly* 20: 579–91.

———. (1959). Schreber: Father and son. *Psychoanalytic Quarterly* 28: 151–69.

———. (1960). Schreber's father. *Journal of the American Psychoanalytic Association* 8: 492–99.

Nietzsche, Friedrich (1887). Third essay: What do ascetic Ideas mean? In *On the Genealogy of Morality: A Polemic*, trans. Maudmarie Clarke and Alan J. Swenson, pp. 67–118. Indianapolis: Hackett Publishers, 1998.

Nunberg, Hans (1932) *Allgemeine Neurosenlehre auf psychoanalytischer Grundlage*. Frankfurt: Fischer Verlag, 1982.

Ogden, Thomas (1994). *Subjects of Analysis*. Northvale, NJ: Jason Aronson.

———. (1997). The perverse subject of analysis. In *Reverie and Interpretation*, ed. Thomas Ogden, pp. 67–104. Northvale, NJ: Jason Aronson.

Oliver, Anne Marie, and Paul F. Steinberg (2006). *The Road to Martyrs' Square: A Journey into the World of the Suicide Bomber*. New York: Oxford University Press.

Ophir, Adi (2005). The Order of Evils: *Towards Ontology of Morals*. Trans. Rela Mazali and Havi Carel. Cambridge, MA: Zone Books.

Oppenheimer, Paul (1996). *Evil and the Demonic: A New Theory of Monstrous Behavior*. New York: New York University Press.

Osman, Marvin P. (2004) The role of an early-life variant of the Oedipus complex in motivating religious endeavors. *Journal of the American Psychoanalytic Association* 52: 975–1007.

Otto, Rudolph (1923). *The Idea of the Holy*. Oxford: Oxford University Press, 1958.

Pagden, Anthony (2008). *Worlds at War: The 2,500-Year Struggle Between East and West*. New York: Random House.

Pandolfo, Stefania (2007). "The burning": Finitude and the politico-theological imagination of illegal migration. *Anthropological Theory* 7: 329–63.

Pape, Robert A. (2006) *Dying to Win: The Strategic Logic of Suicide Terrorism*. New York: Random House.

Peck, M. Scott. 1983. *People of the Lie: The Hope for Healing Human Evil*. New York: Simon and Schuster.

Pecora, Vincent P. (2006). *Secularization and Cultural Criticism: Religion, Nation, and Modernity*. Chicago: University of Chicago Press.

Piven, Jerry (2000). *Death and Delusion: A Freudian Analysis of Mortal Terror*. Greenwich, CT: Information Age Publishing.

————. (2004). *Death and Delusion: A Freudian Analysis of Mortal Terror.* Greenwich, CT: Information Age Publishing.

Piven, Jerry, Chris Boyd, and Henry Lawton, eds. (2004). *Terrorism, Jihad, and Sacred Vengeance.* Giessen: Psychosozial-Verlag.

Polanski, Roman, dir. (1968). *Rosemary's Baby.* Starring Mia Farrow and John Cassavetes. Hollywood: Paramount Pictures.

Pruett, Kyle D. (1983). Infant of primary nurturing fathers. *Psychoanalytic Study of the Child* 38: 257–77.

————. (1992). Latency development in children of primary nurturing fathers: Eight years follow-up. *Psychoanalytic Study of the Child* 47: 85–101.

Pyszczynski, Tom, Jeff Greenberg, and Sheldon Solomon (1997). Why do we need what we need? A terror management perspective on the roots of human social motivation. *Psychological Inquiry* 8(1): 1–20.

————. (2003). *In the Wake of 9/11: The Psychology of Terror.* Washington, DC: American Psychological Association.

Quinby, Lee (forthcoming). Fundamentally gendered and subject to submission. In *The Fundamentalist Mindset: Psychological Perspectives on Religion, Violence, and History,* ed. Charles B. Strozier, David M. Terman, and James W. Jones, chap. 8. New York: Oxford University Press.

Qutb, Sayyid (1953). *Social Justice in Islam.* Trans. John B. Hardie and Hamid Algar. Oneonta, NY: Islamic Publications International.

————. (1964). *Milestones.* New Delhi: Islamic Book Service, 2006.

Rabinbach, Ansor (2000). "Why were the Jews sacrificed?" The place of anti-Semitism in Horkheimer and Adorno's dialectics of enlightenment. *New German Critique* 81: 49–64.

Racker, Heinrich (1968). *Transference and Countertransference.* London: Hogarth Press.

Rangelov, Iavor (2003). Ideology between radical and diabolical evil: Kant's "ethics of the real." *Facta Universitatis* 2: 759–68.

Rapoport, David C. (1990). Sacred terror: A contemporary example from Islam. In *The Origins of Terrorism: Psychologies, Ideologies, Theologies, States of Mind,* ed. Walter Reich, pp. 103–30. Washington DC: Woodrow Wilson Center Press.

Rashid, Ahmed (2008). Jihadi suicide bombers: The new wave. *New York Review of Books,* June 12, pp. 17–22.

Rasoulallah.net (2008). The concept of animal sacrifice in Islam. Rasoulallah Web site, www.rasoulallah.net (December).

Reeder, Jürgen (1995). The uncastrated man: The irrationality of masculinity portrayed in cinema. *American Imago* 52(2): 131–53.

Ricoeur, Paul (1960). *The Symbolism of Evil.* Boston: Beacon Press, 1986.

Rizzolatti, Giacomo, Leonardo Fogassi, and Vittorio Gallese (2001). Neurophysiological mechanisms underlying the understanding and imitation of action. *Neuroscience* 2: 661–70.

———. (2006). Mirrors in the mind. *Scientific American*, November, pp. 30–37.

Robinson, Andrew (2005). The mythology of war. *Peace Review* 17: 33–38.

Rosenfeld, Herbert (1971). A clinical approach to the psychoanalytic theory of the life and death instincts: An investigation into the aggressive aspects of narcissism. *International Journal of Psychoanalysis* 52: 169–78.

Ross, John Munder (1979). Fathering: A review of some psychoanalytic contributions on paternity. *International Journal of Psychoanalysis* 60: 317–27.

Roy, Oliver (2004). *Globalized Islam: The Search for a New Ummah*. New York: Columbia University Press.

Sageman, Marc (2008). *Leaderless Jihad: Terror Networks in the Twenty-First Century*. Philadelphia: University of Pennsylvania Press.

Said, Edward (1978). *Orientalism*. New York: Pantheon Books.

Sargent, William (1957). *Battle for the Mind: A Physiology of Conversion and Brain-Washing*. Cambridge, MA: Malor Books, 1997.

Sartre, Jean-Paul (1945). *Being and Nothingness*. Trans. Hazel Barnes. New York: Washington Square Press, 1966.

Schimmel, Annemarie (1994). *Deciphering the Signs of God: A Phenomenological Approach to Islam*. Albany: State University of New York Press.

Schrag, Calvin O. (1992). *The Resources of Rationality: A Response to the Postmodern Challenge*. Bloomington: Indiana University Press.

———. (2002). *God as Otherwise Than Being: Toward a Semantics of the Gift*. Evanston, IL: Northwestern University Press.

Schwartz, Regina M. (1997). *The Curse of Cain: The Violent Legacy of Monotheism*. Chicago: University of Chicago Press.

Scruton, Roger (2003). *The West and the Rest: Globalization and the Terrorist Threat*. Wilmington, DE: Isi Books.

Sebek, Michael (1996). The fate of the totalitarian object. *International Forum of Psychoanalysis* 5: 289–94.

Shakespeare, William (1953). *Twenty-Three Plays and Sonnets*. Ed. Thomas Marc Parrott. New York: Scribner's.

———. (1982). *Hamlet, Prince of Danemark*. Ed. Harold Jenkins. London: Methuen.

Shengold, Leonard (1989). *Soul Murder: The Effects of Childhood Abuse and Deprivation*. New Haven, CT: Yale University Press.

Shepherdson, Charles (2000). *Vital Signs: Nature, Culture, Psychoanalysis*. New York: Routledge.

Sivan, Emmanuel (1983). Aspects of the enclave culture in fundamentalism. Presentation at the Van Leer Center, Jerusalem, Conference on Fundamentalisms, May.

———. (1985) *Radical Islam: Medieval Theology and Modern Politics*. New Haven, CT: Yale University Press.

———. (2004). The Enclave culture. In *Fundamentalism Comprehended (The Fundamentalism Project)*, ed. Martin E. Marty and R. Scott Appleby. Chicago: University of Chicago Press.

———. (1995). Eavesdropping on radical Islam. *Middle East Quarterly* 2: 13–24.

Sloterdijk, Peter (2007). *Gottes Eifer: Vom Kampf der drei Monotheismen*. Frankfurt: Insel Verlag.

Smart, Ninian (2003). The global future of religion. In *Global Religions: An Introduction*, ed. Mark Juergensmeyer, pp. 124–31. Oxford: Oxford University Press.

Solomon, Robert C. (1987). *From Hegel to Existentialism*. Oxford: Oxford University Press.

Sorkin, Madeleine (2004). Al-Qaeda's defining moment: The prominence of the scapegoat strategy. Religion Department, Colorado College, www.coloradocollege.edu/dept/RE/SrSeminar04/Sorkinpaper.htm (accessed May 18, 2009).

Stein, Ruth (1990). A new look at the theory of Melanie Klein. *International Journal of Psychoanalysis* 71: 499–511.

———. (1991). *Psychoanalytic Theories of Affect*. London: Karnac, 1999.

———. (1992). Schadenfreude. *Iyyun: The Jerusalem Philosophical Quarterly* 41: 83–92.

———. (1995). Analysis of a case of transsexualism. *Psychoanalytic Dialogues* 5: 257–89.

———. (1998a). Two principles of the functioning of the affects. *American Journal of Psychoanalysis* 58: 211–30.

———. (1998b). Un certain style de masculinité "féminine"; ou, Déconstruire le masculin? Trans. Caterine Alicot. *Revue Française de Psychanalyse* 62: 593–606.

———. (1999). The entitlement of the object of perversion. Paper presented at Freud at the Threshold of the Millennium, Hebrew University, Jerusalem, December.

———. (2001). "False Love"—Why Not? Fragments of an Analysis. *Studies in Gender and Sexuality* 1(2): 167–90.

———. (2002). Evil as love and as liberation: The religious terrorist's mind. *Psychoanalytic Dialogues* 12(3): 393–420. Also in *Hating in the First Person Plural: Psychoanalytic Essays on Racism, Homophobia, Misogyny, and Terror*, ed. Donald Moss, pp. 281–310, New York: Other Press, 2003; in *Terrorism, Jihad, and Sacred Vengeance*, ed. Jerry Piven, Chris Boyd, and Henry Lawton, pp. 38–61 (Giessen: Psychosozial-Verlag, 2004); and in *Terrorism and Apocalypse*, vol. 2 of *Psychological Currents in History*, ed. Jerry S. Piven, Paul Ziolo, and Henry W. Lawton. Writer's Showcase, San Jose, New York: 2002.

———. (2003). Vertical mystical homo-eros: An altered form of desire in fundamentalism. *Studies in Gender and Sexuality* 4(1): 38–58.

————. (2005a). Zur psychischen Verfassung religiös motivierter Selbstmordat-tentäter. *Psyche* 59(2): 97–126.

————. (2005b). Why Perversion? "False love" and the perverse pact. *International Journal of Psychoanalysis* 86(3): 775–99.

————. (2006a). Fundamentalism, father and son, and vertical desire. *Psychoanalytic Review* 93(2): 201–29.

————. (2006b). Father regression: Theoretical reflections and clinical narratives. *International Journal of Psychoanalysis* 87(4): 1005–27.

————. (2007). Mind-control: Malevolent uses of emotions, the dark mirror of psychoanalysis. In *First, Do No Harm: Psychoanalysis and Militarism*, ed. Adrienne Harris and Steve Botticelli. London: Taylor & Francis, forthcoming.

Steiner, John (1993). *Psychic Retreats: Pathological Organizations in Psychotic, Neurotic, and Borderline Patients*. New York: Routledge.

Stern, Jessica (2003). *Terror in the Name of God*. New York: HarperCollins.

Stojanović, Svetozar D. (2005). From relative to absolute evil. In *Destined for Evil? The Twentieth-Century Response*, ed. Predrag Cicovacki, pp. 147–54. Rochester, NY: University of Rochester Press.

Stoller, Robert (1986). *Perversion: The Erotic Form of Hatred*. New York: American Psychiatric Club.

Strozier, Charles B. (1994). *Apocalypse: On the Psychology of Fundamentalism in America*. Boston: Beacon Press.

————. (2009). Interview with Ruth Stein, January 12.

Sullivan, Harry Stack (1953). *The Interpersonal Theory of Psychiatry*. New York: W. W. Norton.

Taheri, Amir (1987). *Holy Terror: Inside the World of Islamic Terrorism*. Bethesda, MD: Adler and Adler.

Tanach Hauniversita Haivrit Biyrushalaim [The Old Testament, Hebrew University in Jerusalem Edition] (2000). Jerusalem: Keter Yerushalaim.

Tausk, Victor (1933). On the origin of the "influencing machine" in schizophrenia. *Psychoanalytic Quarterly* 2: 519–56.

Trevarthen, Colwyn (2006). The concept and foundations of infant intersubjectivity. In *Intersubjective Communication and Emotion in Early Ontogeny*, pp. 15–46. New York: Cambridge University Press.

Tronick, Edward, et al. (1999). Dyadically expanded states of consciousness and the process of therapeutic change. *Infant Mental Health Journal* 19: 290–99.

Van Creveld, Martin (1991). *The Transformation of War*. New York: Free Press.

Volkan, Vamik (2004). *Blind Trust: Large Groups and Their Leaders in Times of Crisis*. Charlottesville, VA: Pitchstone Publishing.

Waller, James (2002). *Becoming Evil: How Ordinary People Commit Genocide and Mass Killing*. New York: Oxford University Press.

Waltzer, Michael (1977). *Just and Unjust Wars*. New York: Basic Books.

Weber, Max (1919). Politics as a vocation. In *The Vocation Lectures: Science as a Vocation, Politics as a Vocation*, by Max Weber, David S. Owen, Tracy B. Strong, and Rodney Livingstone. Hackett Publishing, 2004.

Winnicott, Donald W. (1969). The use of an object. *International Journal of Psychoanalysis* 50: 711–16.

The Worm Turns: A cyber-attack alarms the Pentagon (2008). *The Economist*, December 4.

Wright, Lawrence (2006). *The Looming Tower: Al-Qaeda and the Road to 9/11*. New York: Alfred A. Knopf.

Žižek, Slavoj (1997). *The Plague of Fantasies*. London: Verso.

———. (2001). *On Belief*. New York: Routledge.

———. (2002). *Welcome to the Desert of the Real: Five Essays on September 11 and Related Dates*. London: Verso.

———. (2003a). *The Puppet and the Dwarf: The Perverse Core of Christianity*. Cambridge, MA: MIT Press.

———. (2003b). Liberation hurts. Interview with Eric Dean Rasmussen, University of Illinois at Chicago, September 29. *Electronic Book Review*, www.electronicbookreview.com/thread/endconstruction/desublimation (accessed May 27, 2009).

Index

MERIDIAN

Crossing Aesthetics

Jacques Derrida, *H.C. for Life, That Is to Say...*

Ernst Bloch, *Traces*

Elizabeth Rottenberg, *Inheriting the Future: Legacies of Kant, Freud, and Flaubert*

David Michael Kleinberg-Levin, *Gestures of Ethical Life*

Jacques Derrida, *On Touching--Jean-Luc Nancy*

Jacques Derrida, *Rogues: Two Essays on Reason*

Peggy Kamuf, *Book of Addresses*

Giorgio Agamben, *The Time That Remains: A Commentary on the Letter to the Romans*

Jean-Luc Nancy, *Multiple Arts: The Muses II*

Alain Badiou, *Handbook of Inaesthetics*

Jacques Derrida, *Eyes of the University: Right to Philosophy 2*

Maurice Blanchot, *Lautréamont and Sade*

Giorgio Agamben, *The Open: Man and Animal*

Jean Genet, *The Declared Enemy*

Shoshana Felman, *Writing and Madness: (Literature/Philosophy/Psychoanalysis)*

Jean Genet, *Fragments of the Artwork*

Shoshana Felman, *The Scandal of the Speaking Body: Don Juan with J. L. Austin, or Seduction in Two Languages*

Peter Szondi, *Celan Studies*

Neil Hertz, *George Eliot's Pulse*

Maurice Blanchot, *The Book to Come*

Susannah Young-ah Gottlieb, *Regions of Sorrow: Anxiety and Messianism in Hannah Arendt and W. H. Auden*

Jacques Derrida, *Without Alibi*, edited by Peggy Kamuf

Cornelius Castoriadis, *On Plato's 'Statesman'*

Jacques Derrida, *Who's Afraid of Philosophy? Right to Philosophy 1*

Peter Szondi, *An Essay on the Tragic*

Peter Fenves, *Arresting Language: From Leibniz to Benjamin*

Jill Robbins, ed. *Is It Righteous to Be? Interviews with Emmanuel Levinas*

Louis Marin, *Of Representation*

J. Hillis Miller, *Speech Acts in Literature*

Maurice Blanchot, *Faux pas*

Jean-Luc Nancy, *Being Singular Plural*

Maurice Blanchot / Jacques Derrida, *The Instant of My Death / Demeure: Fiction and Testimony*

Niklas Luhmann, *Art as a Social System*

Emmanual Levinas, *God, Death, and Time*

Ernst Bloch, *The Spirit of Utopia*

Giorgio Agamben, *Potentialities: Collected Essays in Philosophy*

Ellen S. Burt, *Poetry's Appeal: French Nineteenth-Century Lyric and the Political Space*

Jacques Derrida, *Adieu to Emmanuel Levinas*

Werner Hamacher, *Premises: Essays on Philosophy and Literature from Kant to Celan*

Aris Fioretos, *The Gray Book*

Deborah Esch, *In the Event: Reading Journalism, Reading Theory*

Winfried Menninghaus, *In Praise of Nonsense: Kant and Bluebeard*

Giorgio Agamben, *The Man Without Content*

Giorgio Agamben, *The End of the Poem: Studies in Poetics*

Theodor W. Adorno, *Sound Figures*

Louis Marin, *Sublime Poussin*

Philippe Lacoue-Labarthe, *Poetry as Experience*

Hans-Jost Frey, *Studies in Poetic Discourse: Mallarmé, Baudelaire, Rimbaud, Hölderlin*

Pierre Bourdieu, *The Rules of Art: Genesis and Structure of the Literary Field*

Nicolas Abraham, *Rhythms: On the Work, Translation, and Psychoanalysis*

Jacques Derrida, *On the Name*

David Wills, *Prosthesis*

Maurice Blanchot, *The Work of Fire*

Jacques Derrida, *Points . . . : Interviews, 1974-1994*

J. Hillis Miller, *Topographies*

Philippe Lacoue-Labarthe, *Musica Ficta (Figures of Wagner)*

Jacques Derrida, *Aporias*

Emmanuel Levinas, *Outside the Subject*

Jean-François Lyotard, *Lessons on the Analytic of the Sublime*

Peter Fenves, *"Chatter": Language and History in Kierkegaard*

Jean-Luc Nancy, *The Experience of Freedom*

Jean-Joseph Goux, *Oedipus, Philosopher*

Haun Saussy, *The Problem of a Chinese Aesthetic*

Jean-Luc Nancy, *The Birth to Presence*